BEST OF
Country Cooking

Taste of Home®

Visit *ShopTasteofHome.com* for other
Taste of Home books and products.

Stamp -of-Approval
Spaghetti Sauce (p. 143)

© 2018 RDA Enthusiast Brands, LLC.
1610 N. 2nd St., Suite 102
Milwaukee, WI 53212-3906

International Standard Book Number: 978-1-61765-770-2

International Standard Serial Number: 2166-0522

Component Number: 117000054H

COVER PHOTOGRAPHY
PHOTOGRAPHER: Jim Wieland
FOOD STYLIST: Dee Dee Schaefer
SET STYLIST: Lauren Knoelke

PICTURED ON THE FRONT COVER:
Lemony Roasted Chicken and Potatoes (p. 93)

PICTURED ON THE BACK COVER:
Cran-Apple Muffins (p. 74), Blackberry Lemonade (p. 16)
and Hot Sausage & Bean Dip (p. 9).

PICTURED ON PAGE 1:
Moist Lemon Chiffon Cake (p. 180).

Down-Home Cooking from the Country's Best Cooks

ACROSS THE COUNTRY, COOKS ARE SERVING UP DELICIOUS RECIPES FOR THEIR FAMILIES. GRAB YOUR SEAT AT THE TABLE!

Country cooking is hearty, delicious and made for sharing. Warming soups and stews, mouthwatering main courses and delicious desserts perfect for passing around the table are the cornerstone of a country kitchen. These are the heirloom recipes that form the foundation of simple, satisfying home-cooked meals. And now the country's home cooks have shared those recipes with you.

This edition of **Best of Country Cooking** is filled with dishes delivering the warmth and tradition of down-home cooking. Farm-fresh ingredients used to their best advantage, home-made jams and jellies to stock the pantry, hot breakfasts to get you started on a busy workday and delicious meals to bring your family together in the evening...all help you set the taste of the country on your table. And nothing says country cooking like home-baked breads, rolls, muffins and cakes!

LOOK INSIDE FOR:

Contest Winner

Blue-Ribbon Recipes
In each chapter, the blue-ribbon icon marks those recipes that have taken the honors in a Taste of Home contest. With these dishes, you're sure to serve up a winner!

Freeze It!
With freezer-friendly recipes, you'll always have a great meal at your fingertips. Recipes with this icon  FREEZE IT can be made in advance and kept in the freezer for your busiest days.

Dish up a meal tonight with all the comfort-food goodness your family craves. Whether you're cooking for two or looking for the perfect dish for a potluck, you'll find what you're after in **Best of Country Cooking!**

CONTENTS

Snacks & Beverages

Let's party! When it comes to setting out an assortment of savory appetizers, quick nibbles and easy drinks, country cooks know how to please a crowd. Turn here for 25 mouthwatering favorites plus a special section dedicated to snack mixes. It's time to celebrate country-style!

GINGER TEA DRINK

Looking for something special to serve to guests? Let this soothing green tea simmer while you prepare other dishes for your gathering.

—Alexandra Marcotty
Cleveland Heights, OH

Prep: 15 min. • **Cook:** 2 hours
Makes: 8 servings (2 quarts)

- 4 cups boiling water
- 15 individual green tea bags
- 4 cups white grape juice
- 1 to 2 tablespoons honey
- 1 tablespoon minced fresh gingerroot
  Crystallized ginger, optional

1. In a 3-qt. slow cooker, combine boiling water and tea bags. Cover and let stand for 10 minutes. Discard the tea bags. Stir in the remaining ingredients. Cover and cook on low for 2-3 hours or until heated through.
2. Serve warm. If desired, strain before serving and garnish each mug with a slice of crystallized ginger.

BACON CHEDDAR POTATO SKINS

Both crisp and hearty, this restaurant-quality snack is one my family requests often—and I'm happy to oblige!
—Trish Perrin Keizer, OR

Start to Finish: 30 min.
Makes: 8 servings

- 4 large baking potatoes, baked
- 3 tablespoons canola oil
- 1 tablespoon grated Parmesan cheese
- ½ teaspoon salt
- ¼ teaspoon garlic powder
- ¼ teaspoon paprika
- ⅛ teaspoon pepper
- 8 bacon strips, cooked and crumbled
- 1½ cups shredded cheddar cheese
- ½ cup sour cream
- 4 green onions, sliced

1. Preheat oven to 475°. Cut potatoes in half lengthwise. Scoop out pulp, leaving a ¼-in. shell. Place the potato skins on a greased baking sheet. (Save the pulp for another use.)
2. Combine oil and next five ingredients; brush over both sides of skins.
3. Bake until crisp, about 7 minutes on each side. Sprinkle bacon and cheddar cheese inside skins. Bake until cheese is melted, about 2 minutes longer. Top with sour cream and onions. Serve immediately.
Note: To save time, instead of prebaking the potatoes in an oven for 50-60 minutes, microwave them for 4 minutes. Scoop out the pulp, then make the potato skins as directed.

SPICY CHICKEN WINGS

These fall-off-the-bone-tender wings have just the right amount of heat, and cool blue cheese dressing creates the perfect flavor combination for dipping.
—**Kevalyn Henderson** Hayward, WI

Prep: 25 min. + marinating • **Bake:** 2 hours
Makes: 2 dozen (1¾ cups dip)

- 1 cup reduced-sodium soy sauce
- ⅔ cup sugar
- 2 teaspoons salt
- 2 teaspoons grated orange peel
- 2 garlic cloves, minced
- ½ teaspoon pepper
- 3 pounds chicken wingettes and drumettes
- 3 teaspoons chili powder
- ¾ teaspoon cayenne pepper
- ¾ teaspoon hot pepper sauce

BLUE CHEESE DIP
- 1 cup mayonnaise
- ½ cup blue cheese salad dressing
- ⅓ cup buttermilk
- 2 teaspoons Italian salad dressing mix

1. In a small bowl, combine the soy sauce, sugar, salt, orange peel, garlic and pepper. Pour half of the marinade into a large resealable plastic bag. Add the chicken; seal bag and turn to coat. Refrigerate for 1 hour. Cover and refrigerate the remaining marinade.
2. Preheat oven to 325°. Drain and discard marinade. Transfer chicken to a greased 13x9-in. baking dish. Cover and bake for 1½ hours or until chicken juices run clear.
3. Using tongs, transfer chicken to a greased 15x10x1-in. baking pan. In a small bowl, combine the chili powder, cayenne, pepper sauce and reserved marinade. Drizzle over chicken.
4. Bake, uncovered, for 30 minutes, turning once. In a small bowl, whisk the dip ingredients. Serve with wings.

ROASTED RED PEPPER TAPENADE

When entertaining, I often rely on my pepper tapenade recipe because it's so delicious, quick and easy. You can use walnuts or pecans instead of almonds.
—**DONNA MAGLIARO** DENVILLE, NJ

Prep: 15 min. + chilling
Makes: 2 cups

- 3 garlic cloves, peeled
- 2 cups roasted sweet red peppers, drained
- ½ cup blanched almonds
- ⅓ cup tomato paste
- 2 tablespoons olive oil
- ¼ teaspoon salt
- ¼ teaspoon pepper
  Minced fresh basil
  Toasted French bread baguette slices or water crackers

1. In a small saucepan, bring 2 cups water to a boil. Add garlic; cook, uncovered, just until tender, 6-8 minutes. Drain and pat dry. Place red peppers, almonds, tomato paste, oil, garlic, salt and pepper in a small food processor; process until blended. Transfer to a small bowl. Refrigerate at least 4 hours to allow the flavors to blend.
2. Sprinkle with basil. Serve with toasted baguette slices or water crackers.

AUSSIE SAUSAGE ROLLS

I was born and raised in Australia but moved to the U.S. when I married my husband. When I long for a taste of my homeland, I bake up a batch of these cute little sausage rolls and share them with my neighbors or co-workers.

—Melissa Landon Port Charlotte, FL

Prep: 30 min. • **Bake:** 20 min.
Makes: 3 dozen

- 1 medium onion, finely chopped
- 2 tablespoons minced fresh chives or 2 teaspoons dried chives
- 2 teaspoons minced fresh basil or ½ teaspoon dried basil
- 2 garlic cloves, minced
- ½ teaspoon salt
- ¼ teaspoon pepper
- 1 teaspoon paprika, divided
- 1¼ pounds bulk pork sausage
- 1 package (17.3 ounces) frozen puff pastry, thawed

1. Preheat oven to 350°. Combine first six ingredients and ¾ teaspoon paprika. Add sausage; mix lightly but thoroughly.
2. On a lightly floured surface, roll each pastry sheet into an 11x10½-in. rectangle. Cut lengthwise into three strips. Spread ½ cup sausage mixture lengthwise down the center of each strip. Fold over sides, pinching the edges to seal. Cut each log into six pieces.
3. Place on a rack in a 15x10x1-in. pan, seam side down. Sprinkle with remaining paprika. Bake until golden brown and sausage is no longer pink, 20-25 minutes.

CHOCOLATE ICE CREAM SODAS

I keep the ingredients for these yummy ice cream sodas on hand so I can enjoy them anytime I want. You can easily make more when feeding a crowd.

—Anna Erickson Silverdale, WA

Start to Finish: 15 min.
Makes: 4 servings

- ¾ cup chocolate syrup
- 1 cup milk
- 4 cups carbonated water, chilled
- 8 scoops chocolate ice cream (about 2⅔ cups), divided
  Whipped cream in a can, optional

Place 3 tablespoons chocolate syrup in each of four 16-oz. glasses. Add ¼ cup milk and 1 cup carbonated water to each; stir until foamy. Add two scoops of ice cream to each glass. Top with whipped cream if desired.

WHITE CHOCOLATE PARTY MIX

You won't be able to stop eating this irresistible mix. The light, sweet coating tatses great with cereal, peanuts, pretzels and M&M's.

—**Norene Wright** Manilla, IN

Start to Finish: 30 min.
Makes: 5 quarts

 5 cups Cheerios
 5 cups Corn Chex
 2 cups salted peanuts
 1 pound chocolate M&M's
 1 package (10 ounces) mini pretzels
 2 packages (12 ounces each) white baking chips
 3 tablespoons canola oil

1. In a large bowl, combine the first five ingredients; set aside. In a microwave-safe bowl, heat chips and oil at 70% power for 1 minute, stirring once. Microwave on high for 5 seconds; stir until smooth.
2. Pour over cereal mixture and mix well. Spread onto three waxed paper-lined baking sheets. Cool; break apart. Store in an airtight container.

HOT SAUSAGE & BEAN DIP

This is a spin-off of a Mexican dip I once had. The original was wicked good, but I decided to switch it up. Take it to a party—I'll bet no one else will bring anything like it!

—**Mandy Rivers** Lexington, SC

Prep: 25 min. • **Bake:** 20 min.
Makes: 16 servings

 1 pound bulk hot Italian sausage
 1 medium onion, finely chopped
 4 garlic cloves, minced
 ½ cup dry white wine or chicken broth
 ½ teaspoon dried oregano
 ¼ teaspoon salt
 ¼ teaspoon dried thyme
 1 package (8 ounces) cream cheese, softened
 1 package (6 ounces) fresh baby spinach, coarsely chopped
 1 can (15 ounces) cannellini beans, rinsed and drained
 1 cup chopped seeded tomatoes
 1 cup shredded part-skim mozzarella cheese
 ½ cup shredded Parmesan cheese
 Assorted crackers or toasted French bread baguette slices

1. Preheat oven to 375°. In a large skillet, cook sausage, onion and garlic over medium heat until sausage is no longer pink, breaking up sausage into crumbles; drain. Stir in wine, oregano, salt and thyme. Bring to a boil; cook until liquid is almost evaporated.
2. Add cream cheese; stir until melted. Stir in spinach, beans and tomatoes; cook and stir until spinach is wilted. Transfer to a greased 8-in. square or if using an oven-proof skillet, leave in skillet. Sprinkle with cheeses.
3. Bake until bubbly, 20-25 minutes. Serve with crackers.

SOUTHWESTERN NACHOS

Guests will go crazy when you serve two heaping pans of this cheesy nacho casserole featuring tender chunks of pork. You don't need to worry about filling the chip bowl...the tortilla chips are baked right in the dish!

—**Kelly Byler** Goshen, IN

Prep: 40 min. • **Cook:** 7¼ hours
Makes: 30 servings

- 2 boneless whole pork loin roasts (3½ pounds each)
- 1 cup unsweetened apple juice
- 6 garlic cloves, minced
- 1 teaspoon salt
- 1 teaspoon liquid smoke, optional
- 2½ cups barbecue sauce
- ⅓ cup packed brown sugar
- 2 tablespoons honey
- 1 package (16 ounces) tortilla chips
- 1½ cups frozen corn
- 1 can (15 ounces) black beans, rinsed and drained
- 1 medium tomato, seeded and chopped
- 1 medium red onion, chopped
- ⅓ cup minced fresh cilantro
- 1 jalapeno pepper, seeded and chopped
- 2 teaspoons lime juice
- 1 package (16 ounces) process cheese (Velveeta), cubed
- ¼ cup 2% milk

1. Cut each roast in half; place in two 5-qt. slow cookers. Combine the apple juice, garlic, salt and, if desired, liquid smoke; pour over meat. Cover and cook on low 7-8 hours or until tender.

2. Preheat oven to 375°. Shred pork with two forks; place in a very large bowl. Stir in barbecue sauce, brown sugar and honey. Divide tortilla chips between two greased 13x9-in. baking dishes; top with pork mixture. Combine corn, beans, tomato, onion, cilantro, jalapeno and lime juice; spoon over pork mixture. Bake, uncovered, for 15-20 minutes or until heated through.

3. Meanwhile, in a small saucepan, melt cheese with milk. Drizzle cheese sauce over nachos.

Note: Wear disposable gloves when cutting hot peppers; the oils can burn exposed skin. Avoid touching your face.

BANANAS FOSTER CRUNCH MIX

Bananas Foster is one of my favorite desserts, so I came up with a crunchy snack mix inspired by the famous dish.
—**David Dahlman** Chatsworth, CA

Prep: 10 min. • **Cook:** 5 min.
Makes: 2½ quarts

     3   cups Honey Nut Chex
     3   cups Cinnamon Chex
    2¼   cups pecan halves
    1½   cups dried banana chips
     ⅓   cup butter, cubed
     ⅓   cup packed brown sugar
     ½   teaspoon ground cinnamon
     ½   teaspoon banana extract
     ½   teaspoon rum extract

1. Place first four ingredients in a large microwave-safe bowl. Place butter, brown sugar and cinnamon in a small microwave-safe bowl; microwave on high for 2 minutes, stirring once. Stir in extracts. Pour over cereal mixture; toss to coat.

2. Microwave cereal mixture on high for 3 minutes, stirring every minute. Spread onto baking sheets to cool. Store in an airtight container.

RISOTTO BALLS (ARANCINI)

My Italian grandma made these for me. I still ask for them when I visit her, and so do my children. These little rice balls freeze well, so I make them ahead of time.
—**Gretchen Whelan** San Francisco, CA

Prep: 35 min. • **Bake:** 25 min.
Makes: about 3 dozen

    1½   cups water
     1   cup uncooked arborio rice
     1   teaspoon salt
     2   large eggs, lightly beaten
     ⅔   cup sun-dried tomato pesto
     2   cups panko (Japanese) bread
         crumbs, divided
         Marinara sauce, warmed

1. Preheat oven to 375°. In a large saucepan, combine water, rice and salt; bring to a boil. Reduce heat; simmer, covered, 18-20 minutes or until liquid is absorbed and rice is tender. Let stand, covered, 10 minutes. Transfer to a large bowl; cool slightly. Add eggs and pesto; stir in 1 cup bread crumbs.

2. Place the remaining bread crumbs in a shallow bowl. Shape the rice mixture into 1¼-in. balls. Roll in bread crumbs, patting to help coating adhere. Place balls on greased 15x10x1-in. baking pans. Bake for 25-30 minutes or until golden brown. Serve with marinara sauce.

CRUNCHY ITALIAN SNACK MIX

Every time my son visits, he asks me to make a batch of this snack mix. It has become a requirement when we all sit down to play board games.
—**Sherry Little** Sherwood, AR

Prep: 10 min. • **Bake:** 30 min. + cooling
Makes: 2½ quarts

- 4 cups Rice Chex
- 4 cups Corn Chex
- 1 package (5 ounces) miniature sesame breadsticks
- 2 cups miniature cheddar cheese fish-shaped crackers
- ½ cup mixed nuts
- ½ cup butter, melted
- ¼ cup grated Parmesan cheese
- 3 tablespoons Italian salad dressing
- 1½ teaspoons Italian seasoning
- ½ teaspoon garlic salt

1. Preheat oven to 300°. In a large bowl, combine cereals, breadsticks, crackers and nuts. In a small bowl, mix butter, cheese, salad dressing, Italian seasoning and garlic salt. Drizzle over cereal mixture; toss to coat.

2. Spread in two greased 15x10x1-in. baking pans. Bake 30 minutes, stirring every 10 minutes. Cool completely in pans on wire racks. Store in an airtight container.

CHUNKY BLUE CHEESE DIP

Every time I make this quick dip, someone asks for the recipe. It only requires a few items, so it's a snap to put together. I often prepare the thick spread with Gorgonzola cheese and serve it with toasted pecans.
—**Sandy Schneider** Naperville, IL

Start to Finish: 15 min.
Makes: 12 servings

- 1 package (8 ounces) cream cheese, softened
- ⅓ cup sour cream
- ½ teaspoon white pepper
- ¼ to ½ teaspoon salt
- 1 cup crumbled blue cheese
- ⅓ cup minced fresh chives
  Toasted chopped pecans, optional
  Apple and pear slices

Beat first four ingredients until blended; gently stir in blue cheese and chives. Transfer to a serving bowl. If desired, sprinkle with pecans. Serve with apple and pear slices.

BRIE APPETIZERS WITH BACON-PLUM JAM

Among my friends, I'm known as the Pork Master because I love to cook just about every cut there is! These appetizers combine soft, mild Brie with a sweet-sour bacon jam that has a touch of Sriracha.
—**Rick Pascocello** New York, NY

Prep: 25 min. • **Cook:** 1¼ hours
Makes: 2½ dozen

- 1 pound bacon strips, chopped
- 1 cup thinly sliced sweet onion
- 1 shallot, finely chopped
- 5 garlic cloves, minced
- 1 cup brewed coffee
- ½ cup water
- ¼ cup cider vinegar

- ¼ cup pitted dried plums, coarsely chopped
- 3 tablespoons brown sugar
- 1 tablespoon maple syrup
- 1 tablespoon Sriracha Asian hot chili sauce
- ½ teaspoon pepper
- 30 slices Brie cheese (¼ inch thick)
- 30 slices French bread baguette (¼ inch thick), toasted

1. In a large skillet, cook bacon over medium heat until partially cooked but not crisp. Remove to paper towels with a slotted spoon; drain, reserving 1 tablespoon of drippings.

2. Add onion and shallot to drippings; cook and stir 5 minutes. Add garlic; cook 2 minutes longer. Stir in coffee, water, vinegar, plums, brown sugar, maple syrup, chili sauce and pepper. Bring to a boil. Stir in bacon. Reduce heat; simmer, uncovered, 1¼-1½ hours or until liquid is syrupy, stirring occasionally. Remove from heat. Cool to room temperature.

3. Transfer mixture to a food processor; pulse until the jam reaches the desired consistency. Place cheese slices on toasted baguette slices. Top each with 2 teaspoons of jam.

Super Snack Mixes

Crunchy and irresistible, a great snack mix is the perfect addition to a game day hangout, cocktail party or family movie night. All the better when the mix is homemade—you can make it your own! Sweet or savory, snack mixes make deliciously thoughtful holiday gifts, too.

CRABBY SNACK MIX

I love boiled Maryland crabs, as well as crab fries dipped in cheese. With those favorites in mind, I created a crunchy snack mix spiced with seafood seasoning. One handful is never enough!

—Karyn Gordon Cinnaminson, NJ

Start to Finish: 10 min.
Makes: 6 cups

- 2 cups Corn Chex
- 2 cups Wheat Chex
- 1 cup cheddar-flavored snack crackers
- 1 cup sourdough pretzel nuggets
- ¼ cup unsalted butter, melted
- 2 tablespoons seafood seasoning
- 1 tablespoon celery seed
- 1 tablespoon lemon-pepper seasoning
- ½ teaspoon dill weed

1. In a large microwave-safe bowl, combine cereals, crackers and pretzels. In a small bowl, combine the butter, seafood seasoning seasoning, celery seed, lemon-pepper and dill weed. Pour over cereal mixture; toss to coat.
2. Microwave on high 3 minutes, stirring three times. Spread onto a baking sheet to cool. Store in an airtight container.

SLOW COOKER SPICED MIXED NUTS

What slow cookers do for soups and stews, they'll do for mixed nuts, too. The scent of spices is delightful, and the nuts are delicious.

—Stephanie Loaiza Layton, UT

Prep: 15 min.
Cook: 1 hour 50 min. + cooling
Makes: 6 cups

- 1 large egg white
- 2 teaspoons vanilla extract
- 1 cup unblanched almonds
- 1 cup pecan halves
- 1 cup shelled walnuts
- 1 cup unsalted cashews
- 1 cup sugar
- 1 cup packed brown sugar
- 4 teaspoons ground cinnamon
- 2 teaspoons ground ginger
- 1 teaspoon ground nutmeg
- ½ teaspoon ground cloves
- ⅛ teaspoon salt
- 2 tablespoons water

1. In a large bowl, whisk egg white and vanilla until blended; stir in nuts. In a small bowl, mix sugars, spices and salt. Add to nut mixture and toss to coat.
2. Transfer to a greased 3-qt. slow cooker. Cook, covered, on high for 1½ hours, stirring every 15 minutes. Gradually stir in water. Cook, covered, on low for 20 minutes.
3. Spread onto waxed paper; cool completely. Store in airtight containers up to 1 week.

ISLAND VACATION PARTY MIX

What's not to love about this taste of the tropics? With a simple no-bake method, you'll be munching on this snack in no time flat.

—**Melissa Talbott** Peoria, IL

Start to Finish: 15 min.
Makes: 3 quarts

- 2½ **cups Corn Chex**
- 2½ **cups Rice Chex**
- 2 **cups macadamia nuts**
- ¼ **cup butter, cubed**
- 2 **tablespoons sugar**
- 2 **tablespoons corn syrup**
- 1 **cup sweetened shredded coconut**
- 1 **package (6 ounces) chopped dried pineapple**
- 1 **cup white baking chips**

1. In a large microwave-safe bowl, combine cereals and nuts; set aside. In a small microwave-safe bowl, combine butter, sugar and corn syrup. Microwave, uncovered, on high for 2 minutes, stirring once. Pour over the cereal mixture and toss to coat.
2. Microwave cereal mixture, uncovered, on high for 2 minutes, stirring once. Add coconut; cook 2 minutes longer, stirring once. Spread onto waxed paper to cool. Stir in pineapple and chips. Store in an airtight container.

CAJUN PARTY MIX

Salty snack mixes are perfect for parties, and this one is no exception. I also pack it in tins to give to friends and family. They all seem to love it, and it's so easy.

—**Twila Burkholder** Middleburg, PA

Prep: 10 min. • **Bake:** 35 min.
Makes: about 5 quarts

- 6 **cups miniature fish-shaped crackers**
- 6 **cups pretzel sticks**
- 3 **cups Rice Chex**
- 3 **cups Corn Chex**
- 1 **can (11½ ounces) mixed nuts**
- 1 **cup butter, melted**
- 1 **teaspoon garlic powder**
- ½ **to 1 teaspoon celery salt**
- ½ **teaspoon cayenne pepper**
- ⅛ **teaspoon hot pepper sauce**

1. Preheat oven to 250°. In a large roasting pan, combine the first five ingredients. Combine butter, garlic powder, celery salt, cayenne and pepper sauce; pour over the cereal mixture and stir to coat.
2. Bake, uncovered, for 35-40 minutes, stirring every 15 minutes. Let cool completely. Store in airtight containers.

BLACKBERRY LEMONADE

This special drink is perfect when blackberries are in season, but works well with frozen fruit, too. It has a tangy, refreshing flavor.

—**Rich Murray** Nevada, MO

Prep: 20 min. + chilling
Makes: about 1½ quarts

- 4 cups water, divided
- 1 cup sugar
- 1 cup lemon juice
- 1 tablespoon grated lemon peel
- 1 cup blackberries
- 1 to 2 drops blue food coloring, optional

1. In a large saucepan, bring 2 cups water and sugar to a boil. Boil for 2 minutes, stirring occasionally. Remove from the heat. Stir in lemon juice, lemon peel and the remaining water; cool slightly.

2. In a blender, combine 1 cup of the lemon mixture and the blackberries; cover and process until blended. Strain and discard seeds. Pour the blackberry mixture and the remaining lemon mixture into a pitcher; stir well. Add food coloring if desired. Refrigerate until chilled. Serve in chilled glasses over ice.

ARTICHOKE & SPINACH DIP PIZZA

When I have it in my pantry, I use garlic oil instead of regular olive oil to make this pizza. It adds a little something extra without overpowering the toppings.

—**Shelly L Bevington** Hermiston, OR

Start to Finish: 20 min.
Makes: 24 pieces

- 1 prebaked 12-inch pizza crust
- 1 tablespoon olive oil
- 1 cup spinach dip
- 1 cup shredded part-skim mozzarella cheese
- 1 jar (7½ ounces) marinated quartered artichoke hearts, drained
- ½ cup oil-packed sun-dried tomatoes, patted dry and chopped
- ¼ cup chopped red onion

1. Preheat oven to 450°. Place pizza crust on an ungreased pizza pan; brush with oil. Spread spinach dip over top. Sprinkle with cheese, artichokes, tomatoes and onion.

2. Bake for 8-10 minutes or until the cheese is melted and edges are lightly browned. Cut into squares.

EASY BUFFALO CHICKEN DIP

Everyone will devour this savory and delicious dip with shredded chicken throughout. The spicy kick makes it perfect football-watching food.
—**Janice Foltz** Hershey, PA

Start to Finish: 30 min.
Makes: 4 cups

- 1 package (8 ounces) reduced-fat cream cheese
- 1 cup (8 ounces) reduced-fat sour cream
- ½ cup Louisiana-style hot sauce
- 3 cups shredded cooked chicken breast
  Assorted crackers

1. Preheat oven to 350°. In a large bowl, beat cream cheese, sour cream and hot sauce until smooth; stir in chicken.
2. Transfer to an 8-in. square baking dish coated with cooking spray. Cover and bake for 18-22 minutes or until heated through. Serve warm with crackers.

MEXICAN SHRIMP COCKTAIL

It's up to you how to enjoy this cocktail—eat it with a spoon as a chilled soup, or use tortilla chips or crackers for scooping.
—**Erin Moreno** Arcadia, WI

Prep: 20 min. + chilling
Makes: 12 servings (¾ cup each)

- 2 medium tomatoes, seeded and finely chopped
- 1 medium onion, finely chopped
- ½ cup chopped fresh cilantro
- 1 tablespoon grated lime peel
- 1 teaspoon salt
- 1 bottle (12½ ounces) mandarin natural flavor soda
- 1½ cups Clamato juice
- ¼ cup lime juice
- ¼ cup ketchup
- 1½ pounds peeled and deveined cooked shrimp (100-150 per pound)
- 2 avocados, finely chopped
  Tortilla chips (optional)

1. In a large bowl, combine the first five ingredients. Stir in soda, Clamato juice, lime juice and ketchup. Add shrimp. Refrigerate, covered, at least 2 hours.
2. Just before serving, add avocados. Serve with tortilla chips, if desired.

FREEZE IT BACON-CHEDDAR POTATO CROQUETTES

Instead of throwing out leftover mashed potatoes, use them to make croquettes. The little baked balls are yummy with ranch dressing, barbecue sauce or Dijon mayonnaise for dipping.

—**Pamela Shank** Parkersburg, WV

Prep: 20 min. + chilling • **Bake:** 20 min.
Makes: about 5 dozen

- 4 cups cold mashed potatoes
  (with added milk and butter)
- 6 bacon strips, cooked and crumbled
- ½ cup shredded cheddar cheese
- 2 large eggs, lightly beaten
- ¼ cup sour cream
- 1 tablespoon minced chives
- ½ teaspoon salt
- ¼ teaspoon pepper
- 40 Ritz crackers, crushed
- ¼ cup butter, melted
- 1 teaspoon paprika
  Barbecue sauce, Dijon-mayonnaise
  blend or ranch salad dressing

1. In a large bowl, combine the first eight ingredients. Shape mixture by tablespoonfuls into balls. Roll balls in cracker crumbs. Place on parchment paper-lined baking sheets. Cover and refrigerate for 2 hours or overnight.

2. Combine butter and paprika; drizzle over croquettes. Bake at 375° until golden brown, 18-20 minutes. Serve with dipping sauce of your choice.

Freeze option: Prepare croquettes as directed, omitting chilling step. Transfer to waxed paper-lined baking sheets. Prepare butter mixture; drizzle over croquettes. Cover and freeze until firm. Transfer to resealable plastic freezer bags; return to freezer. Bake as directed, increasing time to 20-25 minutes.

WHITE CHRISTMAS SANGRIA

This fruity sparkling sangria is alcohol-free, so everyone in your family can feel like a VIP!

—**Taste of Home** Test Kitchen

Start to Finish: 10 min.
Makes: 21 servings (3¾ quarts)

    6 cups white cranberry juice, chilled
    ¾ cup thawed lemonade concentrate
    3 bottles (25.40 ounces each)
       sparkling grape juice
       Pomegranate seeds and sliced
          grapefruit, oranges and kiwi,
          optional

Combine cranberry juice and lemonade concentrate in a punch bowl; pour in sparkling grape juice. If desired, add pomegranate seeds and sliced fruit. Serve immediately.

ARTICHOKE CAPRESE PLATTER

I dressed up the classic Italian trio of mozzarella, tomatoes and basil with marinated artichokes. It looks so yummy set out on a buffet! Fresh mozzarella is the key to its great taste.

—**Margaret Wilson** San Bernardino, CA

Start to Finish: 15 min.
Makes: 12 servings

    2 jars (7½ ounces each) marinated
       artichoke hearts
    2 tablespoons red wine vinegar
    2 tablespoons olive oil
    6 plum tomatoes, sliced
    1 pound fresh mozzarella cheese,
       sliced
    2 cups loosely packed fresh basil
       leaves
       Coarsely ground pepper, optional

1. Drain artichokes, reserving ½ cup marinade. In a small bowl, whisk the vinegar, oil and reserved marinade.
2. On a large serving platter, arrange the artichokes, tomatoes, mozzarella cheese and basil. Drizzle with vinaigrette. If desired, sprinkle with coarsely ground black pepper.
Note: Fresh mozzarella can be found in the deli section of most grocery stores.

CREAMY CARAMEL MOCHA

Indulge in a coffeehouse-quality drink at Christmastime or any time at all. With whipped cream and a butterscotch drizzle, this mocha treat will perk up even the sleepiest person at the table.

—*Taste of Home* Test Kitchen

Start to Finish: 20 min.
Makes: 6 servings

- ½ cup heavy whipping cream
- 1 tablespoon confectioners' sugar
- 1 teaspoon vanilla extract, divided
- ¼ cup Dutch-processed cocoa
- 1½ cups half-and-half cream
- 4 cups hot strong brewed coffee
- ½ cup caramel flavoring syrup
  Butterscotch-caramel ice cream topping

1. In a small bowl, beat whipping cream until it begins to thicken. Add confectioners' sugar and ½ teaspoon vanilla; beat until stiff peaks form.

2. In a large saucepan over medium heat, whisk cocoa and half-and-half cream until smooth. Heat until bubbles form around the sides of pan. Whisk in coffee, caramel syrup and remaining vanilla. Top each serving with whipped cream; drizzle with butterscotch topping.

To prepare in a slow cooker: Prepare whipped cream as directed. Whisk together cocoa, half-and-half, coffee, caramel syrup and the remaining vanilla in a 3-qt. slow cooker. Cook, covered, for 2-3 hours or until heated through. Serve as directed.

Note: This recipe was tested with Torani brand flavoring syrup. Look for it in the coffee section.

BACON CHEESE SPREAD

Each year, I share Christmas cheer by setting up a buffet at my family's hardware store. This cheese spread is always a big hit!
—**Sharon Bickett** Chester, SC

Start to Finish: 15 min.
Makes: 4 cups

- 1 package (12 ounces) bacon strips, chopped
- ½ cup chopped pecans
- 4 cups shredded sharp cheddar cheese
- 2 cups mayonnaise
- 1 small onion, chopped
- 2 tablespoons finely chopped sweet red pepper
- ⅛ teaspoon cayenne pepper
  Assorted crackers

Cook bacon until crisp; drain. Meanwhile, in a large bowl, combine the next six ingredients. Stir in the bacon. Serve with crackers.

BAKED CREAMY SPINACH DIP

I'm a fan of classic dishes but also like to tweak them to suit my family's tastes. Here's my take on cheesy spinach dip.
—**Jenn Tidwell** Fair Oaks, CA

Prep: 25 min. • **Bake:** 30 min.
Makes: 14 servings

- 2 packages (10 ounces each) frozen chopped spinach, thawed
- 1 tablespoon butter
- 2 garlic cloves, minced
- 1 tablespoon all-purpose flour
- 1 can (12 ounces) evaporated milk
- ½ cup grated Parmesan cheese, divided
- ¼ cup cream cheese
- ¼ cup ricotta cheese
- ¼ teaspoon ground nutmeg
- ½ teaspoon salt
- ¼ teaspoon pepper
  Bagel chips

1. Preheat oven to 350°. Place spinach in a colander over a bowl; squeeze dry, reserving 1 cup spinach liquid.
2. In a large saucepan, heat butter over medium heat. Add garlic; cook 1 minute. Stir in flour until blended; gradually whisk in milk and reserved spinach liquid. Bring to a boil, stirring constantly; cook and stir 2-3 minutes or until thickened. Stir in ¼ cup Parmesan cheese, cream cheese, ricotta cheese, seasonings and spinach; cook and stir until blended.
3. Transfer to a 1½-qt. baking dish. Bake 25-30 minutes or until bubbly and top is lightly browned. Remove from oven; top with remaining Parmesan cheese. Bake 4-5 minutes longer or until cheese is melted. Serve with bagel chips.

PICKLED PEPPERONCINI DEVILED EGGS

It's hard to resist these adorable deviled eggs on our buffet table. The avocado filling has pepperoncini and cilantro for extra zip.
—**Carmell Childs** Clawson, UT

Start to Finish: 30 min.
Makes: 1 dozen

- 6 hard-boiled large eggs
- 1 jar (16 ounces) garlic and dill pepperoncini
- 1 medium ripe avocado, peeled and pitted
- 1 tablespoon minced fresh cilantro, divided
- ¼ teaspoon salt
- ⅛ teaspoon pepper
- 1 tablespoon minced sweet red pepper
- ¼ teaspoon chili powder

1. Cut eggs lengthwise in half. Remove yolks, reserving whites. Mash yolks. Stir in 1 teaspoon minced garlic from the pepperoncini jar and 2 teaspoons pepperoncini juice. Add 3 tablespoons minced pepperoncini and the whole avocado; mash with a fork until smooth. Stir in 2 teaspoons cilantro, salt and pepper.
2. Cut a small hole in the tip of a pastry bag or in a corner of a food-safe plastic bag; insert a medium star tip. Transfer avocado mixture to bag. Pipe into egg whites. Sprinkle with minced red pepper, chili powder and remaining cilantro. Cut open and seed one larger pepperoncini; slice and place on top of avocado mixture. Refrigerate, covered, until serving.
Note: If serving at the holidays, pipe avocado mixture upward, to resemble Christmas trees, and place pepperoncini slices to resemble ornaments.

Side Dishes & Condiments

Sweet Onion Pie, Fried Mashed Potato Balls and Garden Risotto...nothing rounds out a hearty menu like side dishes loaded with comforting appeal. Here you'll find the perfect accompaniment to any entree as well as lip-smacking jams, jellies, relishes and flavored butters that make meals extra special.

CHUNKY FRUIT AND NUT RELISH

I tuck a glass jar of this colorful condiment alongside the fudge and cookies in my holiday baskets. Packed with pecans, it's delicious served with ham or poultry.
—**Donna Brockett** Kingfisher, OK

Prep: 5 min. • **Cook:** 10 min. + chilling
Makes: 6 cups

- 2 packages (12 ounces each) fresh or frozen cranberries
- 1½ cups sugar
- 1 cup orange juice
- 1 can (15¼ ounces) sliced peaches, drained and cut up
- 1 cup chopped pecans
- ¾ cup pineapple tidbits
- ½ cup golden raisins

1. In a large saucepan, bring cranberries, sugar and orange juice to a boil, stirring occasionally. Reduce the heat; simmer, uncovered, for 8-10 minutes or until the cranberries pop.

2. Remove from heat; stir in peaches, pecans, pineapple and raisins. Cool. Cover and refrigerate for at least 3 hours.

Contest Winner

PARMESAN ROASTED BROCCOLI

Sure, it's simple and healthy but, oh, is this roasted broccoli delicious! Cutting the stalks into tall trees turns this ordinary veggie into a standout side dish.
—**Holly Sander** Wellesley, MA

Start to Finish: 30 min.
Makes: 4 servings

- 2 small broccoli crowns (about 8 ounces each)
- 3 tablespoons olive oil
- ½ teaspoon salt
- ½ teaspoon pepper
- ¼ teaspoon crushed red pepper flakes
- 4 garlic cloves, thinly sliced
- 2 tablespoons grated Parmesan cheese
- 1 teaspoon grated lemon zest

1. Preheat oven to 425°. Cut broccoli crowns into quarters from top to bottom. Drizzle with oil; sprinkle with seasonings. Place in a parchment paper-lined 15x10x1-in. pan.

2. Roast until crisp-tender, about 10-12 minutes. Sprinkle with garlic; roast for 5 minutes. Sprinkle with cheese; roast until cheese is melted and stalks of broccoli are tender, 2-4 minutes more. Sprinkle with lemon zest.

SUMMER VEGETABLE COBBLER

Here's a comforting vegetarian side that uses a lot of garden produce. Try different squashes like pattypan and crookneck for the zucchini.

—**Elisabeth Larsen** Pleasant Grove, UT

Prep: 40 min. • **Bake:** 25 min.
Makes: 4 servings

- 2 tablespoons butter
- 3 small zucchini, sliced
- 1 small sweet red pepper, finely chopped
- 1 small onion, finely chopped
- 2 garlic cloves, minced
- 2 tablespoons all-purpose flour
- 1 cup 2% milk
- ½ teaspoon salt
- ¼ teaspoon pepper

BISCUIT TOPPING

- 1 cup all-purpose flour
- 1 teaspoon baking powder
- ½ teaspoon salt
- 3 tablespoons cold butter
- ¼ cup shredded Parmesan cheese
- 3 tablespoons minced fresh basil
- ⅔ cup 2% milk

1. Preheat oven to 400°. In a large skillet, heat butter over medium-high heat. Add the zucchini, red pepper and onion; cook and stir 10-12 minutes or until zucchini is crisp-tender. Add the garlic; cook for 1 minute longer.

2. In a small bowl, whisk flour, milk, salt and pepper; stir into the vegetables. Bring to a boil, stirring constantly; cook and stir 2-3 minutes or until sauce is thickened. Spoon vegetable mixture into a greased 8-in. square baking dish.

3. For topping, in a small bowl, whisk flour, baking powder and salt. Cut in butter until mixture resembles coarse crumbs. Stir in cheese and basil. Add milk; stir just until moistened. Drop by rounded tablespoonfuls over filling. Bake 25-30 minutes or until the filling is bubbly and the biscuits are golden brown.

SWEET ONION PIE

Full of sweet onions, this creamy pie makes a scrumptious addition to a brunch buffet. By using less butter to cook the onions and substituting lighter ingredients, I cut calories and fat from this tasty dish.

—**Barbara Reese** Catawissa, PA

Prep: 35 min. • **Bake:** 30 min.
Makes: 8 servings

- 2 sweet onions, halved and sliced
- 1 tablespoon butter
- 1 frozen deep-dish pie shell
- 1 cup egg substitute
- 1 cup fat-free evaporated milk
- 1 teaspoon salt
- ¼ teaspoon pepper

1. Preheat oven to 450°. In a large nonstick skillet, cook onions in butter over medium-low heat until very tender, 30 minutes. Meanwhile, line an unpricked pastry shell with a double thickness of heavy-duty foil.

2. Bake for 6 minutes. Remove foil; cool on a wire rack. Reduce heat to 425°.

3. Spoon onions into the pastry shell. In a small bowl, whisk the egg substitute, milk, salt and pepper; pour over onions. Bake until a knife inserted in the center comes out clean, 30-35 minutes. Let stand for 5-10 minutes before cutting.

Contest Winner

SPANAKOPITA MASHED POTATOES

I learned to cook by watching my mom in the kitchen. This was the first recipe I created by myself, and it's turned out to be my favorite! By not peeling the potatoes, you can save on prep time.
—**Ashley Levy** Clarksville, MD

Prep: 10 min. • **Cook:** 25 min.
Makes: 6 servings

  6 medium red potatoes, quartered
  1 package (6 ounces) fresh baby spinach
  ¼ cup 2% milk
  1 tablespoon butter
  ½ teaspoon salt
  ½ teaspoon pepper
  ¾ cup crumbled feta cheese

1. Place potatoes in a large saucepan and cover with water. Bring to a boil. Reduce heat; cover and cook for 15-20 minutes or until tender.
2. Meanwhile, in another large saucepan, bring ½ in. of water to a boil. Add the spinach; cover and boil for 3-5 minutes or until wilted. Drain and coarsely chop; keep warm.
3. Drain potatoes and return to the saucepan. Add milk, butter, salt and pepper; mash until smooth. Fold in cheese and spinach.

FREEZE IT SWEET & TANGY FREEZER PICKLES

Now you can have all the goodness of crunchy sweet-and-sour pickles without going to the trouble of canning them. A batch of these puckery slices can keep in the freezer for up to six months—but they never last that long at my house!
—**Jean Vance** Charlotte, NC

Prep: 20 min. + chilling
Cook: 5 min. + freezing
Makes: 32 servings

  2 pounds pickling cucumbers (about 8 to 10 medium), trimmed and thinly sliced
  3 medium onions, thinly sliced
  1 large green pepper, chopped
  3 tablespoons salt, divided
  2 cups sugar
  1 cup white vinegar
  3 teaspoons celery seed

1. In a large glass or stainless steel bowl, toss vegetables with 2 tablespoons salt. Cover with crushed ice and mix well. Refrigerate, covered, 8 hours. Drain and rinse; drain well. Return to bowl.
2. In a saucepan, combine sugar, vinegar, celery seed and remaining salt. Bring to a boil; cook and stir 1 minute. Pour over cucumber mixture; stir to combine.
3. Transfer to freezer containers or canning jars, leaving 1 in. of headspace; cool completely. Freeze, covered, up to 6 months.
4. To use, thaw in refrigerator before serving. Store thawed pickles in the refrigerator up to 2 weeks.

Contest Winner

CINNAMON-ORANGE HONEY BUTTER

This sweet and tasty butter spread makes wonderful use of our local honey. It is so easy to mix together and you will receive many compliments!
—**Mary Bates** Cleveland, OH

Start to Finish: 5 min. • **Makes:** ¾ cup
- ½ cup butter, softened
- ¼ cup honey
- 1 teaspoon grated orange peel
- ½ teaspoon ground cinnamon

In a small bowl, combine all ingredients. Serve immediately. Refrigerate leftovers.
Maple Butter: To the butter, mix in 2 tablespoons maple syrup, 1 teaspoon minced fresh parsley and dash pepper.
Rosemary Lemon Butter: To the butter, mix in 4 teaspoons grated lemon peel, 4 teaspoons minced fresh rosemary and dash pepper.
Herb Butter: To butter, mix 2 teaspoons minced fresh chives, 2 teaspoons minced fresh parsley, 2 teaspoons minced fresh basil, ⅛ teaspoon salt, ⅛ teaspoon paprika and dash pepper.
Curry Butter: To the butter, mix in 1½ teaspoons curry powder, ½ teaspoon ground cumin and ¼ teaspoon crushed red pepper flakes.

SAUSAGE SPINACH BAKE

This delicious recipe, which uses a packaged stuffing mix, was given to me some years ago by a friend. Serve it with a salad and bread of your choice for a filling lunch or dinner. It's so versatile, you can even serve it at brunch.
—**Kathleen Grant** Swan Lake, MT

Prep: 20 min. • **Bake:** 40 min.
Makes: 12 servings

- 1 package (6 ounces) savory herb-flavored stuffing mix
- ½ pound bulk pork sausage
- ¼ cup chopped green onions
- ½ teaspoon minced garlic
- 1 package (10 ounces) frozen chopped spinach, thawed and squeezed dry
- 1½ cups shredded Monterey Jack cheese
- 1½ cups half-and-half cream
- 3 large eggs
- 2 tablespoons grated Parmesan cheese

1. Preheat oven to 400°. Prepare stuffing according to package directions. Meanwhile, crumble sausage into a large skillet. Add onions; cook over medium heat until meat is no longer pink. Add garlic; cook 1 minute longer. Drain.
2. In a large bowl, combine the stuffing, sausage mixture and spinach. Transfer to a greased 11x7-in. baking dish; sprinkle with Monterey Jack cheese. In a small bowl, combine cream and eggs; pour over the sausage mixture.
3. Bake for 35-40 minutes or until a thermometer reads 160°. Sprinkle with Parmesan cheese; bake 5 minutes longer or until bubbly.

CHEESE FONDUE MAC & CHEESE

When my husband was a missionary kid in Switzerland, his mom learned to make cheese fondue. I combined that favorite with one of mine—macaroni and cheese!
—**Kathy Lee** Elk Rapids, MI

Prep: 20 min. • **Cook:** 25 min.
Makes: 8 servings

- ¼ cup panko (Japanese) bread crumbs
- 1½ teaspoons plus 1 tablespoon olive oil, divided
- 4 ounces sliced pancetta, finely chopped
- 3 cups uncooked elbow macaroni (about 12 ounces)
- 3 tablespoons butter
- 1 shallot, finely chopped
- 1 garlic clove, minced
- 3 tablespoons all-purpose flour
- ½ teaspoon salt
- ¼ teaspoon pepper
  Dash ground nutmeg
- 1½ cups 2% milk
- ½ cup white wine or chicken broth
- 1 cup shredded Emmenthaler or Swiss cheese
- 1 cup shredded Gruyere or Swiss cheese

1. In a small skillet, toss bread crumbs with 1½ teaspoons oil; cook and stir over medium-high until golden brown. Remove from pan.

2. In same skillet, heat remaining oil over medium heat. Add pancetta; cook until crisp, stirring occasionally. Remove with a slotted spoon; drain on paper towels.

3. Cook the macaroni according to the package directions. Meanwhile, in a large saucepan, heat butter over medium heat. Add shallot and garlic; cook and stir for 1-2 minutes or until tender. Stir in flour and seasonings until blended; gradually whisk in milk and wine. Bring to a boil, stirring constantly; cook and stir for 2-3 minutes or until thickened. Stir in cheeses until melted.

4. Drain macaroni and add to sauce. Add pancetta; toss to combine. Sprinkle with toasted bread crumbs.

VIDALIA ONION RELISH

Burgers and brats get the star treatment with this sweet onion topping. Bourbon adds a lovely caramel note, and the crushed pepper flakes turn up the heat.
—**Janet Roth** Tempe, AZ

Prep: 1 hour • **Cook:** 15 min.
Makes: 3 cups

- 4 large sweet onions, chopped
- 2 tablespoons canola oil
- 3 garlic cloves, minced
- ⅓ cup bourbon
- 4 plum tomatoes, peeled, seeded and chopped
- ½ cup golden raisins
- ¼ cup sugar
- ¼ cup packed dark brown sugar
- ¼ cup cider vinegar
- 1 teaspoon mustard seed
- ½ teaspoon salt
- ½ teaspoon ground turmeric
- ½ teaspoon ground mustard
- ½ teaspoon crushed red pepper flakes
- ¼ teaspoon pepper
  Cooked sausage or meat of your choice

1. In a large saucepan, cook onions in oil over medium heat 40-45 minutes or until onions are golden brown, stirring occasionally. Add garlic; cook 1 minute longer. Remove from heat. Add bourbon, stirring to loosen browned bits from pan.
2. Stir in remaining ingredients; bring to a boil. Reduce heat; simmer, uncovered, 15-20 minutes or until thickened. Store in airtight containers in the refrigerator up to 1 week. Serve with sausage or other meat.

GARDEN RISOTTO

Celebrate spring with a trio of the season's best—peas, asparagus and spinach—tucked inside a creamy white wine risotto. It's perfect paired with pork loin.
—**Kendra Doss** Colorado Springs, CO

Prep: 20 min. • **Cook:** 25 min.
Makes: 8 servings

- ½ pound fresh asparagus, trimmed and cut into ¾-inch pieces
- 4½ cups reduced-sodium chicken broth
- 1 medium onion, chopped
- 2 teaspoons olive oil
- 1½ cups uncooked arborio rice
- ½ cup dry white wine or additional reduced-sodium chicken broth
- ½ teaspoon salt
- ¼ teaspoon pepper
- 3 cups fresh baby spinach
- 1 cup frozen peas
- ¼ cup grated Parmesan cheese

1. Place asparagus in a steamer basket; place in a small saucepan over 1 in. of water. Bring to a boil; cover and steam for 2-3 minutes or until crisp-tender. Set aside.
2. Meanwhile, in a small saucepan, heat broth and keep warm. In a large nonstick skillet, saute onion in oil until tender. Add rice; cook and stir for 2-3 minutes. Reduce heat; stir in the wine, salt and pepper. Cook and stir until all the liquid is absorbed.
3. Add heated broth, ½ cup at a time, stirring constantly. Allow the liquid to absorb between additions. Cook just until risotto is creamy and the rice is almost tender. (Cooking time is about 20 minutes.)
4. Add the spinach, peas, cheese and reserved asparagus; cook and stir until heated through. Serve immediately.

FRIED MASHED POTATO BALLS

The key to this recipe is to use mashed potatoes that are firm from chilling. Serve the potato balls with sour cream or ranch salad dressing on the side.
—***Taste of Home** Test Kitchen*

Prep: 25 min. + standing
Cook: 5 min./batch
Makes: 6 servings

- 2 cups cold mashed potatoes
- 1 large egg, lightly beaten
- ¾ cup shredded cheddar cheese
- ½ cup chopped green onions
- ¼ cup real bacon bits
- ½ cup dry bread crumbs
   Oil for frying

1. Place mashed potatoes in a large bowl; let stand at room temperature for 30 minutes. Stir in the egg, cheese, onions and bacon bits. Shape into 1-in. balls; roll in bread crumbs. Let stand for 15 minutes.
2. In an electric skillet, heat 1 in. of oil to 375°. Fry potato balls, a few at a time, for 2½ to 3 minutes or until golden brown. Remove with a slotted spoon to paper towels to drain. Serve warm.

END-OF-SUMMER RELISH

My family loves this relish and wants it on the table for every meal. My garden can barely keep up with demand!
—**Vivian Conner** Sebring, FL

Prep: 45 min. • **Cook:** 1 hour + chilling
Makes: 12 cups

- 4 each medium green, sweet red and yellow peppers, cut into 1-inch pieces
- 4 medium onions, quartered
- 4 medium carrots, cut into 2-inch pieces
- 2 medium cucumbers, peeled and cut into 2-inch pieces
- 1 small head cabbage, cut into wedges
- 2¾ cups white vinegar
- 1 cup sugar
- ¾ cup water
- 3 tablespoons salt
- 1 tablespoon mustard seed
- 1 tablespoon celery seed
   Cooked sausage or meat of your choice

1. In a food processor, cover and process the vegetables in batches until they are finely chopped. Drain the vegetables and discard liquid.
2. In a stockpot, bring vinegar, sugar, water, salt, mustard seed and celery seed to a boil. Add vegetables; return to a boil. Reduce heat; simmer, uncovered, 1 hour or until thickened. Store in airtight containers in refrigerator up to 1 week. Serve with sausage or other meat.

GOLDEN BEET CURRY RISOTTO WITH CRISPY BEET GREENS

Move over, main dish, this vibrant side will steal the show! When I found golden beets at the farmers market, I knew they'd be perfect in my risotto. Don't forget the crispy beet greens...they're amazing!

—**Merry Graham** Newhall, CA

Prep: 30 min. • **Cook:** 50 min.
Makes: 6 servings

- 3 medium fresh golden beets and beet greens
- 3 tablespoons melted coconut oil, divided
- ¾ teaspoon sea salt, divided
- 5 cups reduced-sodium chicken broth
- 1 cup chopped leeks (white portion only)
- 1 teaspoon curry powder
- 1 teaspoon garlic salt
- 1 cup medium pearl barley
- ½ cup white wine or unsweetened apple juice
- 1 cup grated Manchego cheese
- 3 tablespoons lemon juice (Meyer lemons preferred)
- 4 teaspoons grated lemon zest, divided
- ¼ teaspoon coarsely ground pepper
- ¼ cup chopped fresh parsley
  Lemon slices

1. Preheat oven to 350°. Wash and trim the beet greens, removing the stems; dry with paper towels. Place the greens in a single layer on parchment paper-lined baking sheets. Brush with 1 tablespoon coconut oil; sprinkle with ¼ teaspoon sea salt. Bake until dry and crisp, about 15-18 minutes. Set aside.

2. Meanwhile, peel and dice beets. In a large saucepan, bring chicken broth to a boil. Add beets. Reduce heat; simmer, covered, until beets are tender, 15-18 minutes. Remove beets with a slotted spoon. Keep broth hot.

3. In another large saucepan, heat the remaining coconut oil over medium heat. Add leeks; cook and stir 2-3 minutes. Add curry powder, garlic salt and the remaining sea salt; cook, stirring, until leeks are tender, 2-3 minutes. Increase heat to medium-high. Add the barley; stir constantly until lightly toasted, about 2-3 minutes. Add the wine; stir until the liquid has evaporated.

4. Add enough broth, about 1 cup, to cover barley. Reduce heat to medium; cook and stir until broth is absorbed. Add remaining broth, ½ cup at a time, cooking and stirring until broth is absorbed after each addition. Stir in beets with last addition of broth. Cook until barley is tender but firm to the bite and risotto is creamy, 25-30 minutes.

5. Remove from heat. Stir in cheese, lemon juice, 2½ teaspoons grated lemon zest and pepper. Transfer to a serving dish. Sprinkle with parsley and remaining lemon zest. Serve with crispy beet greens and lemon slices.

Jams & Jellies

Think of it as summer in a jar! Capture delicious fruits and berries at their peak flavor and preserve them year round. Keep these sweet spreads in your pantry to brighten up the winter months, or give them away—a homemade treat makes the perfect personal gift.

THREE-BERRY JAM

I sold jars of this sweet berry jam at craft fairs. It's a wonderful way to preserve summer gems.
—**Bernadette Colvin** Tomball, TX

Prep: 15 min. • **Process:** 10 min. + standing
Makes: 9 pints and 1 half-pint

- 4 cups fresh blueberries
- 3 cups fresh strawberries
- 2 cups fresh raspberries
- ¼ cup bottled lemon juice
- 2 packages (1¾ ounces each) powdered fruit pectin
- 7 cups sugar

1. In a large saucepan, combine berries and lemon juice; crush slightly. Stir in pectin. Bring to a full rolling boil over high heat, stirring constantly. Stir in sugar; return to a full rolling boil. Boil and stir for 1 minute.

2. Remove from the heat; skim off foam. Ladle hot mixture into nine hot pint jars and one hot half-pint jar, leaving ¼-in. headspace. Remove air bubbles and adjust headspace, if necessary, by adding hot mixture. Wipe rims. Center lids on jars; screw on bands until fingertip tight.

3. Place jars into canner with simmering water, ensuring that they are completely covered with water. Bring to a boil; process for 10 minutes. Remove jars and cool.

Note: The processing time listed is for altitudes of 1,000 feet or less. Add 1 minute to the processing time for each 1,000 feet of additional altitude.

CARAMEL APPLE JAM

The flavors of apples, brown sugar, cinnamon and nutmeg come together in this spreadable treat. The jam is a must-have at our breakfast table.
—**Robert Atwood** West Wareham, MA

Prep: 30 min. • **Process:** 10 min.
Makes: 7 half-pints

- 6 cups diced peeled apples (⅛-inch cubes)
- ½ cup water
- ½ teaspoon butter
- ½ teaspoon ground cinnamon
- ¼ teaspoon ground nutmeg
- 1 package (1¾ ounces) powdered fruit pectin
- 3 cups sugar
- 2 cups packed brown sugar

1. In a Dutch oven, combine the apples, water, butter, cinnamon and nutmeg. Cook and stir over low heat until apples are tender. Stir in pectin. Bring to a full rolling boil over high heat, stirring constantly. Stir in sugar; return to a full rolling boil. Boil and stir 1 minute.

2. Remove from heat; skim off foam. Ladle hot mixture into seven hot half-pint jars, leaving ¼-in. headspace. Remove air bubbles and adjust headspace, if necessary, by adding hot mixture. Wipe rims. Center lids on jars; screw on bands until fingertip tight.

3. Place jars into canner with simmering water, ensuring that they are completely covered with water. Bring to a boil; process for 10 minutes. Remove jars and cool.

Note: The processing time listed is for altitudes of 1,000 feet or less. Add 1 minute to the processing time for each 1,000 feet of additional altitude.

CARROT CAKE JAM

For a change of pace from berry jams, try this distinctive option. Spread on a bagel with cream cheese, it tastes almost as good as real carrot cake!

—Rachelle Stratton Rock Springs, WY

Prep: 45 min. • **Process:** 5 min.
Makes: 8 half-pints

- 1 can (20 ounces) unsweetened crushed pineapple, undrained
- 1½ cups shredded carrots
- 1½ cups chopped peeled ripe pears
- 3 tablespoons lemon juice
- 1 teaspoon ground cinnamon
- ¼ teaspoon ground cloves
- ¼ teaspoon ground nutmeg
- 1 package (1¾ ounces) powdered fruit pectin
- 6½ cups sugar

1. Place first seven ingredients in a large saucepan; bring to a boil. Reduce heat; simmer, covered, until pears are tender, 15-20 minutes, stirring occasionally. Stir in pectin. Bring to a full rolling boil over high heat, stirring constantly. Stir in the sugar; return to a full rolling boil. Boil and stir for 1 minute.

2. Remove from heat; skim off foam. Ladle hot mixture into eight hot sterilized half-pint jars, leaving ¼-in. headspace. Remove air bubbles and adjust the headspace, if necessary, by adding hot mixture. Wipe rims. Center lids on jars; screw on bands until fingertip tight.

3. Place jars into canner with simmering water, ensuring that they are completely covered with water. Bring to a boil; process for 5 minutes. Remove the jars and cool.

Note: The processing time listed is for altitudes of 1,000 feet or less. Add 1 minute to the processing time for each 1,000 feet of additional altitude.

Carrot Cake Jam

FREEZE IT RASPBERRY RHUBARB JAM

I love making and enjoying this jam, but I usually end up giving most of it away! It's always a well-received gift.

—LaVonne Van Hoff Rockwell City, IA

Prep: 5 min. + chilling
Cook: 35 min. + chilling
Makes: 6 cups

- 6 cups sliced fresh or frozen rhubarb
- 4 cups sugar
- 1 package (6 ounces) raspberry gelatin
- 1 can (21 ounces) raspberry pie filling

1. In a large saucepan, combine the rhubarb and sugar; cover and refrigerate it overnight.

2. Place saucepan over medium heat; bring to a boil. Reduce heat; simmer, uncovered, for 30-35 minutes or until the rhubarb is tender. Meanwhile, rinse six 1-cup plastic containers and lids with boiling water. Dry thoroughly.

3. Stir in gelatin and pie filling into the rhubarb mixture. Bring to a boil. Remove from heat; cool.

4. Fill all containers to within ½ in. of tops. Wipe off top edges of containers; immediately cover with lids. Refrigerate up to 3 weeks or freeze up to 1 year. Thaw jam in refrigerator before serving.

LOADED RED POTATO CASSEROLE

The flavor of this potato casserole reminds me of the potato skins restaurants offer as an appetizer.
—**Charlane Gathy** Lexington, KY

Prep: 25 min. • **Bake:** 20 min.
Makes: 8 servings

- 16 small red potatoes (about 1¾ pounds)
- ½ cup 2% milk
- ¼ cup butter, cubed
- ½ teaspoon pepper
- ⅛ teaspoon salt
- 1½ cups shredded cheddar cheese, divided
- ½ cup crumbled cooked bacon
- 1 cup (8 ounces) sour cream
- 2 tablespoons minced fresh chives

1. Preheat oven to 350°. Place potatoes in a 6-qt. stockpot; add water to cover. Bring to a boil. Reduce the heat; cook, uncovered, until tender, 15-20 minutes. Drain; return to pot.

2. Mash potatoes, gradually adding milk, butter, pepper and salt. Spread into a greased 13x9-in. baking dish; sprinkle with 1 cup cheese and bacon. Dollop with sour cream; sprinkle with chives and the remaining cheese.

3. Bake, uncovered, until heated through and cheese is melted, 20-25 minutes.

CREAMY SKILLET NOODLES WITH PEAS

I've made this creamy noodle dish for years. Since kids and adults go for it, I keep the ingredients on hand at all times.
—**Anita Groff** Perkiomenville, PA

Start to Finish: 25 min.
Makes: 6 servings

- ¼ cup butter, cubed
- 2 tablespoons canola oil
- 5 cups uncooked fine egg noodles
- 2½ cups frozen peas (about 10 ounces)
- 2½ cups chicken broth
- 1 cup half-and-half cream
- ½ teaspoon salt
- ¼ teaspoon pepper

In a large skillet, heat butter and oil over medium heat. Add noodles; cook and stir 2-3 minutes or until lightly browned. Stir in peas, broth, cream, salt and pepper. Bring to a boil. Reduce heat; simmer, covered, 10-12 minutes or until noodles are tender, stirring occasionally.

CHOCOLATE-HAZELNUT BUTTER

Store varieties of chocolate-hazelnut butter just cannot compete with the homemade kind. Slather it on everything from toast and pretzels to banana chunks and shortbread cookies.
—**Crystal Jo Bruns** Iliff, CO

Start to Finish: 15 min.
Makes: 1½ cups

- 2 cups hazelnuts, toasted
- 1¼ cups confectioners' sugar
- 3 to 4 tablespoons baking cocoa
  Dash salt

Place hazelnuts in a food processor; cover and process about 2-3 minutes or until mixture pulls away from the sides of the processor. Continue processing while gradually adding confectioners' sugar, cocoa and salt to reach the desired consistency. Store in the refrigerator.
Note: To toast nuts, bake in a shallow pan in a 350° oven for 5-10 minutes or cook in a skillet over low heat until lightly browned, stirring occasionally.

CRISPY SMASHED HERBED POTATOES

While scanning a local newspaper, I found a recipe with an intriguing title. Just as advertised, these potatoes are crispy, herbed and smashed.
—**Althea Dye** Howard, OH

Prep: 25 min. • **Bake:** 20 min.
Makes: 4 servings

- 12 small red potatoes (about 1½ pounds)
- 3 tablespoons olive oil
- ¼ cup butter, melted
- ¾ teaspoon salt
- ¼ teaspoon pepper
- 3 tablespoons minced fresh chives
- 1 tablespoon minced fresh parsley

1. Preheat oven to 450°. Place potatoes in a large saucepan; add water to cover. Bring to a boil. Reduce the heat; cook, uncovered, 15-20 minutes or until they are tender. Drain.

2. Drizzle the oil over the bottom of a 15x10x1-in. baking pan; arrange potatoes over oil. Using a potato masher, flatten potatoes to ½-in. thickness. Brush the potatoes with butter; sprinkle with salt and pepper.

3. Roast 20-25 minutes or until golden brown. Sprinkle with chives and parsley.

Lemon-Rosemary Smashed Potatoes: Boil and flatten the potatoes; add 1 small halved and sliced lemon and 1½ teaspoons minced fresh rosemary. Butter, season and roast. Omit herbs.

Dill Smashed Potatoes: Boil, flatten and season potatoes, adding ¼ teaspoon garlic powder. Butter, season and roast. Sprinkle with 2 to 3 teaspoons snipped fresh dill instead of the chives and parsley.

Artichoke Smashed Potatoes: Boil, flatten and season the potatoes, adding ¾ teaspoon dried thyme. Butter, season and roast, adding a drained 7½-ounce jar of marinated quartered artichoke hearts during last 5 minutes. Omit herbs.

Contest Winner

FRUITED GOAT CHEESE STUFFING

This sweet and savory side dish incorporates creamy goat cheese for an unexpected twist on a seasonal favorite. Your guests will be impressed!
—Jennifer Coduto Kent, OH

Prep: 20 min. • **Bake:** 30 min.
Makes: 10 servings

- 1 pound whole wheat bread, cubed
- 1 cup chopped dates
- 1 medium onion, chopped
- ¼ cup minced fresh sage
- 1 tablespoon minced fresh rosemary or 1 teaspoon dried rosemary, crushed
- 1 teaspoon minced fresh marjoram or ¼ teaspoon dried marjoram
- 2 tablespoons butter
- 1 cup dried cherries, chopped
- ¼ teaspoon salt
- ¼ teaspoon pepper
- 3 cups reduced-sodium chicken broth
- ¾ cup crumbled goat cheese

1. Place bread cubes in an ungreased 15x10x1-in. baking pan. Bake at 350° for 10 minutes or until toasted; set aside to cool. Meanwhile, in a large skillet, saute the dates, onion, sage, rosemary and marjoram in butter until onion is tender. Remove from the heat.
2. Place bread cubes in a large bowl. Stir in the onion mixture, cherries, salt and pepper. Add broth; toss to coat. Sprinkle with cheese; toss gently.
3. Transfer to 13x9-in. baking dish coated with cooking spray. Bake, uncovered, at 350° for 30-35 minutes or until the top is lightly browned.

DUO TATER BAKE

Cut down on holiday prep time with this creamy potato dish that combines sweet potatoes with regular spuds. I served this for Thanksgiving, and it was a winner with my family.
—Joan McCulloch Abbotsford, BC

Prep: 40 min. • **Bake:** 20 min.
Makes: 2 casseroles (10 servings each)

- 4 pounds russet or Yukon Gold potatoes, peeled and cubed
- 3 pounds sweet potatoes, peeled and cubed
- 2 cartons (8 ounces each) spreadable chive and onion cream cheese
- 1 cup (8 ounces) sour cream
- ¼ cup shredded Colby-Monterey Jack cheese
- ⅓ cup whole milk
- ¼ cup shredded Parmesan cheese
- ½ teaspoon salt
- ½ teaspoon pepper

TOPPING

- 1 cup shredded Colby-Monterey Jack cheese
- ½ cup chopped green onions
- ¼ cup shredded Parmesan cheese

1. Place russet potatoes in a Dutch oven and cover with water. Bring to a boil. Reduce heat; cover and cook for 10-15 minutes or until tender.
2. Meanwhile, place sweet potatoes in a large saucepan; cover with water. Bring to a boil. Reduce heat; cover and cook for 10-15 minutes or until tender. Drain; mash with half of the cream cheese and sour cream and all of Colby cheese.
3. Drain russet potatoes; mash with the remaining cream cheese and sour cream. Stir in the milk, Parmesan cheese, salt and pepper.
4. Spread 2⅔ cups of the russet potato mixture into each of two greased 11x7-in. baking dishes. Layer with 4 cups of the sweet potato mixture. Repeat the layers. Spread with the remaining russet potato mixture.
5. Bake, uncovered, at 350° for 15 minutes or until heated through. Combine the topping ingredients; sprinkle over casseroles. Bake for 2-3 minutes longer or until the cheese is melted.

ROSEMARY SWEET POTATO FRIES

A local restaurant got me hooked on sweet potato fries. I started experimenting at home, trying to make them taste like theirs, but baked, not fried. I'm thrilled with these results!

—**Jackie Gregston** Hallsville, TX

Prep: 15 min. • **Bake:** 30 min.
Makes: 4 servings

- 3 tablespoons olive oil
- 1 tablespoon minced fresh rosemary
- 1 garlic clove, minced
- 1 teaspoon cornstarch
- ¾ teaspoon salt
- ⅛ teaspoon pepper
- 3 large sweet potatoes, peeled and cut into ¼-inch julienned strips (about 2¼ pounds)

1. Preheat oven to 425°. In a large resealable plastic bag, combine the first six ingredients. Add sweet potatoes; shake to coat.

2. Arrange in a single layer on two 15x10x1-in. baking pans coated with cooking spray. Bake, uncovered, for 30-35 minutes or until tender and lightly browned, turning occasionally.

Should I Peel It?

You don't have to peel sweet potatoes: The skins are edible and high in nutrients, including potassium, iron and Vitamins C and E. Be sure to wash them thoroughly; the skins retain dirt.

FREEZE IT RHUBARB-CHERRY CHUTNEY

I love surprising recipes like this chutney with rhubarb, apple and cherries. Try it with cream cheese and crackers or as a condiment for grilled chicken.

—Sue Gronholz Beaver Dam, WI

Prep: 20 min. • **Cook:** 35 min.
Makes: 6 cups

- 7 cups chopped fresh or frozen rhubarb (about 2 pounds)
- 2 cups packed brown sugar
- 2 cups fresh or frozen pitted tart cherries, chopped
- 1 large tart apple, peeled and chopped
- 1 cup red wine vinegar
- 1 medium red onion, chopped
- 1 celery rib, chopped
- 1 tablespoon finely chopped crystallized ginger
- 3 garlic cloves, minced
- ¾ teaspoon ground cinnamon
- ½ teaspoon ground coriander
- ¼ teaspoon ground cloves

1. In a 6-qt. stockpot, combine all ingredients; bring to a boil. Reduce heat; simmer, uncovered, for 25-30 minutes or until the mixture has thickened.
2. Transfer to covered containers. (If freezing, use freezer-safe containers and fill to within ½ in. of tops.) Refrigerate up to 3 weeks or freeze up to 12 months. Thaw frozen chutney in refrigerator before serving.

ROASTED BALSAMIC SWEET POTATOES

By the end of summer, I'm done with the usual potato salad. This warm, spicy side kicks off cozy season.

—Karen Vande Slunt Watertown, WI

Prep: 30 min. • **Cook:** 30 min.
Makes: 12 servings

- 6 medium sweet potatoes, cubed
- 1 teaspoon olive oil
- ½ teaspoon salt
- ½ teaspoon pepper
- 1 pound bacon strips, chopped
- 4 celery ribs, chopped
- 1 medium onion, thinly sliced
- 3 garlic cloves, minced
- 1 cup beef stock
- ⅔ cup balsamic vinegar
- 4 teaspoons paprika
- ¾ teaspoon ground cumin, optional
- 6 green onions, chopped
  Minced fresh parsley, optional

1. Preheat oven to 375°. Place sweet potatoes in a 15x10-in. pan; drizzle with olive oil and sprinkle with salt and pepper. Turn to coat. Bake until tender, about 30-35 minutes.
2. Meanwhile, in a large skillet, cook the bacon over medium-low heat until it is crisp; drain. Discard all but 4 teaspoons of the drippings.
3. Cook the celery and onion in drippings over medium heat until tender, about 6-8 minutes. Stir in garlic; cook 1 minute. Add beef stock and balsamic vinegar; simmer until liquid is reduced by half, 5-8 minutes. Add paprika and, if desired, cumin; cook 1 minute longer.
4. Pour balsamic mixture over the sweet potatoes; add bacon. Toss to coat. Top with green onions and, if desired, minced fresh parsley; serve immediately.

HERBED RICE PILAF

This savory side dish has been a family favorite for years. Our 12-year-old daughter, Jennifer, is an expert with this recipe, which is a great help for a busy working mom like me. We sure enjoy this rice dish in the summer with a grilled entree.

—Jeri Dobrowski Beach, ND

....

Prep: 15 min. • **Cook:** 15 min. + standing
Makes: 6 servings

- 1 cup uncooked long grain rice
- 1 cup chopped celery
- ¾ cup chopped onion
- ¼ cup butter, cubed
- 2½ cups water
- 1 package (2 to 2½ ounces) chicken noodle soup mix
- 1 teaspoon dried thyme
- ¼ teaspoon rubbed sage
- ¼ teaspoon pepper
- 2 tablespoons fresh minced parsley
- 1 tablespoon chopped pimientos, optional

1. In a large skillet, cook the rice, celery and onion in butter, stirring constantly, until rice is browned. Stir in the next five ingredients; bring to a boil. Reduce the heat; cover and simmer for 15 minutes. Sprinkle with parsley; stir in pimientos if desired.

2. Remove from heat and let it stand, covered, for 10 minutes. Fluff with a fork.

CHEESY SAUSAGE POTATOES

For a satisfying brunch, try these tender potato slices with lots of sausage and cheese. I never have to worry about leftovers—everyone loves them and the pan is always empty. You can also serve these as a side dish at Sunday supper or for potlucks.

—Linda Hill Marseilles, IL

....

Start to Finish: 25 min.
Makes: 6-8 servings

- 3 pounds potatoes, peeled and cut into ¼-inch slices
- 1 pound bulk pork sausage
- 1 medium onion, chopped
- ¼ cup butter, melted
- 2 cups shredded cheddar cheese

1. Place potatoes in a large saucepan and cover with water. Bring to a boil. Reduce heat; simmer, uncovered, for 8-10 minutes or until tender. Meanwhile, crumble sausage into a large skillet; add onion. Cook over medium heat until meat is no longer pink; drain if necessary.

2. Drain the potatoes; arrange in an ungreased 13x9-in. baking dish. Drizzle with butter. Add sausage mixture and stir gently. Sprinkle with cheese.

3. Bake, uncovered, at 350° for 5-7 minutes or until cheese is melted.

Soups, Salads & Sandwiches

Serve them on their own, or mix and match for a complete meal—these soups, salads and sandwiches go together naturally. Pair cool, garden-fresh ingredients in the summer, or dish up rich harvest vegetables when the weather turns colder. These great recipes put the taste of the season on your table all year!

OPEN-FACED GRILLED SALMON SANDWICHES

My family loves to fish. What better reward from a day of fishing than eating what you just caught? We make salmon several different ways, and this one is the family favorite.

—**Stephanie Hanisak** Port Murray, NJ

Start to Finish: 30 min.
Makes: 4 servings

- 4   salmon fillets (1 inch thick and 5 ounces each), skin removed
- ¾   cup mesquite marinade
- ¼   teaspoon pepper
- 4   slices sourdough bread (½ inch thick)
- ¼   cup tartar sauce
- 4   iceberg lettuce leaves
- 4   lemon wedges, optional

1. Place fillets in an 8-in. square dish. Pour marinade over fillets; turn fish to coat. Let stand 15 minutes.
2. Drain salmon, discarding marinade. Sprinkle salmon with pepper.
3. Grill salmon, covered, on an oiled grill rack over medium heat or broil 4 in. from heat. Grill 4-6 minutes on each side or until fish just begins to flake easily with a fork.
4. Grill bread, covered, over medium heat for 1-2 minutes on each side or until lightly toasted. Spread with tartar sauce; top with lettuce and salmon. If desired, serve with lemon wedges.

GARDEN VEGETABLE BEEF SOUP

This soup is my go-to healthy lunch option. It's a great way to eat my vegetables, and it's so comforting during the cold winter months.

—**Dawn Donald** Herron, MI

Prep: 20 min. • **Cook:** 55 min.
Makes: 8 servings (3½ quarts)

- 1½   pounds lean ground beef (90% lean)
- 1   medium onion, chopped
- 2   garlic cloves, minced
- 1   package (10 ounces) julienned carrots
- 2   celery ribs, chopped
- ¼   cup tomato paste
- 1   can (14½ ounces) diced tomatoes, undrained
- 1½   cups shredded cabbage
- 1   medium zucchini, coarsely chopped
- 1   medium red potato (about 5 ounces), finely chopped
- ½   cup fresh or frozen cut green beans
- 1   teaspoon dried basil
- ½   teaspoon dried oregano
- ¼   teaspoon salt
- ¼   teaspoon pepper
- 4   cans (14½ ounces each) reduced-sodium beef broth
  Grated Parmesan cheese, optional

1. In a 6-qt. stockpot, cook beef, onion and garlic over medium heat 6-8 minutes or until beef is no longer pink, breaking up beef into crumbles; drain. Add carrots and celery; cook and stir 6-8 minutes or until tender. Stir in tomato paste; cook 1 minute longer.
2. Add tomatoes, cabbage, zucchini, potato, green beans, seasonings and broth; bring to a boil. Reduce heat; simmer, covered, 35-45 minutes or until vegetables are tender. If desired, top each serving with cheese.

CURRIED CHICKEN SOUP

This was one of my favorite recipes that my grandmother used to make. I've added my own touches to it, such as chickpeas, coconut milk and fresh cilantro.
—**Deanna Hindenach** Paw Paw, MI

Prep: 25 min. • **Cook:** 45 min.
Makes: 8 servings

  4 teaspoons curry powder
  ½ teaspoon salt
  ½ teaspoon pepper
  ½ teaspoon cayenne pepper
  1 pound boneless skinless chicken
      breasts, cut into 1-inch cubes
  3 medium carrots, chopped
  1 medium sweet red pepper, chopped
  1 small onion, chopped
  2 tablespoons olive oil
  1 garlic clove, minced
  1 can (15 ounces) garbanzo beans or
      chickpeas, rinsed and drained
  1 can (14½ ounces) chicken broth
  1 can (14½ ounces) diced tomatoes,
      drained
  1 cup water
  1 can (13.66 ounces) coconut milk
  ¾ cup minced fresh cilantro

1. In a large resealable plastic bag, combine the curry, salt, pepper and cayenne. Add chicken, a few pieces at a time, and shake to coat.
2. In a large saucepan over medium heat, cook the chicken, carrots, red pepper and onion in oil for 4 minutes. Add garlic; cook 1-2 minutes longer or until the chicken is browned and the vegetables are tender; drain.
3. Stir in the garbanzo beans, broth, tomatoes and water. Bring to a boil. Reduce heat; cover and simmer for 30 minutes. Stir in coconut milk; heat through. Garnish servings with cilantro.

HOT SPINACH APPLE SALAD

With a light sweet-tangy dressing, the spinach doesn't wilt and the apples retain their crunch. We serve this salad with homemade bread.
—**Denise Albers** Freeburg, IL

Start to Finish: 20 min.
Makes: 10 servings

  6 bacon strips, diced
  ¼ cup cider vinegar
  3 tablespoons brown sugar
  9 cups fresh baby spinach
  2 unpeeled large red apples, thinly
      sliced
  1 medium red onion, chopped
      (about ¾ cup)

1. In a large skillet, cook the bacon until crisp. Remove to paper towels. Drain, reserving 2 tablespoons of the drippings.
2. In the same skillet, combine vinegar, brown sugar and the reserved drippings. Bring to a boil; cook and stir until the sugar is dissolved. Cool slightly.
3. Meanwhile, in a serving bowl, combine spinach, apples, onion and bacon. Drizzle with warm dressing; toss to coat. Serve immediately.

GRILLED STEAK AND PORTOBELLO STACKS

You don't need a special panini maker for these bistro-style sandwiches. They may take some time to prepare, but it's well worth it!

—**Judy Murphy** Coeur d' Alene, ID

Prep: 45 min. + marinating
Grill: 20 min. + standing
Makes: 8 servings

- 2 **tablespoons plus ¼ cup olive oil, divided**
- 1 **tablespoon herbes de Provence**
- 1 **beef tenderloin roast (1¼ pounds)**
- 4 **large portobello mushrooms**
- 2 **tablespoons balsamic vinegar**

BALSAMIC ONION

- 1 **large onion, halved and thinly sliced**
- 4½ **teaspoons sugar**
- ½ **teaspoon salt**
- ½ **teaspoon pepper**
- 1 **tablespoon olive oil**
- 2 **tablespoons balsamic vinegar**

HORSERADISH SAUCE

- ½ **cup sour cream**
- 1½ **teaspoons prepared horseradish**
- ¼ **teaspoon Worcestershire sauce**

SANDWICHES

- 12 **slices white bread**
- ¼ **cup butter, melted**
- 4 **cups spring mix salad greens**
- 2 **tablespoons red wine vinaigrette**
- ¾ **cup julienned roasted sweet red peppers**

1. Combine 2 tablespoons oil and herbes de Provence. Rub over tenderloin; cover and refrigerate for 2 hours. Place the mushrooms in a small bowl; toss with vinegar and the remaining oil. Cover and refrigerate until grilling.

2. In a large skillet, cook the onion, sugar, salt and pepper in oil over medium heat for 15-20 minutes or until golden brown, stirring frequently. Remove from the heat; stir in vinegar. Set aside.

3. In a small bowl, combine the sauce ingredients. Cover and refrigerate until serving.

4. Grill tenderloin and mushrooms, covered, over medium heat 8-10 minutes on each side or until the meat reaches desired doneness (for medium-rare, a thermometer should read 135°; medium, 140°; medium-well, 145°) and the mushrooms are tender. Let tenderloin stand for 10 minutes.

5. Meanwhile, brush both sides of bread with butter. Grill over medium heat for 1 minute on each side or until browned. Toss salad greens with the vinaigrette. Cut the tenderloin and mushrooms into thin slices.

6. Divide the mushrooms among four slices of bread. Layer with roasted peppers, greens and another slice of bread. Top each with onion mixture and beef. Spread sauce over remaining slices of bread; place over beef. Cut each sandwich diagonally in half.

ONION BEEF AU JUS

Garlic, sweet onions and soy sauce make a flavorful juice for dipping these savory open-faced sandwiches. Any leftover beef makes delicious cold sandwiches, too.
—**Blake Brown** West Union, IA

Prep: 20 min. • **Bake:** 2½ hours + standing
Makes: 12 servings

- 1 beef rump roast or bottom round roast (4 pounds)
- 2 tablespoons canola oil
- 2 large sweet onions, cut into ¼-inch slices
- 6 tablespoons butter, softened, divided
- 5 cups water
- ½ cup reduced-sodium soy sauce
- 1 envelope onion soup mix
- 1 garlic clove, minced
- 1 teaspoon browning sauce, optional
- 1 loaf (1 pound) French bread
- 1 cup shredded Swiss cheese

1. Preheat oven to 325°. In a Dutch oven over medium-high heat, brown roast on all sides in oil; drain. In a large skillet, saute the onions in 2 tablespoons of butter until tender. Add water, soy sauce, soup mix, garlic and, if desired, browning sauce. Pour over roast.

2. Cover and bake for 2½ hours or until the meat is tender.

3. Let meat stand for 10 minutes, then thinly slice. Return meat to pan juices. Split bread lengthwise; cut into 3-in. sections. Spread with the remaining butter. Place on a baking sheet.

4. Broil bread 4-6 in. from the heat for 2-3 minutes or until golden brown. Top with beef and onions; sprinkle with cheese. Broil for 1-2 minutes or until cheese is melted. Serve with pan juices.

Contest Winner

COLD-DAY CHICKEN NOODLE SOUP

When I was sick, my mom would make me this heartwarming chicken noodle soup. It was soothing when I had a cold, but this soup is a bowlful of comfort on any chilly day.
—**Anthony Graham** Ottawa, IL

Prep: 15 min. • **Cook:** 25 min.
Makes: 8 servings (3 quarts)

- 1 tablespoon canola oil
- 2 celery ribs, chopped
- 2 medium carrots, chopped
- 1 medium onion, chopped
- 8 cups reduced-sodium chicken broth
- ½ teaspoon dried basil
- ¼ teaspoon pepper
- 3 cups uncooked whole wheat egg noodles (about 4 ounces)
- 3 cups coarsely chopped rotisserie chicken
- 1 tablespoon minced fresh parsley

1. In a 6-qt. stockpot, heat oil over medium-high heat. Add celery, carrots and onion; cook and stir 5-7 minutes or until tender.

2. Add broth, basil and pepper; bring to a boil. Stir in noodles; cook 12-14 minutes or until al dente. Stir in chicken and parsley; heat through.

Tasty Grilled Cheese

Year-round, for any occasion, no comfort food compares to a classic grilled cheese sandwich. Try these fabulous new spins on a tried-and-true family favorite.

BACON & CHEESE SANDWICHES

This mean melt, with bacon, Dijon mustard and two kinds of cheese, is the perfect combo of creamy-melty filling and crispy, buttery bread.

—Sharon Delaney-Chronis
South Milwaukee, WI

....

Start to Finish: 25 min.
Makes: 4 servings

- ¼ cup mayonnaise
- 2 teaspoons Dijon mustard
- 8 slices sourdough bread
- 8 slices Swiss cheese (¾ ounce each)
- 8 slices cheddar cheese (¾ ounce each)
- 8 slices tomato
- 4 slices sweet onion
- 8 cooked bacon strips
- 2 tablespoons butter, softened

1. In a small bowl, mix mayonnaise and mustard; spread over four bread slices. Layer with cheeses, tomato, onion and bacon. Top with remaining bread. Butter outsides of sandwiches.
2. On a griddle, toast sandwiches over medium heat 2-3 minutes on each side or until the bread is golden brown and the cheese is melted.

GREEN CHILI GRILLED CHEESE MELT

My daughter created a masterpiece with her ultimate grilled cheese and chilies. Want more heat? Use a 4-ounce can of diced jalapenos instead of chilies.

—Julia Huntington Cheyenne, WY

....

Start to Finish: 25 min.
Makes: 6 servings

- 4 ounces cream cheese, softened
- 1 cup shredded Colby-Monterey Jack cheese
- 1 cup shredded part-skim mozzarella cheese
- 1 can chopped green chilies, drained
- 2 tablespoons mayonnaise
- ¼ teaspoon garlic powder
  Dash seasoned salt
- 12 slices white bread
- 6 slices tomato
- ¼ cup butter, melted

1. In a small bowl, mix the first seven ingredients until blended. Spread over half of the bread slices. Top with tomato and remaining bread.
2. Brush outsides of sandwiches with melted butter. In a large skillet, toast sandwiches in batches over medium-low heat 3-4 minutes on each side or until golden brown and heated through.

GRILLED PESTO HAM AND PROVOLONE SANDWICHES

These Italian-style sandwiches are packed with zesty flavors. If you want to lighten them a little, use fat-free mayo. We serve them with minestrone soup or a crisp green salad.

—Priscilla Yee Concord, CA

....

Start to Finish: 20 min.
Makes: 4 servings

- 2 tablespoons mayonnaise
- 4 teaspoons prepared pesto
- 8 slices sourdough bread
- 8 ounces thinly sliced deli ham
- ½ cup loosely packed basil leaves
- 4 pickled sweet cherry peppers, chopped
- 1 plum tomato, thinly sliced
- ¾ cup shredded provolone cheese
- 2 tablespoons butter, softened

1. In a small bowl, mix mayonnaise and pesto; spread over four slices of bread. Layer with ham, basil, peppers, tomato and cheese. Top with the remaining bread. Spread outsides of sandwiches with butter.

2. On a griddle, toast sandwiches over medium heat 2-3 minutes on each side or until golden brown and cheese is melted.

GREEK SANDWICH BITES

Here's an appetizer that tastes like traditional spanakopita, but is easier to make.

—Lynn Scully Rancho Santa Fe, CA

....

Start to Finish: 25 min.
Makes: 16 appetizers

- 1 medium onion, finely chopped
- 1 tablespoon olive oil
- 2 garlic cloves, minced
- 1 pound fresh baby spinach

- 1 cup crumbled feta cheese
- ¼ cup pine nuts, toasted
- ¼ teaspoon salt
- ¼ teaspoon pepper
- ⅛ teaspoon ground nutmeg
- 8 slices Italian bread (½ inch thick)
- 4 teaspoons butter, softened

1. In a large nonstick skillet, saute onion in oil until tender. Add garlic; cook for 1 minute longer. Stir in the spinach; cook and stir until wilted. Drain. Stir in the feta, pine nuts, salt, pepper and nutmeg.

2. Spread over four bread slices; top with the remaining bread. Spread outsides of sandwiches with butter. Grill, uncovered, over medium heat for 3-4 minutes or until the bread is browned and the cheese is melted, turning once. Cut each sandwich into quarters.

> ### Baby Spinach
> *Baby spinach has flat leaves, is harvested earlier than regular spinach, and is more tender, with milder flavor. For stronger flavor, use regular spinach and cut the leaves in pieces.*

BUTTERNUT SQUASH CHILI

Add butternut squash to chili for a tasty, filling, energy-packed dish your whole family will love.

—**Jeanne Larson** Mission Viejo, CA

Prep: 20 min. • **Cook:** 30 min.
Makes: 8 servings (2 quarts)

- 1 pound ground beef or turkey
- ¾ cup chopped red onion
- 5 garlic cloves, minced
- 3 tablespoons tomato paste
- 1 tablespoon chili powder
- 1 teaspoon ground cumin
- ½ to 1 teaspoon salt
- 1¾ to 2 cups water
- 1 can (15 ounces) black beans, rinsed and drained
- 1 can (15 ounces) pinto beans, rinsed and drained
- 1 can (14½ ounces) diced tomatoes
- 1 can (14½ to 15 ounces) tomato sauce
- 3 cups peeled butternut squash, cut into ½-inch cubes
- 2 tablespoons cider vinegar
  Chopped avocado, plain Greek yogurt and shredded mozzarella cheese, optional

1. In a Dutch oven over medium heat, cook beef and onion, crumbling meat, until the beef is no longer pink and the onion is tender, 6-8 minutes.

2. Add next five ingredients; cook for 1 minute longer. Stir in water, both types of beans, diced tomatoes and tomato sauce. Bring to a boil; reduce heat. Stir in squash; simmer, covered, until squash is tender, 20-25 minutes. Stir in vinegar.

3. If desired, serve with chopped avocado, Greek yogurt and shredded mozzarella cheese.

HEIRLOOM TOMATO & ZUCCHINI SALAD

Tomato wedges give this salad a juicy bite. It's a smart way to use the fresh herbs and veggies from your own garden or the farmers market.
—**Matthew Hass** Franklin, WI

Start to Finish: 25 min.
Makes: 12 servings

- 7 large heirloom tomatoes (about 2½ pounds), cut into wedges
- 3 medium zucchini, halved lengthwise and thinly sliced
- 2 medium sweet yellow peppers, thinly sliced
- ⅓ cup cider vinegar
- 3 tablespoons olive oil
- 1 tablespoon sugar
- 1½ teaspoons salt
- 1 tablespoon each minced fresh basil, parsley and tarragon

1. In a large bowl, combine tomatoes, zucchini and peppers. In a small bowl, whisk vinegar, oil, sugar and salt until blended. Stir in herbs.

2. Just before serving, drizzle dressing over salad; toss gently to coat.

BERRY-BEET SALAD

Here's a delightfully different salad that balances the earthy flavor of beets with the natural sweetness of berries. If you prefer, substitute crumbled feta for the goat cheese.
—**Amy Lyons** Mounds View, MN

Prep: 20 min. • **Bake:** 30 min. + cooling
Makes: 4 servings

- 1 each fresh red and golden beets
- ¼ cup balsamic vinegar
- 2 tablespoons walnut oil
- 1 teaspoon honey
  Dash salt
  Dash pepper
- ½ cup sliced fresh strawberries
- ½ cup fresh raspberries
- ½ cup fresh blackberries
- 3 tablespoons chopped walnuts, toasted
- 1 shallot, thinly sliced
- 4 cups torn mixed salad greens
- 1 ounce fresh goat cheese, crumbled
- 1 tablespoon fresh basil, thinly sliced

1. Preheat oven to 400°. Place beets in an 8-in. square baking dish; add 1 in. of water. Cover and bake for 30-40 minutes or until tender.

2. Meanwhile, in a small bowl, whisk the vinegar, oil, honey, salt and pepper; set aside. Cool the beets; peel and cut into thin slices.

3. In a large bowl, combine the beets, berries, walnuts and shallot. Pour the dressing over the beet mixture and toss gently to coat. Divide the salad greens among four serving plates. Top with the beet mixture; sprinkle with goat cheese and basil.

1. In a large stockpot, cook beef over medium heat until no longer pink; drain. Add broth, tomatoes, spaghetti sauce, onions, celery, carrots, beans, oregano, pepper and pepper sauce.

2. Bring to a boil. Reduce heat; simmer, covered, 30 minutes. Add pasta and parsley; simmer, covered, 10-14 minutes or until pasta is tender.

SPICY CHICKEN TOMATO PITAS

I'm not sure if this is a Mediterranean dish with a southwestern flair or the other way around. All I know is that it's ideal for a summer dinner. The tomato relish is yummy as an appetizer with tortilla chips, so you may want to double it.

—Cori Cooper Boise, ID

Start to Finish: 30 min.
Makes: 4 servings

TOMATO RELISH
- ¼ cup lemon juice
- 1 tablespoon olive oil
- 1 teaspoon ground coriander
- 1 teaspoon ground cumin
- ¼ teaspoon crushed red pepper flakes
- 4 medium tomatoes, seeded and chopped
- 1 small onion, chopped
- ¼ cup minced fresh parsley

CHICKEN PITAS
- 1 tablespoon ground cumin
- 1 tablespoon paprika
- 1½ teaspoons dried oregano
- 1½ teaspoons ground coriander
- ½ teaspoon crushed red pepper flakes
- ¼ teaspoon salt
- 4 boneless skinless chicken breast halves (4 ounces each)
- 8 whole wheat pita pocket halves

1. In a bowl, whisk the first five ingredients. Add tomatoes, onion and parsley; toss to coat. Refrigerate until serving.

2. Combine cumin, paprika, oregano, coriander, pepper flakes and salt; rub onto both sides of the chicken. Grill chicken, covered, on an oiled grill rack over medium heat or broil 4 in. from heat 4-7 minutes on each side or until a thermometer reads 165°.

3. Cut chicken into slices. Serve in pita halves with relish.

HEARTY PASTA FAJIOLI

Here's a classic Italian favorite. Canned broth and spaghetti sauce form the flavorful base.

—Cindy Garland Limestone, TN

Prep: 40 min. • **Cook:** 40 min.
Makes: 24 servings (7½ quarts)

- 2 pounds ground beef
- 6 cans (14½ ounces each) beef broth
- 2 cans (28 ounces each) diced tomatoes, undrained
- 2 jars (26 ounces each) spaghetti sauce
- 3 large onions, chopped
- 8 celery ribs, diced
- 3 medium carrots, sliced
- 2 cups canned cannellini beans, rinsed and drained
- 2 cups canned kidney beans, rinsed and drained
- 3 teaspoons minced fresh oregano or 1 teaspoon dried oregano
- 2½ teaspoons pepper
- 1½ teaspoons hot pepper sauce
- 8 ounces uncooked medium pasta shells
- 5 teaspoons minced fresh parsley

SMOKY CHEDDAR CORN CHOWDER

When I'm making a pot of this delicious and hearty soup, no one misses dinner! Smoked cheese takes the flavor to another level.

—**Danielle Crawford** Pelzer, SC

Prep: 20 min. • **Cook:** 30 min.
Makes: 6 servings (2 quarts)

- 1 fully cooked boneless ham steak (1½ pounds), cubed
- 2 large baking potatoes, peeled and cubed
- 2 cups 2% milk
- 1 can (15¼ ounces) whole kernel corn, drained
- 1 can (14¾ ounces) cream-style corn
- 1 medium onion, finely chopped
- 1½ cups shredded smoked cheddar cheese

1. In a Dutch oven, cook and stir ham over medium-high heat until browned. Add potatoes, milk, corn and onion. Bring to a boil. Reduce heat; simmer, uncovered, for 20-25 minutes or until the potatoes are tender.
2. Remove from heat; stir in the cheese until melted.

FREEZE IT SAUSAGE BREAD SANDWICHES

I make these sandwiches in my spare time and freeze them so they're ready when needed, like for tailgating when we attend Kansas State football games.

—**Donna Roberts** Manhattan, KS

Prep: 30 min. • **Bake:** 20 min.
Makes: 4 sandwich loaves (3 pieces each)

- 1 package (16 ounces) hot roll mix
- 2 pounds reduced-fat bulk pork sausage
- 2 tablespoons dried parsley flakes
- 2 teaspoons garlic powder
- 1 teaspoon onion powder
- ½ teaspoon dried oregano
- 2 cups shredded part-skim mozzarella cheese
- ½ cup grated Parmesan cheese
- 1 large egg
- 1 tablespoon water

1. Preheat oven to 350°. Prepare roll mix dough according to package directions.
2. Meanwhile, in a large skillet, cook sausage over medium heat 8-10 minutes or until no longer pink, breaking into crumbles; drain. Stir in seasonings.
3. Divide dough into four portions. On a lightly floured surface, roll each into a 14x8-in. rectangle. Top each with 1¼ cups sausage mixture to within 1 inch of edges; sprinkle with ½ cup mozzarella cheese and 2 tablespoons Parmesan cheese. Roll up jelly-roll style, starting with a long side; pinch seams and ends to seal.
4. Transfer to greased baking sheets, seam side down. In a small bowl, whisk egg with water; brush over loaves. Bake 20-25 minutes or until golden brown and heated through. Cool loaves 5 minutes before slicing.
Freeze option: Cool cooked sandwiches 1 hour on wire racks. Cut each sandwich into thirds; wrap each securely in foil. Freeze until serving. To reheat in the oven, place wrapped frozen sandwiches on a baking sheet. Heat in a preheated 375° oven for 20-25 minutes or until heated through.

CINNAMON APPLE-NUT SALAD

This sensational apple salad features lots of color, taste and texture. But don't wait for a party to enjoy it—treat your clan to this tasty delight on weeknights, too. The cinnamon in the dressing is a fantastic accent to the crisp apples.

—**Jessica Lin** West Hartford, CT

Prep: 25 min. + chilling
Makes: 12 servings

- 3 medium red apples, chopped
- 3 medium Granny Smith apples, chopped
- 1 cup chopped pecans, toasted
- ½ cup dried cranberries
- 2 green onions, chopped
- ¼ cup plus 1½ teaspoons mayonnaise
- 3 tablespoons cider vinegar
- 3 tablespoons honey
- 1 tablespoon plus 1½ teaspoons orange juice
- 1 tablespoon grated orange peel
- ¾ teaspoon ground cinnamon
- ¼ teaspoon pepper

In a large bowl, combine apples, pecans, cranberries and onions. In a small bowl, whisk the remaining ingredients until blended. Pour over apple mixture; toss to coat. Refrigerate salad for 1 hour before serving.

Note: To toast nuts, bake in a shallow pan in a 350° oven for 5-10 minutes or cook in a skillet over low heat until lightly browned, stirring occasionally.

CUBAN SLIDERS

It's easy to make these delicious Cuban-style sliders by the panful, which is great because they go fast! Bake the pan until the rolls are lightly toasted and the cheese melts, then set them out and just watch them disappear.

—**Serene Herrera** Dallas, TX

Start to Finish: 30 min.
Makes: 2 dozen

- 2 packages (12 ounces each) Hawaiian sweet rolls
- 1¼ pounds thinly sliced deli ham
- 9 slices Swiss cheese (about 6 ounces)
- 24 dill pickle slices

TOPPING
- ½ cup butter, cubed
- 2 tablespoons finely chopped onion
- 2 tablespoons Dijon mustard

1. Preheat oven to 350°. Without separating rolls, cut each package of rolls in half horizontally; arrange bottom halves in a greased 13x9-in. baking pan. Layer with ham, cheese and pickles; replace top halves of rolls.

2. In a microwave, melt butter; stir in onion and mustard. Drizzle over rolls. Bake, covered, 10 minutes. Uncover; bake until golden brown and heated through, 5-10 minutes longer.

SPICY SAUSAGE SOUP WITH TORTELLINI

This soup is such a family treasure, both my daughters asked for the recipe when they moved out on their own.
—**Cynthia Krakowiak** Langhorne, PA

Start to Finish: 30 min.
Makes: 8 servings (3 quarts)

- 2 cartons (32 ounces each) chicken broth
- 1 pound bulk hot or mild Italian sausage
- 1 package (9 ounces) refrigerated cheese tortellini
- 1 can (14½ ounces) fire-roasted or Italian diced tomatoes
- 1 teaspoon Italian seasoning
- 3 cups fresh spinach, thinly sliced

1. In a 6-qt. stockpot, bring broth to a boil. Carefully drop sausage by heaping teaspoonfuls into boiling broth. Add tortellini, tomatoes and Italian seasoning; return to a boil.

2. Reduce heat; simmer, uncovered, for 8-10 minutes or until the sausage is cooked through and the pasta is tender. Stir in spinach until wilted.

Freeze option: Freeze cooled soup in freezer containers. To use, partially thaw in refrigerator overnight. Heat through in a saucepan, stirring occasionally and adding a little broth if necessary.

Slicing Spinach

To cut spinach leaves into thin slices, stack them neatly in the same direction, then roll the stack into a cigar shape. Slice across the rolled leaves to create thin strips.

BACON MACARONI SALAD

This pleasing pasta salad is like eating a BLT in a bowl. Filled with crispy bacon, chopped tomato, celery and green onion, the sensational salad is coated with a tangy mayonnaise and vinegar dressing. It's a real crowd-pleaser!

—**Norene Wright** Manilla, IN

Prep: 20 min. + chilling
Makes: 12 servings

- 2 cups uncooked elbow macaroni
- 1 large tomato, finely chopped
- 2 celery ribs, finely chopped
- 5 green onions, finely chopped
- 1¼ cups mayonnaise
- 5 teaspoon white vinegar
- ¼ teaspoon salt
- ⅛ to ¼ teaspoon pepper
- 1 pound bacon strips, cooked and crumbled

1. Cook macaroni according to package directions; drain and rinse in cold water. Transfer to a large bowl; stir in tomato, celery and green onions.

2. In a small bowl, whisk mayonnaise, vinegar, salt and pepper. Pour over macaroni mixture and toss to coat. Refrigerate, covered, at least 2 hours. Just before serving, stir in the bacon.

ALL-AMERICAN HAMBURGERS

We do a lot of camping and outdoor cooking. Hamburgers are on our menu more than any other food.

—**Diane Hixon** Niceville, FL

Start to Finish: 20 min.
Makes: 4 servings

- 1 pound ground beef
- 2 tablespoons finely chopped onion
- 2 tablespoons chili sauce
- 2 teaspoons Worcestershire sauce
- 2 teaspoons prepared mustard
- 4 slices process American cheese or cheddar cheese, halved diagonally
- 2 slices Swiss cheese, halved diagonally
- 4 hamburger buns, split and toasted
  Lettuce leaves, sliced tomato and onion, cooked bacon strips, ketchup and mustard, optional

1. Combine the first five ingredients, mixing lightly but thoroughly. Shape into four patties. Grill burgers, covered, on a greased rack over medium direct heat until a thermometer reads 160° and juices run clear, about 6 minutes on each side.

2. During the last minute of cooking, top each patty with two triangles of American cheese and one triangle of Swiss cheese. Serve on buns; if desired, top with lettuce, tomato, onion, bacon, ketchup or mustard.

BACON & SWISS CHICKEN SANDWICHES

I created this sandwich based on one my daughter ordered at a restaurant. She likes to dip her sandwich in the extra honey-mustard sauce.
—**Marilyn Moberg** Papillion, NE

Start to Finish: 25 min.
Makes: 4 servings

- ¼ cup reduced-fat mayonnaise
- 1 tablespoon Dijon mustard
- 1 tablespoon honey
- 4 boneless skinless chicken breast halves (4 ounces each)
- ½ teaspoon Montreal steak seasoning
- 4 slices Swiss cheese
- 4 whole wheat hamburger buns, split
- 2 bacon strips, cooked and crumbled
  Lettuce leaves and tomato slices, optional

1. In a small bowl, mix mayonnaise, mustard and honey. Pound chicken with a meat mallet to ½-in. thickness. Sprinkle the chicken with steak seasoning. Grill chicken, covered, over medium heat or broil 4 in. from heat 4-6 minutes on each side or until a thermometer reads 165°. Top with cheese during the last 1 minute of cooking.
2. Grill buns over medium heat, cut side down, for 30-60 seconds or until toasted. Serve chicken on buns with bacon, mayonnaise mixture and, if desired, lettuce and tomato.

QUICK CALZONES

We came up with this recipe to use up leftover meat sauce. You can use your favorite sauce or make your own. Frozen bread dough makes these calzones a snap to assemble and creates a tasty crust, thanks to the Parmesan topping.
—***Taste of Home** Test Kitchen*

Start to Finish: 30 min.
Makes: 4 servings

- 1 loaf (1 pound) frozen bread dough, thawed
- 1 cup pasta sauce with meat
- ¼ cup shredded part-skim mozzarella cheese
- 1 to 2 tablespoons 2% milk
- ½ teaspoon Italian seasoning
- 1 tablespoon grated Parmesan cheese

1. Preheat oven to 350°. On a lightly floured surface, divide dough into four portions. Roll each into a 6-in. circle. Spread ¼ cup sauce over half of each circle to within ½ in. of edge; top with 1 tablespoon mozzarella cheese. Fold dough over filling; pinch edges to seal. Place on a greased baking sheet.
2. Brush milk over tops; sprinkle with Italian seasoning and Parmesan cheese. Bake for 20-25 minutes or until crust is golden brown.

TARRAGON ASPARAGUS SALAD

I love asparagus, and I love it even more when it's drizzled with my light, lemony vinaigrette dressing with a touch of tarragon. It's perfect as a side for fresh spring meals.
—**Linda Lacek** Winter Park, FL

Prep: 15 min. + chilling • **Cook:** 5 min.
Makes: 4 servings

- 2 tablespoons lemon juice
- 2 tablespoons olive oil
- 1 teaspoon minced fresh tarragon or ¼ teaspoon dried tarragon
- 1 garlic clove, minced
- ½ teaspoon Dijon mustard
- ¼ teaspoon pepper
  Dash salt
- 1 pound fresh asparagus, cut into 2-inch pieces

1. Place the first seven ingredients in a jar with a tight-fitting lid; shake well. Refrigerate at least 1 hour.
2. In a large skillet, bring ½ in. of water to a boil. Add asparagus; cook, covered, until crisp-tender, 1-3 minutes. Remove asparagus and immediately drop into ice water. Drain and pat dry. Refrigerate, covered, until serving.
3. To serve, shake dressing again. Spoon over asparagus.

DILLY POTATO & EGG SALAD

Everyone has a favorite potato salad, and this is mine. As a young bride 36 years ago, I was eager to learn how to cook and make things my husband would love. I merged my mom's and his mom's recipes, and this is the delicious result.
—**Angela Leinenbach** Mechanicsvlle, VA

Prep: 20 min. + chilling
Cook: 20 min. + cooling
Makes: 12 servings

- 4 pounds medium red potatoes (about 14), peeled and halved
- 5 hard-boiled large eggs
- 1 cup chopped dill pickles
- 1 small onion, chopped
- 1½ cups mayonnaise
- 1 teaspoon celery seed
- ½ teaspoon salt
- ¼ teaspoon pepper
  Paprika

1. Place potatoes in a large saucepan; add water to cover. Bring to a boil. Reduce heat; cook, uncovered, until tender, 15-20 minutes. Drain; cool completely.
2. Cut potatoes into ¾-in. cubes; place in a large bowl. Peel and chop four eggs; peel and slice remaining egg. Add the chopped eggs, pickles and onion to potatoes. Mix mayonnaise, celery seed, salt and pepper; stir gently into potato mixture.
3. Sprinkle with paprika; top with the sliced egg. Refrigerate, covered, for at least 2 hours before serving.

ROASTED AUTUMN VEGETABLE SOUP

Roasting sweet potatoes, carrots and parsnips brings out their best features. Blend them, and you have a warm, healthy soup for a cool fall night.
—**Stephanie Flaming** Woodland, CA

Prep: 35 min. • **Bake:** 40 min.
Makes: 12 servings (4 quarts)

2 pounds sweet potatoes (about 4 medium)
2 pounds carrots (about 8 large)
1½ pounds parsnips (about 6 medium)
2 large onions, quartered
6 garlic cloves, peeled
¼ cup canola oil
3 cartons (32 ounces each) chicken broth
1 cup fat-free evaporated milk
1 teaspoon salt
½ teaspoon pepper
Minced fresh parsley and sage

1. Preheat oven to 400°. Peel and cut sweet potatoes, carrots and parsnips into 1½-in. pieces; place in a large bowl. Add onions and garlic cloves; drizzle with oil and toss to coat. Divide mixture between two greased 15x10x1-in. baking pans. Roast 40-50 minutes or until tender, stirring occasionally.

2. Transfer vegetables to a Dutch oven. Add broth, milk, salt and pepper. Bring to a boil; simmer, uncovered, 10-15 minutes to allow flavors to blend.

3. Puree the soup using an immersion blender. Or, cool soup slightly and puree in batches in a blender; return to pan and heat through. Sprinkle servings with minced herbs.

Breads, Rolls & More

When it comes to country cooking, it doesn't get better than golden loaves, buttery biscuits and aromatic muffins fresh from the oven. And don't forget coffee cakes, sticky buns and pull-aparts! Whether you're an ace baker or simply like to surprise your family on weekends, these flaky treats will become new favorites in your home!

AUNT BETTY'S BLUEBERRY MUFFINS

My Aunt Betty bakes many items each Christmas, but I look forward to these mouthwatering muffins the most!
—**Sheila Raleigh** Kechi, KS

Prep: 15 min. • **Bake:** 20 min.
Makes: about 1 dozen

- ½ cup old-fashioned oats
- ½ cup orange juice
- 1 large egg
- ½ cup canola oil
- ½ cup sugar
- 1½ cups all-purpose flour
- 1¼ teaspoons baking powder
- ½ teaspoon salt
- ¼ teaspoon baking soda
- 1 cup fresh or frozen blueberries

TOPPING

- 2 tablespoons sugar
- ½ teaspoon ground cinnamon

1. Preheat oven to 400°. In a large bowl, combine oats and orange juice; let stand for 5 minutes. Beat in egg, oil and sugar until blended. Combine the flour, baking powder, salt and baking soda; stir into oat mixture just until moistened. Fold in the blueberries.

2. Fill greased or paper-lined muffin cups two-thirds full. Combine topping ingredients; sprinkle over batter. Bake for 20-25 minutes or until a toothpick inserted in the center comes out clean. Cool for 5 minutes before removing from pan to a wire rack. Serve warm.

Note: If using frozen blueberries, use without thawing to avoid discoloring the batter.

Contest Winner

I LIKE TO EAT APPLES AND BANANAS BREAD

My children love to bake (and eat) all kinds of banana bread. They make this all by themselves, with just a little help from me to put it in the oven.
—**Kristin Metcalf** Charlton, MA

Prep: 20 min. • **Bake:** 50 min. + cooling
Makes: 1 loaf (16 slices)

- 1½ cups mashed ripe bananas (4-5 medium)
- 1½ cups chopped peeled apples (2 medium)
- ½ cup granulated sugar
- ½ cup packed brown sugar
- 2 tablespoons water
- 2 tablespoons butter, melted
- 1½ cups all-purpose flour
- 1 teaspoon baking soda
- 1 teaspoon baking powder
- ¼ teaspoon salt
- 1 cup sweetened shredded coconut
- ½ cup caramel sundae syrup
- ¼ teaspoon sea salt

1. Preheat oven to 350°. Combine bananas, apples, sugars and water. Stir in melted butter. In another bowl, whisk flour, baking soda, baking powder and salt. Stir into banana mixture. Transfer to a greased and floured 9x5-in. loaf pan.

2. Bake until a toothpick inserted in center comes out clean, 50-60 minutes. Cool in pan 10 minutes before removing to a wire rack to cool completely.

3. Meanwhile, toast coconut, stirring occasionally, in a shallow pan at 350° until golden brown, 4-6 minutes. Cool slightly. Mix coconut with caramel syrup and sea salt; spread over loaf.

SOUR CREAM CHIVE BREAD

This savory loaf mildly flavored with chives is delicious when served warm with a meal, soup, salad or stew. It also tastes wonderful toasted the next day for breakfast.

—Deborah Plank West Salem, OH

Prep: 10 min. • **Bake:** 3 hours
Makes: 1 loaf (16 slices)

⅔ cup milk (70° to 80°)
¼ cup water (70° to 80°)
¼ cup sour cream
2 tablespoons butter
1½ teaspoons sugar
1½ teaspoons salt
3 cups bread flour
⅛ teaspoon baking soda
¼ cup minced chives
2¼ teaspoons active dry yeast

In bread machine pan, place all the ingredients in the order suggested by manufacturer. Select the basic bread setting. Choose crust color and loaf size if available. Bake according to the bread machine directions (check the dough after 5 minutes of mixing; add 1-2 tablespoons of water or flour if needed).

Note: We recommend you do not use a bread machine's time-delay feature for this recipe.

FREEZE IT PUMPKIN CHOCOLATE LOAF

These moist chocolate loaves with hints of pumpkin and spice have been a favorite in our family for years. They can be sliced to serve as snacks or dessert.

—Kathy Gardner Rockville, MD

Prep: 15 min. • **Bake:** 55 min. + cooling
Makes: 3 loaves (16 slices each)

3¾ cups all-purpose flour
3½ cups sugar
1½ teaspoons salt
1½ teaspoons baking powder
1¼ teaspoons baking soda
1¼ teaspoons ground cinnamon
1 to 1¼ teaspoons ground cloves
½ teaspoon ground nutmeg
3 large eggs
1 can (29 ounces) solid-pack pumpkin
1¼ cups canola oil
3 ounces unsweetened chocolate, melted and cooled
1½ teaspoons vanilla extract
2 cups (12 ounces) semisweet chocolate chips

1. Preheat oven to 350°. In a large bowl, combine the flour, sugar, salt, baking powder, baking soda, cinnamon, cloves and nutmeg. In another large bowl, whisk the eggs, pumpkin, oil, chocolate and vanilla. Stir into the dry ingredients just until moistened. Fold in the chips.

2. Transfer to three greased 9x5-in. loaf pans. Bake for 55-65 minutes or until a toothpick inserted in the center comes out clean. Cool for 10 minutes before removing from pans to wire racks. Wrap and freeze for up to 6 months.

SWEDISH TEA RING

This showstopper will add a special touch to any holiday spread. It's absolutely spectacular, and tastes as good as it looks.

—**Elsie Epp** Newton, KS

Prep: 30 min. + rising
Bake: 20 min. + cooling
Makes: 1 ring (24 slices)

- 1 tablespoon active dry yeast
- 1½ cups warm water (110° to 115°)
- ¼ cup sugar
- ¼ cup canola oil
- 2 large egg whites, lightly beaten
- 1¼ teaspoons salt
- 5½ to 6 cups all-purpose flour
- ½ cup chopped walnuts
- ½ cup chopped maraschino cherries, patted dry
- ¼ cup packed brown sugar
- 1 teaspoon ground cinnamon
- 2 tablespoons butter, melted

ICING

- 1 cup confectioners' sugar
- 1 to 2 tablespoons fat-free milk

1. Dissolve yeast in warm water. Add sugar, oil, egg whites, salt and 1 cup flour; beat until smooth. Stir in enough remaining flour to form a soft dough.

2. Turn dough onto a lightly floured surface; knead until smooth, about 6-8 minutes. Place in a bowl coated with cooking spray, turning once to coat the top. Cover and let rise until doubled, about 1 hour.

3. Combine the walnuts, cherries, brown sugar and cinnamon; set aside. Punch dough down; roll into an 18x12-in. rectangle. Brush with butter; sprinkle with nut mixture to within ½ in. of edges. Roll up jelly-roll style, starting with a long side; pinch seam to seal.

4. Place roll seam-side down on a 14-in. pizza pan coated with cooking spray; pinch the ends together to form a ring. With scissors, cut from outside edge two-thirds of the way toward center of ring at scant 1-in. intervals. Separate strips slightly; twist to allow filling to show. Cover and let rise until doubled, about 40 minutes.

5. Bake at 400° for 20-25 minutes or until golden brown. Remove from pan to a wire rack to cool.

6. In a small bowl, combine the confectioners' sugar and enough milk to achieve desired consistency; drizzle over tea ring.

MONKEY BREAD BISCUITS

Classic monkey bread is a sweetly spiced breakfast treat. I came up with an easy dinner version featuring garlic and Italian seasoning the crowd will love.

—**Dana Johnson** Scottsdale, AZ

Start to Finish: 20 min.
Makes: 1 dozen

- 1 tube (16.3 ounces) large refrigerated flaky biscuits
- 3 tablespoons butter, melted
- 1 garlic clove, minced
- ½ teaspoon Italian seasoning
- ¼ cup grated Parmesan cheese
  Additional Italian seasoning

1. Preheat oven to 425°. Separate the biscuits; cut each into six pieces. In a large bowl, combine butter, garlic and Italian seasoning; add biscuit pieces and toss to coat.

2. Place four pieces in each of 12 greased muffin cups. Sprinkle with cheese and additional Italian seasoning. Bake for 8-10 minutes or until golden brown. Serve warm.

NEW ORLEANS BEIGNETS

These sweet French doughnuts are square instead of round and have no hole in the middle. They're a traditional part of breakfast in New Orleans.
—Beth Dawson Jackson, LA

Prep: 25 min. + chilling • **Cook:** 5 min./batch
Makes: 4 dozen

- 1 package (¼ ounce) active dry yeast
- ¼ cup warm water (110° to 115°)
- 1 cup evaporated milk
- ½ cup canola oil
- ¼ cup sugar
- 1 large egg
- 4½ cups self-rising flour
  Oil for deep-fat frying
  Confectioners' sugar

1. In a large bowl, dissolve yeast in warm water. Add milk, oil, sugar, egg and 2 cups flour. Beat until smooth. Stir in enough remaining flour to form a soft dough (dough will be sticky). Do not knead. Cover and refrigerate overnight.
2. Punch dough down. Turn onto a floured surface; roll into a 16x12-in. rectangle. Cut into 2-in. squares.
3. In an electric skillet or deep-fat fryer, heat oil to 375°. Fry squares, a few at a time, until golden brown on both sides. Drain on paper towels. Roll warm beignets in confectioners' sugar.
Note: As a substitute for each cup of self-rising flour, place 1½ teaspoons baking powder and ½ teaspoon salt in a measuring cup. Add all-purpose flour to measure 1 cup.

ICEBOX ROLLS

These rolls get their name because the first rise happens overnight in the refrigerator. The next day, just shape, let rise again, and bake.
—Jean Fox Welch, MN

Prep: 30 min. + rising • **Bake:** 15 min.
Makes: 36 rolls

- 1 package (¼ ounce) active dry yeast
- 2½ cups water, divided
- ½ cup shortening
- 2 large eggs, beaten
- 1½ teaspoons salt
- ½ cup sugar
- 8½ to 9 cups all-purpose flour
- ⅓ cup butter, melted

1. Dissolve yeast in ½ cup warm water (110°-115°). In a separate bowl, combine 1 cup boiling water and shortening. Add the remaining water, eggs, salt, sugar and yeast mixture.
2. Stir in 1 cup of flour at a time, mixing well after each addition, until a soft dough forms. Turn the dough onto a floured surface; knead until smooth and elastic, about 6-8 minutes. Place in a greased bowl, turning once to grease top. Cover and refrigerate overnight.
3. Turn dough onto a lightly floured surface. Divide into nine portions, then divide and shape each portion into 12 balls. Place three balls in each greased muffin cup. Cover with kitchen towels; let rise in a warm place until doubled, about 1 hour.
4. Preheat oven to 375°. Brush rolls with half of the melted butter; bake until golden brown, about 15-20 minutes. Remove from the oven; brush with the remaining butter.

ALMOND BEAR CLAWS

These bear claws are absolutely melt-in-your-mouth delicious! It's impossible to resist the delicate pastry, rich almond filling and pretty fanned tops sprinkled with sugar and almonds.
—**Aneta Kish** La Crosse, WI

Prep: 45 min. + chilling • **Bake:** 15 min.
Makes: 1½ dozen

- 1½ **cups cold butter, cut into**
  ½-inch pieces
- 5 **cups all-purpose flour, divided**
- 1 **package (¼ ounce) active dry yeast**
- 1¼ **cups half-and-half cream**
- ¼ **cup granulated sugar**
- ¼ **teaspoon salt**
- 2 **large eggs**
- 1 **large egg white**
- ¾ **cup confectioners' sugar**
- ½ **cup almond paste, cubed**
- 1 **tablespoon water**
  Coarse or granulated sugar
  Sliced almonds

1. In a bowl, toss butter with 3 cups flour until well coated; refrigerate. In a large bowl, combine yeast and remaining flour.
2. In a saucepan, heat cream, sugar and salt to 120°-130°. Add to yeast mixture with 1 egg. Beat until smooth. Stir in butter mixture just until moistened.
3. Place dough onto a well-floured surface; roll into a 21x12-in. rectangle. Starting at a short side, fold dough in thirds, forming a 12x7-in. rectangle. Give the dough a quarter turn; roll into a 21x12-in. rectangle. Fold into thirds, starting with a short side. Repeat, flouring surface as needed. (Do not chill dough between each rolling and folding.) Cover and chill for 4 to 24 hours or until firm.
4. For filling, in a bowl, beat egg white until foamy. Gradually add confectioners' sugar and almond paste; beat until smooth. Cut dough in half widthwise. Roll each portion into a 12-in. square; cut each square into three 12x4-in. strips. Spread about 2 tablespoons filling down

center of each strip. Fold long edges together over filling; seal edges and ends. Cut into three pieces.
5. Place on parchment paper-lined baking sheets with folded edge facing away from you. With scissors, cut strips four times to within ½ in. of folded edge; separate slightly. Repeat with remaining dough and filling. Cover and let rise in a warm place until doubled, about 1 hour.
6. Preheat oven to 375°. Lightly beat water and remaining egg; brush over dough. Sprinkle with sugar and almonds. Bake for 15 minutes or until golden brown. Remove from pans to wire racks to cool.

IRISH SODA BREAD

This traditional Irish soda bread can be made with an assortment of mix-ins such as dried fruit and nuts, but I like it with a handful of raisins. It's the perfect change-of-pace item to bring to a get-together.
—**Gloria Warczak** Cedarburg, WI

Prep: 15 min. • **Bake:** 30 min.
Makes: 8 servings

- 2 cups all-purpose flour
- 2 tablespoons brown sugar
- 1 teaspoon baking powder
- 1 teaspoon baking soda
- ½ teaspoon salt
- 3 tablespoons cold butter, cubed
- 2 large eggs, divided use
- ¾ cup buttermilk
- ⅓ cup raisins

1. Preheat oven to 375°. Whisk together the first five ingredients. Cut in butter until mixture resembles coarse crumbs. In another bowl, whisk together 1 egg and buttermilk. Add to flour mixture; stir just until moistened. Stir in raisins.
2. Turn dough onto a lightly floured surface; knead gently 6-8 times. Shape into a 6½-in. round loaf; place on a greased baking sheet. Using a sharp knife, make a shallow cross in top of loaf. Whisk the remaining egg; brush over top.
3. Bake loaf until golden brown, about 30-35 minutes. Remove from pan to a wire rack. Serve warm.
Caraway Irish Soda Bread: Add 1-2 tablespoons of caraway seeds to the dry ingredients.

FREEZE IT
RHUBARB & STRAWBERRY COFFEE CAKE

Vanilla cake with cream cheese filling and strawberry rhubarb sauce makes a grand finale for a Mother's Day brunch.
—**Danielle Lee** Sewickley, PA

Prep: 50 min. • **Bake:** 50 min. + cooling
Makes: 12 servings

- 1½ teaspoons cornstarch
- 3 tablespoons sugar
- ¾ cup chopped fresh strawberries
- ¾ cup chopped fresh or frozen rhubarb
- 1 tablespoon water

FILLING
- 1 package (8 ounces) cream cheese, softened
- ¼ cup sugar
- 1 large egg, lightly beaten

CAKE
- 2 cups all-purpose flour
- ¾ cup sugar
- ½ cup cold butter, cubed
- ½ teaspoon baking powder
- ½ teaspoon baking soda
- ¼ teaspoon salt
- 1 large egg, lightly beaten
- ¾ cup fat-free sour cream
- 1 teaspoon vanilla extract

1. Preheat oven to 350°. Line the bottom of a greased 9-in. springform pan with parchment paper; grease paper. In a small saucepan, mix cornstarch and sugar; stir in strawberries, rhubarb and water. Bring to a boil. Reduce heat; simmer, uncovered, 6-8 minutes or until thickened, stirring occasionally. For filling, in a small bowl, beat cream cheese and sugar until smooth. Beat in egg.
2. In a large bowl, combine flour and sugar; cut in butter until crumbly. Reserve ¾ cup for topping. Stir baking powder, baking soda and salt into remaining flour mixture. In a small bowl, whisk egg, sour cream and vanilla until blended; gently stir into flour mixture (do not overmix).
3. Spread batter onto bottom and ½ in. up sides of prepared pan. Spread filling over crust, leaving a ½-in. border. Spoon strawberry mixture over top; sprinkle with reserved crumb mixture.
4. Bake 50-60 minutes or until edges are golden brown. Cool on a wire rack 20 minutes. Loosen sides from pan with a knife. Cool completely. Remove rim from pan. Refrigerate leftovers.
Freeze option: Securely wrap cooled cake in plastic wrap and foil, then freeze. To use, thaw in refrigerator.

ORANGE CRANBERRY BREAD

The beauty of this festive quick bread is that it makes a delicious post-dinner snack as well as breakfast the next day. I like to toast leftover slices and spread them with cream cheese or butter for breakfast.
—**Ron Gardner** Grand Haven, MI

Prep: 20 min. • **Bake:** 50 min. + cooling
Makes: 2 loaves (16 slices each)

- 2¾ cups all-purpose flour
- ⅔ cup sugar
- ⅔ cup packed brown sugar
- 3½ teaspoons baking powder
- 1 teaspoon salt
- ½ teaspoon ground cinnamon
- ¼ teaspoon ground nutmeg
- 1 large egg
- 1 cup 2% milk
- ½ cup orange juice
- 3 tablespoons canola oil
- 2 to 3 teaspoons grated orange peel
- 2 cups coarsely chopped fresh or frozen cranberries
- 1 large apple, peeled and chopped

1. Preheat oven to 350°. In a large bowl, combine flour, sugars, baking powder, salt, cinnamon and nutmeg. Whisk egg, milk, orange juice, oil and orange peel; stir into dry ingredients just until blended. Fold in the cranberries and apple.
2. Pour into two greased 8x4-in. loaf pans. Bake for 50-55 minutes or until a toothpick inserted in the center comes out clean. Cool for 10 minutes before removing from pans to wire racks.
Freeze option: Securely wrap and freeze cooled loaves in plastic wrap and foil. To use, thaw at room temperature.

OVERNIGHT CHERRY DANISH

These rolls with their cherry-filled centers melt in your mouth and make the perfect morning treat.
—**Leann Sauder** Tremont, IL

Prep: 1½ hours + chilling
Bake: 15 min. + cooling
Makes: 3 dozen

- 2 packages (¼ ounce each) active dry yeast
- ½ cup warm 2% milk (110° to 115°)
- 6 cups all-purpose flour
- ⅓ cup sugar
- 2 teaspoons salt
- 1 cup cold butter, cubed
- 1½ cups warm half-and-half cream (70° to 80°)
- 6 large egg yolks
- 1 can (21 ounces) cherry pie filling

ICING
- 3 cups confectioners' sugar
- 2 tablespoons butter, softened
- ¼ teaspoon vanilla extract
  Dash salt
- 4 to 5 tablespoons half-and-half cream

1. Dissolve yeast in warm milk. In a large bowl, combine flour, sugar and salt. Cut in butter until crumbly. Add yeast mixture, cream and egg yolks; stir until mixture forms a soft dough (dough will be sticky). Refrigerate, covered, overnight.
2. Punch down dough. Turn onto a lightly floured surface; divide into four portions. Roll each into an 18x4-in. rectangle; cut into 4x1-in. strips.
3. Place two strips side by side; twist together. Shape into a ring and pinch ends together. Place 2 in. apart on greased baking sheets. Repeat with remaining strips. Cover with kitchen towels; let rise in a warm place until doubled, about 45 minutes.
4. Preheat oven to 350°. Using the end of a wooden spoon handle, make a ½-in.-deep indentation in the center of each Danish. Fill each with 1 tablespoon pie filling. Bake 14-16 minutes or until lightly browned. Remove from pans to wire racks to cool.
5. For icing, in a medium bowl, beat confectioners' sugar, butter, vanilla, salt and enough cream to reach desired consistency. Drizzle over Danish.

GRAHAM STREUSEL COFFEE CAKE

This sweet coffee cake is so quick and easy to make, it makes a regular appearance on our table!

—Blanche Whytsell Arnoldsburg, WV

....

Prep: 20 min. • **Bake:** 40 min. + cooling
Makes: 16 servings

1½ cups graham cracker crumbs
¾ cup packed brown sugar
¾ cup chopped pecans
1½ teaspoons ground cinnamon
⅔ cup butter, melted
1 package yellow cake mix (regular size)
½ cup confectioners' sugar
1 tablespoon milk

1. Preheat oven to 350°. In a small bowl, combine the cracker crumbs, brown sugar, pecans and cinnamon. Stir in butter; set aside. Prepare cake mix according to package directions.

2. Pour half of the batter into a greased 13x9-in. baking pan. Sprinkle with half the graham cracker mixture. Carefully spoon the remaining batter on top. Sprinkle with the remaining graham cracker mixture.

3. Bake for 40-45 minutes or until a toothpick inserted in center comes out clean. Cool on a wire rack. Combine confectioners' sugar and milk; drizzle over coffee cake.

Good-Morning Muffins

What could be better than your family waking up to the tantalizing aroma of fresh-baked muffins, still warm from the oven? These tasty morsels make the perfect breakfast treat!

GRANDMA'S HONEY MUFFINS

I can remember my Grandma Wheeler making these delicious muffins—we'd eat them nice and warm! She was a "pinch of this and handful of that" kind of cook, so getting the recipe correct was a challenge. Now it's a family treasure!

—Darlis Wilfer West Bend, WI

....

Start to Finish: 30 min.
Makes: 1 dozen

- 2 **cups all-purpose flour**
- ½ **cup sugar**
- 3 **teaspoons baking powder**
- ½ **teaspoon salt**
- 1 **large egg**
- 1 **cup 2% milk**
- ¼ **cup butter, melted**
- ¼ **cup honey**

1. Preheat oven to 400°. In a large bowl, combine flour, sugar, baking powder and salt. In a small bowl, combine egg, milk, butter and honey. Stir into dry ingredients just until moistened.
2. Fill greased or paper-lined muffin cups three-fourths full. Bake 15-18 minutes or until a toothpick inserted in center comes out clean. Cool 5 minutes before removing from pan to a wire rack. Serve warm.

PUMPKIN-APPLE MUFFINS WITH STREUSEL TOPPING

My mother always made these muffins whenever our family got together at her house. Now they're a family favorite at my house, and my in-laws love them, too!

—Carolyn Riley Carlisle, PA

....

Prep: 20 min. • **Bake:** 30 min. + cooling
Makes: about 1½ dozen

- 2½ **cups all-purpose flour**
- 2 **cups sugar**
- 1 **tablespoon pumpkin pie spice**
- 1 **teaspoon baking soda**
- ½ **teaspoon salt**
- 2 **large eggs, lightly beaten**
- 1 **cup canned pumpkin**
- ½ **cup vegetable oil**
- 2 **cups finely chopped peeled apples**

TOPPING
- ¼ **cup sugar**
- 2 **tablespoons all-purpose flour**
- ½ **teaspoon ground cinnamon**
- 1 **tablespoon butter or margarine**

1. Preheat oven to 350°. In a large bowl, combine flour, sugar, pumpkin pie spice, baking soda and salt. Combine eggs, pumpkin and oil; stir into dry ingredients just until moistened. Fold in apples. Fill greased or paper-lined muffin cups three-fourths full.
2. For topping, combine sugar, flour and cinnamon. Cut in butter until mixture resembles coarse crumbs; sprinkle 1 teaspoon over each muffin. Bake until muffins test done, 30-35 minute. Cool in pan 10 minutes; remove to a wire rack.

SWEET POTATO MUFFINS

This is my own recipe, and I make it often. My five grandchildren think these are absolutely delicious.
—**Christine Johnson** Ricetown, KY

Start to Finish: 25 min.
Makes: 2 dozen

- 2 **cups self-rising flour**
- 2 **cups sugar**
- 2 **teaspoons ground cinnamon**
- 1 **large egg**
- 2 **cups cold mashed sweet potatoes** (**without added butter or milk**)
- 1 **cup canola oil**

GLAZE

- 1 **cup confectioners' sugar**
- 2 **tablespoons plus 1½ teaspoons 2% milk**
- 1½ **teaspoons butter, melted**
- 1 **teaspoon vanilla extract**
- ½ **teaspoon ground cinnamon**

1. Preheat oven to 375°. In a small bowl, combine flour, sugar and cinnamon. In another bowl, whisk egg, sweet potatoes and oil. Stir into dry ingredients just until moistened.
2. Fill greased muffin cups two-thirds full. Bake 15-18 minutes or until a toothpick comes out clean. Cool 5 minutes before removing from pans to wire racks.
3. In a small bowl, combine the glaze ingredients; drizzle over warm muffins.
Freeze option: Freeze unglazed cooled muffins in resealable plastic freezer bags. Thaw at room temperature or microwave each muffin on high until heated through, 20-30 seconds. Glaze.
Note: As a substitute for each cup of self-rising flour, place 1½ teaspoons baking powder and ½ teaspoon salt in a measuring cup. Add all-purpose flour to measure 1 cup.

BANANA MACADAMIA MUFFINS

These muffins taste even better the next day, so to save time, I often make them the night before. They stay moist for days.
—**Stasha Wampler** Clinchport, VA

Prep: 15 min. • **Bake:** 20 min.
Makes: 2 dozen

- 3 **cups all-purpose flour**
- 2 **cups sugar**
- 2 **teaspoons ground cinnamon**
- 1 **teaspoon baking soda**
- 1 **teaspoon salt**
- 3 **large eggs**
- 1 **cup canola oil**
- 1 **teaspoon vanilla extract**
- 3 **medium ripe bananas, mashed**
- 1 **cup sweetened shredded coconut**
- 1 **can (8 ounces) crushed pineapple, drained**
- 1 **cup macadamia nuts, coarsely chopped**

1. Preheat oven to 375°. In a large bowl, combine the flour, sugar, cinnamon, baking soda and salt. In another bowl, combine the eggs, oil and vanilla. Stir into dry ingredients just until moistened. Fold in the bananas, coconut and pineapple.
2. Fill greased or paper-lined muffin cups two-thirds full. Sprinkle with nuts. Bake for 18-20 minutes or until a toothpick comes out clean. Cool for 5 minutes before removing from pans to wire racks.
Freeze option: Freeze cooled muffins in resealable plastic freezer bags. To use, thaw at room temperature or microwave each muffin on high until heated through, 20-30 seconds.

PUMPKIN SCONES WITH BERRY BUTTER

My delightful scones are perfect on a cold winter day with a steaming hot cup of coffee. They also make a wonderful hostess gift arranged in a basket.

—Judy Wilson Sun City West, AZ

Prep: 25 min. + chilling • **Bake:** 15 min.
Makes: 8 scones (about ½ cup butter)

- 2 tablespoons dried cranberries
- ½ cup boiling water
- ½ cup butter, softened
- 3 tablespoons confectioners' sugar

DOUGH

- 2¼ cups all-purpose flour
- ¼ cup packed brown sugar
- 2 teaspoons baking powder
- 1½ teaspoons pumpkin pie spice
- ¼ teaspoon salt
- ¼ teaspoon baking soda
- ½ cup cold butter, cubed
- 1 large egg
- ½ cup canned pumpkin
- ⅓ cup 2% milk
- 2 tablespoons chopped pecans, optional

1. Place cranberries in a small bowl; add boiling water. Let stand for 5 minutes; drain and chop. Beat butter until light and fluffy. Add confectioners' sugar and cranberries; mix well. Cover and refrigerate for at least 1 hour.

2. In a large bowl, combine the flour, brown sugar, baking powder, pie spice, salt and baking soda. Cut in butter until mixture resembles coarse crumbs. In a small bowl, whisk the egg, pumpkin and milk; add to the crumb mixture just until moistened. Stir in pecans if desired.

3. Turn dough onto a floured surface; knead 10 times. Pat into an 8-in. circle. Cut into eight wedges; separate wedges and place on a greased baking sheet.

4. Bake at 400° for 12-15 minutes or until golden brown. Serve warm with berry butter.

CHEESE & PESTO BISCUITS

Biscuits always liven up a meal, especially when they're golden brown and filled with pesto, garlic and cheese for extra zip.

—Liz Bellville Jacksonville, NC

Start to Finish: 25 min.
Makes: 1 dozen

- 2 cups all-purpose flour
- 2 teaspoons baking powder
- ½ teaspoon salt
- ¼ teaspoon baking soda
- ⅓ cup cold butter, cubed
- 1 cup shredded Italian cheese blend
- 1¼ cups buttermilk
- 1 tablespoon prepared pesto
- 1 tablespoon butter, melted
- 1 garlic clove, minced

1. Preheat oven to 450°. In a large bowl, whisk flour, baking powder, salt and baking soda. Cut in butter until mixture resembles coarse crumbs. Stir in cheese. In a small bowl, whisk buttermilk and pesto until blended; stir into the flour mixture just until moistened.

2. Drop dough by ¼ cupfuls 2 in. apart onto an ungreased baking sheet. Bake 10-12 minutes or until golden brown.

3. Mix melted butter and garlic; brush over biscuits. Serve warm.

Contest Winner

LEMON/RASPBERRY STREUSEL MUFFINS

These attractive, delicious muffins make a great accompaniment to any breakfast or brunch. I usually double the recipe because they seem to disappear the minute I set them out!
—**Marie Herr** Berea, OH

Prep: 15 min. • **Bake:** 20 min. + cooling
Makes: about 1 dozen

- 2 cups all-purpose flour
- ½ cup sugar
- 2 teaspoons baking powder
- ½ teaspoon baking soda
- ½ teaspoon salt
- 2 large eggs, lightly beaten
- 1 cup (8 ounces) lemon yogurt
- ½ cup vegetable oil
- 1 teaspoon grated lemon zest
- 1 cup fresh or frozen raspberries

TOPPING
- ⅓ cup sugar
- ¼ cup all-purpose flour
- 2 tablespoons butter or margarine

1. In a large bowl, combine flour, sugar, baking powder, baking soda and salt. Combine eggs, yogurt, oil and lemon zest; mix well. Stir into dry ingredients just until moistened. Fold in raspberries. Fill greased or paper-lined muffin cups three-fourths full.
2. For topping, combine the sugar and flour. Cut in butter until the mixture resembles coarse crumbs; sprinkle about 1 tablespoon over each muffin. Bake at 400° for 18-20 minutes or until muffins test done. Cool in pan 10 minutes before removing to a wire rack.

HONEY WHOLE WHEAT PAN ROLLS

With their pleasant wheat flavor and a honey of a glaze, these rolls impress my guests. When I take them to potlucks, I come home with an empty pan.
—**Nancye Thompson** Paducah, KY

Prep: 35 min. + chilling • **Bake:** 20 min.
Makes: 5 dozen (1¼ cups honey butter)

- 4 to 5 cups bread flour
- ¼ cup sugar
- 2 packages (¼ ounce each) active dry yeast
- 1 teaspoon salt
- 1 cup 2% milk
- 1 cup butter, cubed
- ½ cup water
- 2 large eggs
- 2 cups whole wheat flour

HONEY BUTTER
- 1 cup butter, softened
- 7 tablespoons honey

HONEY GLAZE
- 2 tablespoons honey
- 1 tablespoon butter, melted

1. In a large bowl, combine 2 cups bread flour, sugar, dry yeast and salt. In a small saucepan, heat the milk, butter and water to 120°-130°. Add to dry ingredients; beat just until moistened. Beat in eggs. Stir in the whole wheat flour and enough of the remaining bread flour to form a soft dough.
2. Turn onto a floured surface; knead dough until smooth and elastic, about 10 minutes. Cover; let rest 15 minutes.
3. Divide dough into thirds. Roll each portion into a 20-in. rope. Cut each rope into 20 pieces; shape each piece into a ball. Grease three 9-in. round baking pans; arrange 20 balls in each pan. Cover and refrigerate overnight.
4. Let rise in a warm place until doubled, about 1¼ hours. Bake at 350° until golden brown, 18-22 minutes.
5. Meanwhile, in a small bowl, cream butter. Add honey; beat until light and fluffy. Remove rolls from pans to wire racks. Combine glaze ingredients; brush over warm rolls. Serve with honey butter.

PECAN STICKY BUNS

My homemade caramel rolls have the old-fashioned goodness we crave. Tender and nutty, the buns disappear fast!
—**Julia Spence** New Braunfels, TX

Prep: 45 min. + rising • **Bake:** 20 min.
Makes: 1 dozen

- 4 to 4½ cups all-purpose flour
- ⅓ cup sugar
- 1 package (¼ ounce) active dry yeast
- ½ teaspoon salt
- 1 cup 2% milk
- ¼ cup butter, cubed
- 2 large eggs

TOPPING
- ⅓ cup butter, cubed
- ⅔ cup packed brown sugar
- 2 tablespoons light corn syrup
- 1 cup chopped pecans

FILLING
- 3 tablespoons butter, melted
- ½ cup packed brown sugar
- ⅓ cup sugar
- 2 tablespoons ground cinnamon

1. In a large bowl, combine 2 cups flour, sugar, yeast and salt. In a small saucepan, heat milk and butter to 120°-130°. Add to the dry ingredients; beat just until moistened. Add eggs; beat until smooth. Stir in enough remaining flour to form a soft dough (dough will be sticky).

2. Turn onto a floured surface; knead until smooth and elastic, about 6-8 minutes. Place in a greased bowl, turning once to grease top. Cover and let rise in a warm place until doubled, about 1 hour.

3. In a small saucepan, melt butter over medium heat. Stir in brown sugar and corn syrup until combined. Pour into a well-greased 13x9-in. baking dish. Sprinkle with pecans.

4. Punch dough down. Turn onto a floured surface. Roll into a 12x8-in. rectangle; brush with melted butter. Combine sugars and cinnamon; sprinkle over dough to within ½ in. of edges and press into dough. Roll up jelly-roll style, starting with a long side; pinch seam to seal.

5. Cut into 12 slices. Place cut side down in prepared pan. Cover and let rise until doubled, about 30 minutes. Preheat oven to 375°.

6. Bake 20-25 minutes or until golden brown. Immediately invert onto a serving platter. Serve warm.

Cinnamon Rolls: Omit topping. Frost warm rolls with vanilla frosting: 1½ cups confectioners' sugar, 3 tablespoons softened butter, ¾ teaspoon vanilla extract and 1 tablespoon milk.

Chocolate Chip Cinnamon Rolls: Omit topping and filling. Brush dough with 2 tablespoons melted butter. Combine ¼ cup packed brown sugar, ½ teaspoon ground cinnamon and ⅔ cup miniature semisweet chocolate chips; sprinkle over dough. Frost warm rolls with vanilla frosting (see Cinnamon Rolls recipe variation above).

Hot Butter Rum Rolls: Add ½ teaspoon rum extract to topping. Omit cinnamon from filling. Add ⅓ cup chopped pecans and ½ teaspoon rum extract to filling.

DILLY ROLLS

These versatile rolls are great served warm alongside any dinner. I always make a big batch since my family enjoys the rolls after they're cool, too, stuffed with filling like egg salad or ham salad.

—**Mary Bickel** Terre Haute, IN

Prep: 25 min. + rising • **Bake:** 20 min.
Makes: 2 dozen

- 2 cups 4% cottage cheese
- 2 tablespoons butter
- 2 packages (¼ ounce each) active dry yeast
- ½ cup warm water (110° to 115°)
- 2 large eggs
- ¼ cup sugar
- 2 tablespoons dried minced onion
- 1 to 2 tablespoons dill weed
- 1 tablespoon salt
- ½ teaspoon baking soda
- 4½ to 5 cups all-purpose flour

1. In a large saucepan over medium heat, cook cottage cheese and butter until butter is melted. Cool to 110° to 115°. In a large bowl, dissolve yeast in water. Add eggs, sugar, onion, dill, salt, baking soda and cottage cheese mixture. Add 3 cups of flour; beat until smooth. Add enough remaining flour to form a soft dough.
2. Turn dough onto a floured surface; knead until smooth and elastic, 6-8 minutes. Place in a greased bowl, turning once to grease top. Cover and let rise in a warm place until doubled, about 1 hour.
3. Punch dough down. Form into 24 balls; place in a 13x9-in. baking pan that has been sprayed with cooking spray. Cover and let rise until doubled, about 45 minutes.
4. Bake at 350° for 20-25 minutes.

GARLIC BUBBLE LOAF

Complete your next spaghetti dinner with this eye-catching loaf. Family and friends will have fun pulling off each rich and buttery piece.

—**Lynn Nichols** Bartlett, NE

Prep: 35 min. + rising
Bake: 35 min. + cooling
Makes: 2 loaves

- 2 packages (¼ ounce each) active dry yeast
- ¼ cup warm water (110° to 115°)
- 2 cups warm milk (110° to 115°)
- 2 tablespoons sugar
- 1 tablespoon shortening
- 2 teaspoons salt
- 6¼ to 6½ cups all-purpose flour
- ½ cup butter, melted
- 1 tablespoon dried parsley flakes
- 2 teaspoons garlic powder

1. In a large bowl, dissolve yeast in warm water. Add milk, sugar, shortening, salt and 2 cups flour; beat until smooth. Stir in enough of the remaining flour to form a soft dough. Turn out on a floured surface; knead until smooth and elastic, about 6-8 minutes. Place in a greased bowl, turning once to grease top. Cover and let rise in a warm place until doubled, about 1 hour.
2. Punch dough down. Turn onto a lightly floured surface; divide into fourths. Divide each portion into 12 pieces. In a shallow bowl, combine butter, parsley and garlic powder. Shape each piece into a ball; dip in the butter mixture. Place in two greased 9x5-in. loaf pans. Pour any remaining butter mixture over dough. Cover and let rise until doubled, about 30 minutes.
3. Bake at 375° for 35-40 minutes or until golden brown. Cool for 10 minutes before removing from pans to wire racks. Serve warm.

CRAN-APPLE MUFFINS

I like to pile a fresh batch of these muffins on a plate when friends drop in for coffee. Even my grandkids enjoy the cranberry and apple flavor combination.
—**Millie Westland** Hayward, MN

Prep: 20 min. • **Bake:** 20 min.
Makes: about 1 dozen

- ½ cup whole-berry cranberry sauce
- ½ teaspoon grated orange peel
- 1½ cups all-purpose flour
- ½ cup sugar
- 1 teaspoon ground cinnamon
- ½ teaspoon baking soda
- ¼ teaspoon baking powder
- ¼ teaspoon salt
- 1 large egg
- ⅓ cup 2% milk
- ⅓ cup canola oil
- 1 cup shredded peeled tart apple
- ½ cup confectioners' sugar
- 1 tablespoon orange juice

1. Preheat oven to 375°. Combine cranberry sauce and orange peel; set aside.

2. In a large bowl, combine flour, sugar, cinnamon, baking soda, baking powder and salt. Beat egg, milk and oil; stir into dry ingredients just until moistened. Fold in apple.

3. Fill greased or paper-lined muffin cups half full. Make a well in the center of each muffin; fill with about 2 teaspoons of reserved cranberry mixture.

4. Bake 18-20 minutes or until a toothpick comes out clean. Cool for 5 minutes; remove from pan to a wire rack. Combine confectioners' sugar and orange juice; drizzle over warm muffins.

MOM'S ITALIAN BREAD

Mom used to bake at least four of these tender loaves at once, and they never lasted long. She served the bread with every Italian meal. I love it toasted, too.
—**Linda Harrington** Windham, NH

Prep: 30 min. + rising
Bake: 20 min. + cooling
Makes: 2 loaves (12 slices each)

- 1 package (¼ ounce) active dry yeast
- 2 cups warm water (110° to 115°)
- 1 teaspoon sugar
- 2 teaspoons salt
- 5½ cups all-purpose flour

1. In a large bowl, dissolve yeast in warm water. Add sugar, salt and 3 cups flour. Beat on medium speed for 3 minutes. Stir in remaining flour to form a soft dough.

2. Turn dough onto a floured surface; knead until smooth and elastic, about 6-8 minutes. Place in a greased bowl, turning once to grease the top. Cover and let rise in a warm place until doubled, about 1 hour.

3. Punch dough down. Turn onto a floured surface; divide in half. Shape each portion into a loaf. Place each loaf seam side down on a greased baking sheet. Cover and let rise until doubled, about 30 minutes.

4. Meanwhile, preheat oven to 400°. With a sharp knife, make four shallow slashes across top of each loaf. Bake 20-25 minutes or until golden brown. Remove from pans to wire racks to cool.

Note: To ensure a light texture, be sure to take the time to knead well. After kneading the first few minutes, press your thumb into the dough. If the indent stays, you're done. If not, knead a few more minutes.

KEY LIME BREAD

The first time I tasted this deliciously different bread was at a friend's house, and she graciously shared the recipe. It's so easy to make and absolutely yummy!
—**Joan Hallford** North Richland Hills, TX

Prep: 15 min. • **Bake:** 50 min. + cooling
Makes: 2 loaves (16 slices each)

- ⅔ **cup butter, softened**
- 2 **cups sugar**
- 4 **large eggs**
- 2 **tablespoons grated lime peel**
- 2 **tablespoons Key lime juice**
- 1 **teaspoon vanilla extract**
- 3 **cups all-purpose flour**
- 3 **teaspoons baking powder**
- 1 **teaspoon salt**
- 1 **cup milk**
- 1 **cup chopped walnuts**

GLAZE
- ⅔ **cup confectioners' sugar**
- 1 **to 2 tablespoons Key lime juice**

1. Preheat oven to 350°. In a large bowl, cream butter and sugar until light and fluffy. Beat in eggs. Beat in lime peel, juice and vanilla. Combine flour, baking powder and salt; gradually add to creamed mixture alternately with milk, beating well after each addition. Fold in walnuts.

2. Transfer to two greased 9x5-in. loaf pans. Bake for 50-55 minutes or until a toothpick inserted in the center comes out clean. Cool for 10 minutes before removing from pans to wire racks.

3. Combine confectioners' sugar and enough lime juice to achieve desired consistency; drizzle over warm bread. Cool completely.

Freeze option: Securely wrap unglazed, cooled loaves in plastic wrap and foil, then freeze. To use, thaw at room temperature. Prepare glaze as directed.

Contest Winner

PULL-APART CARAMEL COFFEE CAKE

When I made this delightful breakfast treat for a brunch party, it was a huge hit. Now I get requests every time family or friends do anything around the breakfast hour! That's why I always keep the four simple ingredients on hand.
—**Jaime Keeling** Keizer, OR

Prep: 10 min. • **Bake:** 25 min.
Makes: 1 loaf (16 servings)

- 2 **tubes (12 ounces each) refrigerated buttermilk biscuits**
- 1 **cup packed brown sugar**
- ½ **cup heavy whipping cream**
- 1 **teaspoon ground cinnamon**

1. Preheat oven to 350°. Cut each biscuit into four pieces; arrange evenly in a 10-in. fluted tube pan coated with cooking spray. In a small bowl, mix the remaining ingredients until blended; pour over the biscuits.

2. Bake for 25-30 minutes or until golden brown. Cool in pan for 5 minutes before inverting onto a serving plate.

Main Dishes

Get ready to dig in to all the goodness country cooking offers! With 40 stick-to-your-ribs entrees, this chapter is one you'll turn to time and again. Turkey Biscuit Stew, Big John's Chili-Rubbed Ribs and Creamy Braised Chicken are just a few of the unbeatable meals you'll find here. Ring the dinner bell, and let's eat!

MY MOTHER'S LEMONY CHICKEN WITH BROCCOLI

My mom used to make super succulent chicken with broccoli for our family in Montana. The lucky guests invited for supper could not stop raving.
—Jessy Drummond Springfield, TN

Prep: 15 min. • **Cook:** 20 min.
Makes: 4 servings

- 1 pound boneless skinless chicken breasts, cut into 1-inch strips
- ½ teaspoon salt
- ¼ teaspoon pepper
- ½ cup all-purpose flour
- ¼ teaspoon garlic powder
- ¼ teaspoon paprika
- 1 large egg
- 3 tablespoons lemon juice, divided
- ¼ cup butter, cubed
- 1 cup chicken broth
- ½ teaspoon grated lemon peel
- 4 cups fresh broccoli florets
  Lemon wedges
  Hot cooked rice, optional

1. Sprinkle chicken with salt and pepper. In a shallow bowl, mix flour, garlic powder and paprika. In another shallow bowl, whisk egg and 1 tablespoon lemon juice. Dip chicken in egg mixture, then in flour mixture; shake off excess.
2. In a large skillet, heat butter over medium heat. Add the chicken; cook 4-6 minutes on each side or until no longer pink. Remove and keep warm. Add broth, lemon peel and remaining lemon juice to skillet; bring to a boil. Stir in broccoli. Reduce heat; simmer, covered, 8-10 minutes or until broccoli is tender. Serve with chicken, lemon wedges and, if desired, rice.

PUFF PASTRY CHICKEN BUNDLES

Inside these golden puff pastry packages, there's a savory surprise—chicken breasts rolled with spinach, herbed cream cheese and walnuts. I serve this elegant entree when we have guests or are celebrating a holiday or special occasion.
—Brad Moritz Limerick, PA

Prep: 30 min. • **Bake:** 20 min.
Makes: 8 servings

- 8 boneless skinless chicken breast halves (about 6 ounces each)
- 1 teaspoon salt
- ½ teaspoon pepper
- 40 large spinach leaves
- 1 carton (8 ounces) spreadable chive and onion cream cheese
- ½ cup chopped walnuts, toasted
- 2 sheets frozen puff pastry, thawed
- 1 large egg
- ½ teaspoon cold water

1. Preheat oven to 400°. Cut a lengthwise slit in each chicken breast half to within ½ in. of the other side; open meat so it lies flat. Cover chicken with plastic wrap; pound with a meat mallet to ⅛-in. thickness. Remove plastic wrap. Sprinkle with salt and pepper.
2. Place five spinach leaves on each chicken breast half. Spoon a scant 2 tablespoons of cream cheese down the center of each chicken breast half; sprinkle with 1 tablespoon walnuts. Roll up chicken; tuck in ends. Repeat with remaining chicken.
3. Unfold puff pastry; cut into eight portions. Roll each portion into a 7-in. square. Place chicken on one half of each square; fold other half of pastry over chicken. Crimp edges with fork. Combine egg and cold water; brush over edges of pastry. Repeat with remaining pastry.
4. Bake on a greased 15x10x1-in. baking sheet until a thermometer reads 165°, 20-25 minutes.

HAM & SWISS POTATO CASSEROLE

When I wanted to use up ingredients I had on hand, I started experimenting—and hit a home run! The classic trio of potatoes, ham and Swiss comes together in this comforting bake, which is now one of my go-to recipes to feed a crowd.
—**Sarah Wilham** Elkhart, IL

Prep: 25 min. • **Bake:** 20 min.
Makes: 8 servings

- 5 large potatoes (about 4 pounds), peeled and cut into ¾-inch pieces
- ¼ cup butter, cubed
- 1 medium onion, chopped
- 1 garlic clove, minced
- ⅓ cup all-purpose flour
- 2 cups 2% milk
- 1⅓ cups roasted red pepper Alfredo sauce
- 1 teaspoon dried basil
- ¼ teaspoon salt
- ¼ teaspoon dill weed
- ¼ teaspoon pepper
- 2 cups cubed fully cooked ham
- 2 cups shredded Swiss cheese
- ¼ cup seasoned bread crumbs
- 1 tablespoon butter, melted

1. Preheat oven to 375°. Place potatoes in a large saucepan; add water to cover. Bring to a boil. Reduce heat; simmer, covered, for 8-10 minutes or until crisp-tender. Meanwhile, in a large skillet, heat butter over medium-high heat. Add onion; cook and stir 6-8 minutes or until tender. Add garlic; cook and stir 1 minute. Stir in flour until blended; gradually whisk in milk. Bring to a boil, stirring constantly; cook and stir for 1-2 minutes or until thickened. Stir in Alfredo sauce and seasonings; heat through.

2. Drain potatoes; transfer to a greased 13x9-in. baking dish. Layer with ham, cheese and sauce. In a small bowl, combine bread crumbs and butter. Sprinkle over top. Bake, uncovered, for 18-22 minutes or until topping is golden brown and cheese is melted. Let stand 5 minutes before serving.

To make ahead: Can be made a day in advance. Prepare recipe as directed, layering ham, cheese and sauce in baking dish. Cover and refrigerate overnight. Remove from the refrigerator 30 minutes before baking. Prepare crumb topping; sprinkle over top. Bake as directed.

GLAZED CORNISH HENS

If you're looking to add a touch of elegance to your dinner table, try these Cornish game hens topped with a sweet apricot glaze.
—*Taste of Home* Test Kitchen

Prep: 5 min. • **Bake:** 1 hour
Makes: 4 servings

- 2 Cornish game hens (20 to 24 ounces each), split lengthwise
- ¼ teaspoon salt
- ⅛ teaspoon white pepper
- ⅓ cup apricot spreadable fruit
- 1 tablespoon orange juice

1. Preheat oven to 350°. Place hens, breast side up, on a rack in a shallow roasting pan. Sprinkle with salt and pepper. Bake, uncovered, 30 minutes.

2. In a small bowl, combine spreadable fruit and orange juice. Spoon some of the apricot mixture over the hens. Bake until golden brown and juices run clear, 30-35 minutes, basting several times with remaining apricot mixture. Let stand for 5 minutes before serving.

HEARTY JAMBALAYA

This meaty, satisfying jambalaya freezes nicely, so I can serve half and put the rest away for another day when time is tight.
—**Mel Miller** Perkins, OK

Prep: 25 min. • **Cook:** 10 min.
Makes: 8 servings

- 1 pound smoked kielbasa or Polish sausage, cut into ½-inch slices
- 1 pound boneless skinless chicken breasts, cubed
- 1 large onion, chopped
- ½ cup chopped celery
- ½ cup chopped green pepper
- 4 garlic cloves, minced
- 2 tablespoons butter
- 1 can (14½ ounces) diced tomatoes, undrained
- 1 can (6 ounces) tomato paste
- ½ teaspoon hot pepper sauce
- ¼ to ½ teaspoon cayenne pepper
- ⅛ teaspoon garlic powder
- ⅛ teaspoon white pepper
- ⅛ teaspoon pepper
- ½ pound uncooked medium shrimp, peeled and deveined
  Hot cooked rice, optional

1. In a Dutch oven, saute the sausage, chicken, onion, celery, green pepper and garlic in butter until chicken is browned. Stir in the tomatoes, tomato paste and seasonings. Bring to a boil. Reduce heat; cover and simmer for 6-8 minutes or until chicken is no longer pink.

2. Stir in shrimp; cover and simmer for 4 minutes or until shrimp turn pink. Serve over rice if desired; or cool, cover and freeze for up to 2 months.

SPINACH & TURKEY TURNOVERS

Never toss any leftovers from a holiday meal when you can make turnovers using turkey, gravy and cranberries! We serve these as a quick meal or an appetizer.
—**Anjli Sabharwal** Marlboro, NJ

Prep: 25 min. • **Bake:** 15 min.
Makes: 8 servings

- 1½ teaspoons olive oil
- 2 green onions, chopped
- 1 garlic clove, minced
- ½ teaspoon dried rosemary, crushed
- ¼ teaspoon dried thyme
- 1 cup cubed cooked turkey
- 1 package (10 ounces) frozen chopped spinach, thawed and squeezed dry
- ½ cup shredded Monterey Jack cheese
- ¼ cup turkey gravy
- ¼ teaspoon salt
- ¼ teaspoon pepper
- 1 package (17.3 ounces) frozen puff pastry, thawed
- 1 large egg, lightly beaten
- 1 tablespoon water

SAUCE
- 1 cup whole-berry cranberry sauce
- ¼ cup orange juice
- 1 tablespoon grated orange peel

1. Preheat oven to 400°. In a large skillet, heat oil over medium-high heat. Add green onions, garlic, rosemary and thyme; cook and stir 1 minute. Remove from heat. Stir in turkey, spinach, cheese, gravy, salt and pepper.

2. Unfold puff pastry; cut each sheet into four squares. Transfer to greased baking sheets. Spoon turkey mixture onto center of each square. In a small bowl, whisk egg and water; brush over the edges of the pastry. Fold one corner of the dough diagonally over the filling, forming triangles; press edges with a fork to seal. Brush tops with egg mixture. Bake 12-14 minutes or until golden brown.

3. Meanwhile, in a small saucepan, combine cranberry sauce and orange juice. Bring to a boil; cook and stir for 3-4 minutes or until slightly thickened. Stir in orange peel. Serve with turnovers.

TURKEY BISCUIT STEW

This chunky stew makes a hearty supper, especially in the fall and winter. It's also a great way to use extra turkey during the holiday season.
—Lori Schlecht Wimbledon, ND

Prep: 15 min. • **Bake:** 20 min.
Makes: 8 servings

- ⅓ cup chopped onion
- ¼ cup butter, cubed
- ⅓ cup all-purpose flour
- ½ teaspoon salt
- ⅛ teaspoon pepper
- 1 can (10½ ounces) condensed chicken broth, undiluted
- ¾ cup whole milk
- 2 cups cubed cooked turkey
- 1 cup cooked peas
- 1 cup cooked whole baby carrots
- 1 tube (10 ounces) refrigerated buttermilk biscuits

1. In a 10-in. ovenproof skillet, saute onion in butter until tender. Stir in the flour, salt and pepper until blended. Gradually add broth and milk. Bring to a boil. Cook and stir for 2 minutes or until thickened and bubbly. Add the turkey, peas and carrots; heat through. Separate biscuits and arrange over the stew.
2. Bake at 375° for 20-25 minutes or until biscuits are golden brown.

STEAK & NEW POTATO TOSS

I usually use leftover barbecued steak to make this fabulous main dish salad. It's pretty, too, with the red pepper, green broccoli and white potatoes.
—Deyanne Davies Rossland, BC

Prep: 20 min. • **Cook:** 20 min.
Makes: 4 servings

- 1 pound small red potatoes, cut into 1-inch wedges
- 1 beef top sirloin steak (1 inch thick and about 1¼ pounds)
- 3 cups fresh broccoli florets
- ¼ cup olive oil
- 2 tablespoons cider vinegar
- 2 garlic cloves, minced
- ½ teaspoon ground mustard
- ½ teaspoon paprika
- ¼ teaspoon pepper
- 2 green onions, thinly sliced
- 1 medium sweet red pepper, chopped

1. Place potatoes in a large saucepan; add water to cover. Bring to a boil. Reduce heat; cook, uncovered, for 10-15 minutes or until tender. Drain.
2. Meanwhile, grill the steak, covered, over medium heat 7-9 minutes on each side or until meat reaches the desired doneness (for medium-rare, a thermometer should read 135°; medium, 140°; medium-well, 145°).
3. In a large saucepan, place steamer basket over 1 in. of water. Place broccoli in basket. Bring water to a boil. Reduce the heat to maintain a low boil; steam, covered, 2-3 minutes or until broccoli is crisp-tender. Remove from heat.
4. In a small bowl, whisk oil, vinegar, garlic and seasonings until blended; stir in green onions. Cut steak into thin slices.
5. In a large bowl, combine potatoes, steak, broccoli and red pepper. Drizzle with vinaigrette; toss to combine. Serve warm or refrigerate and serve cold.

BIG JOHN'S CHILI-RUBBED RIBS

When my family thinks of summer grilling, it's ribs all the way. Our Asian-inspired recipe is a welcome change from the usual barbecue-sauce versions.

—Ginger Sullivan Cutler Bay, FL

Prep: 20 min. + chilling • **Grill:** 1½ hours
Makes: 10 servings

3 tablespoons packed brown sugar
2 tablespoons paprika
2 tablespoons chili powder
3 teaspoons ground cumin
2 teaspoons garlic powder
1 teaspoon salt
6 pounds pork baby back ribs

GLAZE

1 cup reduced-sodium soy sauce
1 cup packed brown sugar
⅔ cup ketchup
⅓ cup lemon juice
1½ teaspoons minced fresh gingerroot

1. Mix the first six ingredients; rub over ribs. Refrigerate, covered, 30 minutes.
2. Wrap rib racks in large pieces of heavy-duty foil; seal tightly. Grill, covered, over indirect medium heat 1-1½ hours or until tender.
3. In a large saucepan, combine glaze ingredients; cook, uncovered, over medium heat 6-8 minutes or until heated through and sugar is dissolved, stirring occasionally.
4. Carefully remove the ribs from the foil. Place ribs over direct heat; brush with some of the glaze. Grill, covered, over medium heat for 25-30 minutes or until browned, turning and brushing ribs occasionally with remaining glaze.

FAVORITE CHICKEN POTPIE

Chock-full of chicken, potatoes, peas and corn, this autumn favorite makes two golden pies, so you can serve one at supper and freeze the other to save for a busy night.

—**Karen Johnson** Bakersfield, CA

Prep: 40 min. • **Bake:** 35 min. + standing
Makes: 2 potpies (8 servings each)

- 2 cups diced peeled potatoes
- 1¾ cups sliced carrots
- 1 cup butter, cubed
- ⅔ cup chopped onion
- 1 cup all-purpose flour
- 1¾ teaspoons salt
- 1 teaspoon dried thyme
- ¾ teaspoon pepper
- 3 cups chicken broth
- 1½ cups milk
- 4 cups cubed cooked chicken
- 1 cup frozen peas
- 1 cup frozen corn
- 2 packages (14.1 ounces each) refrigerated pie pastry

1. Preheat oven to 425°. Place potatoes and carrots in a large saucepan; add water to cover. Bring to a boil. Reduce heat; cook, covered, 8-10 minutes or until crisp-tender; drain.
2. In a large skillet, heat butter over medium-high heat. Add onion; cook and stir until tender. Stir in flour and seasonings until blended. Gradually stir in broth and milk. Bring to a boil, stirring constantly; cook and stir 2 minutes or until thickened. Stir in chicken, peas, corn and potato mixture; remove from heat.
3. Unroll a pastry sheet into each of two 9-in. pie plates; trim even with rims. Add chicken mixture. Unroll remaining pastry; place over filling. Trim, seal and flute the edges. Cut slits in tops.
4. Bake 35-40 minutes or until crust is lightly browned. Let stand 15 minutes before cutting.

Freeze option: Cover and freeze unbaked pies. To use, remove pies from freezer 30 minutes before baking (do not thaw). Preheat oven to 425°. Place pies on baking sheets; cover edges loosely with foil. Bake 30 minutes. Reduce oven setting to 350°; bake 70-80 minutes longer or until the crust is golden brown and a thermometer inserted in center reads 165°.

SIMPLE CREAMY CHICKEN ENCHILADAS

This is one of the first recipes I created and cooked for my husband after we got married. He was so impressed! Now we fix these enchiladas regularly for friends.

—**Melissa Rogers** Tuscaloosa, AL

Prep: 30 min. • **Bake:** 30 min.
Makes: 2 casseroles (5 servings each)

- 2 cans (14½ ounces each) diced tomatoes with mild green chilies, undrained
- 2 cans (10½ ounces each) condensed cream of chicken soup, undiluted
- 1 can (10¾ ounces) condensed cheddar cheese soup, undiluted
- ¼ cup 2% milk
- 1 tablespoon ground cumin
- 1 tablespoon chili powder
- 2 teaspoons garlic powder
- 2 teaspoons dried oregano
- 5 cups shredded rotisserie chicken
- 1 package (8 ounces) cream cheese, cubed and softened
- 20 flour tortillas (8 inches), warmed
- 4 cups shredded Mexican cheese blend

1. Preheat oven to 350°. For sauce, mix first eight ingredients. For filling, in a large bowl, mix chicken and cream cheese until blended; stir in 3½ cups sauce.
2. Spread ¼ cup sauce into each of two greased 13x9-in. baking dishes. Place ⅓ cup filling down the center of each tortilla; roll up and place seam side down in baking dishes. Pour remaining sauce over tops; sprinkle with cheese.
3. Bake, uncovered, 30-35 minutes or until heated through and cheese is melted.

Freeze option: Cover and freeze unbaked casseroles up to 3 months. To use, partially thaw in refrigerator overnight. Remove from refrigerator 30 minutes before baking. Preheat oven to 350°. Cover the casserole with greased foil; bake until heated through and a thermometer inserted in center reads 165°, about 45 minutes. Uncover; bake until cheese is melted, 5-10 minutes longer.

SHORT RIB COBBLER

My family's love of beef stew and biscuits inspired me to create this savory meal. After years of making the two separately, I put the biscuits on top of the stew like a cobbler. This supper's as down-home as it gets.
—**Janine Talley** Orlando, FL

Prep: 45 min. • **Bake:** 3 hours
Makes: 8 servings

- ½ cup plus 3 tablespoons all-purpose flour, divided
- 1¼ teaspoons salt, divided
- ½ teaspoon pepper
- 2 pounds well-trimmed boneless beef short ribs, cut into 1½-in. pieces
- 5 tablespoons olive oil, divided
- 1 large onion, chopped
- 1 medium carrot, chopped
- 1 celery rib, chopped
- 1 garlic clove, minced
- 2 tablespoons tomato paste
- 5 cups beef stock
- 1 cup dry red wine or additional beef stock
- 1 teaspoon poultry seasoning
- 1 bay leaf
- 1 package (14 ounces) frozen pearl onions, thawed
- 4 medium carrots, cut into 2-inch pieces

COBBLER TOPPING
- 2 cups biscuit/baking mix
- ⅔ cup 2% milk
- Fresh thyme leaves

1. Preheat oven to 350°. In a shallow bowl, mix ½ cup flour, ¾ teaspoon salt and pepper. Dip short ribs in flour mixture to coat all sides; shake off excess.
2. In an ovenproof Dutch oven, heat 3 tablespoons oil over medium heat. Brown beef in batches. Remove from pan.
3. In same pan, heat remaining oil over medium heat. Add onion, chopped carrot and celery; cook and stir 2-3 minutes or until tender. Add garlic; cook 1 minute longer. Stir in tomato paste and remaining flour until blended. Gradually stir in stock and wine until smooth. Return beef to pan; stir in poultry seasoning, bay leaf and remaining salt. Bring to a boil.
4. Bake, covered, 1¾ hours. Stir in pearl onions and carrot pieces. Bake, covered, 30-45 minutes longer or until beef and onions are tender. Skim fat and remove bay leaf.
5. In a small bowl, mix biscuit mix and milk just until a soft dough forms. Drop by scant ¼ cupfuls over beef mixture. Bake, uncovered, 40-45 minutes longer or until topping is golden brown. Sprinkle with thyme.

SPINACH-PESTO TURKEY TENDERLOINS

My husband and I are avid trail runners who get hungry after long runs. We love the taste of turkey tenderloin stuffed with spinach and goat cheese.
—**Hayley Long** Oxford, AL

Prep: 20 min. • **Bake:** 25 min.
Makes: 4 servings

- 6 cups fresh baby spinach (about 6 ounces), coarsely chopped
- 1 cup crumbled goat cheese
- 2 garlic cloves, minced
- 2 turkey breast tenderloins (8 ounces each)
- ⅓ cup prepared pesto
- ¼ cup shredded Parmesan cheese

1. Preheat oven to 350°. In a large saucepan, bring ½ in. of water to a boil. Add spinach; cover and boil 3-5 minutes or until wilted. Drain well.
2. In a small bowl, combine spinach, cheese and garlic. Cut a pocket in each tenderloin by slicing horizontally to within ½ in. of opposite side. Fill with cheese mixture; secure with kitchen string if necessary.
3. Place tenderloins on a greased 15x10x1-in. baking pan; brush with pesto. Bake 20 minutes. Sprinkle with Parmesan cheese. Bake 5-10 minutes longer or until a thermometer reads 165°. Cut each tenderloin into four slices.

TRADITIONAL MEAT LOAF

Homemade meat loaf is a must-have comfort food. We always increase the recipe and freeze a loaf for a crazy day.
—**Gail Graham** Maple Ridge, BC

Prep: 15 min. • **Bake:** 1 hour + standing
Makes: 6 servings

- 3 **slices bread**
- 1 **large egg, lightly beaten**
- ⅔ **cup 2% milk**
- 1 **cup shredded cheddar cheese**
- 1 **medium onion, finely chopped**
- ½ **cup finely shredded carrot**
- 1 **teaspoon salt**
- ¼ **teaspoon pepper**
- 1½ **pounds ground beef**

GLAZE
- ¼ **cup packed brown sugar**
- ¼ **cup ketchup**
- 1 **tablespoon prepared mustard**

1. Preheat oven to 350°. Tear bread into 2-inch pieces; place in a blender. Cover and pulse to form coarse crumbs; transfer to a large bowl. Stir in egg, milk, cheese, onion, carrot, salt and pepper. Add beef; mix lightly but thoroughly. Transfer to a greased 9x5-in. loaf pan.
2. In a small bowl, mix glaze ingredients; spread over loaf. Bake 60-75 minutes or until a thermometer reads 160°. Let stand 10 minutes before slicing.
Freeze option: Bake meat loaf without glaze. Securely wrap cooled meat loaf in plastic wrap and foil, then freeze. To use, partially thaw meat loaf in refrigerator overnight. Prepare and spread glaze over top; reheat on a greased shallow baking pan in a preheated 350° oven until heated through and a thermometer inserted in center reads 165°.
Savory Meat Loaf: Omit shredded carrot. Saute ½ cup chopped green pepper with onion in 2 teaspoon canola oil until tender. Add 2 minced garlic cloves and cook for 1 minute. Cool slightly. Combine with the egg, milk, bread, cheese, salt and pepper. Add 1 teaspoon crushed dried rosemary. Proceed as recipe directs.

Hearty Home-Cooked Stews

The ultimate in comfort food, a delicious stew is hearty, filling and everything we love about home cooking in one bowl. Spoon up the perfect combination of veggies, meat and rich flavor in a one-dish main course.

TUSCAN PORTOBELLO STEW

This one-skillet meal is quick and easy to prepare yet elegant enough for company. I take this to my school's potlucks, where it is devoured by vegetarian teachers and students alike.

—**Jane Siemon** Viroqua, WI

Prep: 20 min. • **Cook:** 20 min.
Makes: 4 servings

- 2 large portobello mushrooms, coarsely chopped
- 1 medium onion, chopped
- 3 garlic cloves, minced
- 2 tablespoons olive oil
- ½ cup white wine or vegetable broth
- 1 can (28 ounces) diced tomatoes, undrained
- 2 cups chopped fresh kale
- 1 bay leaf
- 1 teaspoon dried thyme
- ½ teaspoon dried basil
- ½ teaspoon dried rosemary, crushed
- ¼ teaspoon salt
- ¼ teaspoon pepper
- 2 cans (15 ounces each) white kidney or cannellini beans, rinsed and drained

1. In a large skillet, saute the mushrooms, onion and garlic in oil until tender. Add the wine. Bring to a boil; cook until liquid is reduced by half. Stir in the tomatoes, kale and seasonings. Bring to a boil. Reduce heat; cover and simmer for 8-10 minutes.

2. Add the beans; heat through. Discard bay leaf.

WEST AFRICAN CHICKEN STEW

I really love authentic African flavors, but they can be hard to come by in the U.S. This recipe features a delicious combination of traditional African ingredients like peanut butter, sweet potatoes and black-eyed peas, all of which are readily available.

—**Michael Cohen** Los Angeles, CA

Prep: 20 min. • **Cook:** 30 min.
Makes: 8 servings (2½ quarts)

- 1 pound boneless skinless chicken breasts, cut into 1-inch cubes
- ½ teaspoon salt
- ¼ teaspoon pepper
- 3 teaspoons canola oil, divided
- 1 medium onion, thinly sliced
- 6 garlic cloves, minced
- 2 tablespoons minced fresh gingerroot
- 2 cans (15½ ounces each) black-eyed peas, rinsed and drained
- 1 can (28 ounces) crushed tomatoes
- 1 large sweet potato, peeled and cut into 1-inch cubes
- 1 cup reduced-sodium chicken broth
- ¼ cup creamy peanut butter
- 1½ teaspoons minced fresh thyme or ½ teaspoon dried thyme, divided
- ¼ teaspoon cayenne pepper
  Hot cooked brown rice, optional

1. Sprinkle the chicken with salt and pepper. In a Dutch oven, cook chicken over medium heat in 2 teaspoons oil for 4-6 minutes or until no longer pink; remove and set aside.

2. In the same pan, saute onion in the remaining oil until tender. Add garlic and ginger; cook 1 minute longer.

3. Stir in peas, tomatoes, sweet potato, broth, peanut butter, 1¼ teaspoons thyme and the cayenne. Bring to a boil. Reduce heat; cover and simmer for 15-20 minutes or until potato is tender. Add chicken; heat through.

4. Serve with rice if desired. Sprinkle with the remaining thyme.

ITALIAN PORK STEW

Don't skip the anchovy paste in this stew! It gives a savory, salty flavor, but doesn't taste fishy at all. Add a salad and artisan bread for a wholesome meal.
—**Lynne German** Woodland Hills, CA

Prep: 30 min. • **Cook:** 2¼ hours
Makes: 8 servings (2 quarts)

- ⅔ cup all-purpose flour
- 2 pounds boneless pork loin, cut into 1-inch pieces
- 4 tablespoons olive oil, divided
- 1 large onion, chopped
- 5 garlic cloves, crushed
- 1 can (28 ounces) diced tomatoes, undrained
- 1 cup dry red wine or beef broth
- 3 bay leaves
- 1 cinnamon stick (3 inches)
- 1 tablespoon tomato paste
- 1 tablespoon red wine vinegar
- 1 teaspoon anchovy paste
- 1 teaspoon each dried oregano, basil and sage leaves
- ½ teaspoon salt
- ½ teaspoon crushed red pepper flakes
- ¼ teaspoon pepper
- ¼ cup minced fresh parsley
  Hot cooked bow tie pasta
  Grated Parmesan cheese

1. Place flour in a large resealable plastic bag. Add pork, a few pieces at a time, and shake to coat. In a Dutch oven, brown pork in 3 tablespoons oil in batches. Remove and keep warm.
2. In the same pan, saute onion in the remaining oil until crisp-tender. Add garlic; cook 1 minute longer. Stir in the tomatoes, wine, bay leaves, cinnamon, tomato paste, vinegar, anchovy paste, herbs, salt, pepper flakes, pepper and pork; bring to a boil.
3. Reduce heat; cover and simmer for 1½ hours, stirring occasionally. Stir in parsley. Cover and cook 30-40 minutes longer or until meat is tender. Skim fat; discard bay leaves and cinnamon stick.
4. Serve with pasta; sprinkle with cheese.
Freeze option: Place individual portions of cooled stew in freezer containers and freeze. To use, partially thaw in refrigerator overnight. Heat through in a saucepan, stirring occasionally and adding a little water if necessary.

SLOW-SIMMERED BURGUNDY BEEF STEW

My mother-in-law shared this recipe with me almost 25 years ago. Ever since then, it's been a go-to whenever I need a lot of food without a lot of fussing.
—**Mary Lou Timpson** Colorado City, AZ

Prep: 30 min. • **Bake:** 1¾ hours
Makes: 4 servings

- 1½ pounds beef stew meat (1¼-inch pieces)
- 3 tablespoons all-purpose flour
- ¾ teaspoon salt
- 2 to 4 teaspoons canola oil, divided
- 2 teaspoons beef bouillon granules
- 2 teaspoons dried parsley flakes
- 1½ teaspoons Italian seasoning
- 2 cups water
- 1 cup Burgundy wine or beef stock
- 3 medium potatoes (about 1⅓ pounds), peeled and quartered
- 1 cup fresh mushrooms, halved
- 1 medium onion, cut into eight wedges
- 2 medium carrots, cut into 1-inch pieces
- 2 celery ribs, cut into ½-inch pieces
  Additional water, optional

1. Preheat oven to 350°. Toss beef with flour and salt to coat lightly; shake off excess. In an ovenproof Dutch oven, heat 2 teaspoons oil over medium heat. Brown beef in batches, adding additional oil as needed. Remove from pan.
2. Add bouillon, herbs, 2 cups water and the wine to same pan; bring to a boil, stirring to loosen browned bits from pan. Add beef; return to a boil. Transfer to oven; bake, covered, 1 hour.
3. Stir in the vegetables and, if desired, thin with additional water. Bake, covered, until the beef and vegetables are tender, 45-60 minutes.

BEST LASAGNA

For a casual holiday meal, you can't go wrong with this rich and meaty lasagna. My grown sons and daughter-in-law request it for their birthdays, too.
—**Pam Thompson** Girard, IL

Prep: 1 hour • **Bake:** 50 min. + standing
Makes: 12 servings

- 9 lasagna noodles
- 1¼ pounds bulk Italian sausage
- ¾ pound ground beef
- 1 medium onion, diced
- 3 garlic cloves, minced
- 2 cans (one 28 ounces, one 15 ounces) crushed tomatoes
- 2 cans (6 ounces each) tomato paste
- ⅔ cup water
- 2 to 3 tablespoons sugar
- 3 tablespoons plus ¼ cup minced fresh parsley, divided
- 2 teaspoons dried basil
- ¾ teaspoon fennel seed
- ¾ teaspoon salt, divided
- ¼ teaspoon coarsely ground pepper
- 1 large egg, lightly beaten
- 1 carton (15 ounces) ricotta cheese
- 4 cups shredded part-skim mozzarella cheese
- ¾ cup grated Parmesan cheese

1. Cook noodles according to package directions; drain. Meanwhile, in a Dutch oven, cook sausage, beef and onion over medium heat for 8-10 minutes or until the meat is no longer pink, breaking up meat into crumbles. Add garlic; cook for 1 minute. Drain.
2. Stir in tomatoes, tomato paste, water, sugar, 3 tablespoons parsley, basil, fennel, ½ teaspoon salt and pepper; bring to a boil. Reduce heat; simmer, uncovered, 30 minutes, stirring occasionally.
3. In a small bowl, mix egg, ricotta cheese, and remaining parsley and salt.
4. Preheat oven to 375°. Spread 2 cups meat sauce into an ungreased 13x9-in. baking dish. Layer with three noodles and a third of the ricotta mixture. Sprinkle with 1 cup mozzarella cheese and 2 tablespoons Parmesan cheese. Repeat layers twice. Top with remaining meat sauce and cheeses (dish will be full).
5. Bake, covered, 25 minutes. Bake, uncovered, 25 minutes longer or until bubbly. Let stand 15 minutes before serving.

BEEF SHORT RIBS IN BURGUNDY SAUCE

My stepdad—an Army general—got this recipe from his aide, who said it was his mother's best Sunday meal. It's now a mouthwatering favorite in our family, too.
—**Judy Batson** Tampa, FL

Prep: 35 min. • **Cook:** 2¼ hours
Makes: 6 servings

- 3 pounds bone-in beef short ribs
- 3 tablespoons butter
- 1 large sweet onion, halved and sliced
- 2 celery ribs, thinly sliced
- 1 medium carrot, thinly sliced
- 1 garlic clove, minced
  Dash dried thyme
- 2 tablespoons all-purpose flour
- 1 cup water
- 1 cup dry red wine or beef broth
- 1 beef bouillon cube or 1 teaspoon beef bouillon granules
- 2 tablespoons minced fresh parsley
- ½ teaspoon Worcestershire sauce
- ¼ teaspoon salt
- ¼ teaspoon browning sauce, optional
- ⅛ teaspoon pepper

1. Preheat oven to 450°. Place short ribs on a rack in a shallow roasting pan. Roast for 30-40 minutes or until browned, turning once.
2. Meanwhile, in a Dutch oven, heat butter over medium heat. Add onion, celery and carrot; cook and stir until tender, 10-12 minutes. Add garlic and thyme; cook 1 minute longer. Stir in flour until blended; gradually stir in water and wine. Add bouillon and parsley, stirring to dissolve bouillon.
3. Transfer ribs to Dutch oven; bring to a boil. Reduce heat; simmer, covered, 2-2½ hours or until meat is tender.
4. Remove short ribs; keep warm. Skim fat from the sauce; stir in the remaining ingredients. Serve sauce with ribs.

ENCHILADA CHICKEN

We enjoy southwestern flavors and this six-ingredient recipe never gets boring. The chicken sizzles in the skillet before being baked and comes out tender and juicy every time.
—**Nancy Sousley** Lafayette, IN

Prep: 15 min. • **Bake:** 20 min.
Makes: 4 servings

- 4 boneless skinless chicken breast halves (6 ounces each)
- 2 teaspoons salt-free Southwest chipotle seasoning blend
- 1 tablespoon olive oil
- ¼ cup enchilada sauce
- ½ cup shredded sharp cheddar cheese
- 2 tablespoons minced fresh cilantro

Preheat oven to 350°. Sprinkle chicken with seasoning blend. In an ovenproof skillet, brown chicken in oil. Top with enchilada sauce, cheese and cilantro. Bake for 18-20 minutes or until a thermometer reads 170°.

BLACK BEAN AND RICE ENCHILADAS

I love Mexican food, but I am always looking for ways to make it more healthy. I reworked a dish that I have enjoyed in restaurants to suit my taste and lifestyle.
—**Christie Ladd** Mechanicsburg, PA

Prep: 40 min. • **Bake:** 30 min.
Makes: 8 servings

- 1 tablespoon olive oil
- 1 green pepper, chopped
- 1 medium onion, chopped
- 3 garlic cloves, minced
- 1 can (15 ounces) black beans, rinsed and drained
- 1 can (14½ ounces) diced tomatoes and green chilies
- ¼ cup picante sauce
- 1 tablespoon chili powder
- 1 teaspoon ground cumin
- ¼ teaspoon crushed red pepper flakes
- 2 cups cooked brown rice
- 8 flour tortillas (6 inches), warmed
- 1 cup salsa
- 1 cup shredded reduced-fat cheddar cheese
- 3 tablespoons chopped fresh cilantro leaves

1. Preheat oven to 350°. In a large nonstick skillet, heat oil over medium heat. Add green pepper, onion and garlic; saute until tender. Add the next six ingredients; bring to a boil. Reduce heat; simmer, uncovered, until heated through. Add rice; cook 5 minutes longer.
2. Spoon a rounded ½ cup of rice mixture down center of each tortilla. Fold sides over filling and roll up. Place rolls seam side down in a 13x9-in. baking dish coated with cooking spray. Spoon remaining rice mixture along sides of dish. Top tortillas with salsa. Bake, covered, for 25 minutes. Uncover; sprinkle with cheese. Bake until the cheese is melted, 2-3 minutes longer. Sprinkle with cilantro before serving.

CREAMY BRAISED CHICKEN

A smooth, delicate cream sauce gives a special taste to these tender chicken breasts accompanied by sweet pearl onions and sauteed mushrooms. This dish is so rich-tasting, you'll want to serve it to company.

—Margaret Haugh Heilman Houston, TX

Prep: 10 min. • **Cook:** 30 min.
Makes: 6 servings

- ½ pound pearl onions
- 1 cup thinly sliced onion
- ½ cup thinly sliced carrot
- ½ cup thinly sliced celery
- 1 tablespoon plus 2 teaspoons butter, divided
- 6 boneless skinless chicken breast halves (4 ounces each)
- 1 cup chardonnay or other dry white wine or reduced-sodium chicken broth
- 1⅓ cups reduced-sodium chicken broth
- 1 tablespoon minced fresh parsley
- 1 teaspoon salt
- 1 teaspoon dried thyme
- ⅛ teaspoon white pepper
- 1 bay leaf
- 3 tablespoons all-purpose flour
- ½ cup fat-free evaporated milk
- ½ pound fresh mushrooms, quartered

1. In a Dutch oven or large kettle, bring 6 cups of water to a boil. Add pearl onions; boil for 3 minutes. Drain and rinse in cold water; peel and set aside. In the same pan, saute sliced onion, carrot and celery in 1 tablespoon butter until tender. Remove vegetables; set aside.

2. Add chicken to pan; brown on both sides. Remove and keep warm. Add wine; simmer until reduced to ½ cup. Stir in broth and seasonings. Return chicken to pan; cover and simmer for 5 minutes or until juices run clear. Remove chicken to a serving platter; keep warm.

3. Combine flour and milk until smooth; gradually stir into pan. Bring to a boil; cook and stir for 2 minutes or until thickened. Return the vegetables to the pan. Remove from the heat; cover and set aside.

4. In a nonstick skillet, saute the reserved pearl onions in the remaining butter until tender. Remove and set aside. In the same pan, saute mushrooms until tender. Add onions and mushrooms to serving platter. Discard bay leaf from sauce; spoon over chicken and vegetables.

CREAMY CAVATAPPI & CHEESE

Dive fork-first into oodles of noodles coated with a to-die-for sharp cheddar cheese sauce in this grown-up mac and cheese. Hot sauce lends mild heat that's delectable with the smoky topping.
—**Barbara Colucci** Rockledge, FL

Prep: 30 min. • **Bake:** 20 min.
Makes: 10 servings

- 6 cups uncooked cavatappi or spiral pasta
- 3 garlic cloves, minced
- ⅓ cup butter
- ¼ cup all-purpose flour
- 1 tablespoon hot pepper sauce
- 4 cups 2% milk
- 6 cups shredded sharp cheddar cheese
- 1 cup cubed process cheese (Velveeta)
- 3 green onions, chopped

TOPPINGS
- ½ cup panko (Japanese) bread crumbs
- 3 thick-sliced bacon strips, cooked and coarsley crumbled
- 1 tablespoon butter, melted
- 1 green onion, chopped
  Coarsely ground pepper, optional

1. Cook cavatappi according to the package directions.
2. Meanwhile, in a Dutch oven, saute garlic in butter. Stir in flour and pepper sauce until blended; gradually add milk. Bring to a boil; cook and stir for 2 minutes or until thickened.
3. Stir in cheeses until melted; add green onions. Drain the cavatappi; stir into the cheese mixture.
4. Transfer to a greased 13x9-in. baking dish. Combine the bread crumbs, bacon and melted butter; sprinkle over top.
5. Bake, uncovered, at 350° until bubbly, 20-25 minutes. Sprinkle with green onion and, if desired, pepper.

Make It a Main!

If you want to serve the Creamy Cavatappi & Cheese as a main dish, add some protein. Try cubed ham, grilled chicken breast or sliced sausage—kielbasa for a mild dish, or andouille for a bit of spice.

FREEZE IT CHICKEN & SWISS STUFFING BAKE

I love to cook but just don't have much time. This casserole is both good and fast—which makes it my favorite kind of recipe! I serve it with a green salad.
—**Jena Coffey** Sunset Hills, MO

Prep: 20 min. • **Bake:** 25 min.
Makes: 8 servings

- 1 can (10¾ ounces) condensed cream of mushroom soup, undiluted
- 1 cup whole milk
- 1 package (6 ounces) stuffing mix
- 2 cups cubed cooked chicken breast
- 2 cups fresh broccoli florets, cooked
- 2 celery ribs, finely chopped
- 1½ cups shredded Swiss cheese, divided

1. Preheat oven to 375°. In a large bowl, combine soup and milk until blended. Add the stuffing mix with contents of seasoning packet, chicken, broccoli, celery and 1 cup cheese. Transfer to a greased 13x9-in. baking dish.
2. Bake, uncovered, for 20 minutes or until heated through. Sprinkle with remaining cheese; bake 5 minutes longer or until cheese is melted.

Freeze option: Sprinkle remaining cheese over unbaked casserole. Cover and freeze. To use, partially thaw in refrigerator overnight. Remove from refrigerator 30 minutes before baking. Bake casserole as directed, increasing time as necessary to heat through and for a thermometer inserted in center to read 165°.

CARIBBEAN-SPICED PORK TENDERLOIN WITH PEACH SALSA

I love this recipe because of the depth of flavors and burst of colors. It's quick and easy to make. It's best when peaches are in season, but you could try strawberries or pineapple instead.
—**Holly Bauer** West Bend, WI

Prep: 15 min. • **Grill:** 20 min.
Makes: 4 servings (1⅓ cups salsa)

- ¾ cup chopped peeled fresh peaches
- 1 small sweet red pepper, chopped
- 1 jalapeno pepper, seeded and chopped
- 2 tablespoons finely chopped red onion
- 2 tablespoons minced fresh cilantro
- 1 tablespoon lime juice
- 1 garlic clove, minced
- ⅛ teaspoon salt
- ⅛ teaspoon pepper
- 2 tablespoons olive oil
- 1 tablespoon brown sugar
- 1 tablespoon Caribbean jerk seasoning
- 1 teaspoon dried thyme
- 1 teaspoon dried rosemary, crushed
- ½ teaspoon seasoned salt
- 1 pork tenderloin (1 pound)

1. In a small bowl, combine the first nine ingredients; set aside. In another small bowl, combine the oil, brown sugar, jerk seasoning, thyme, rosemary and seasoned salt. Rub over pork.
2. Grill, covered, over medium heat for 9-11 minutes on each side or until a thermometer reads 145°. Let stand for 5 minutes before slicing. Serve with salsa.
Note: Wear disposable gloves when cutting hot peppers; the oils can burn exposed skin. Avoid touching your face.

RICOTTA GNOCCHI WITH SPINACH & GORGONZOLA

In this special dish, tender pillows of dumplinglike pasta are treated to a creamy white sauce with butternut squash, spinach and Gorgonzola cheese.
—**Brud Holland** Watkins Glen, NY

Prep: 2 hours • **Cook:** 10 min.
Makes: 8 servings

- 3 large potatoes
- 3 cups reduced-fat ricotta cheese
- ¼ cup grated Romano cheese
- 2 tablespoons olive oil
- 1 tablespoon kosher salt
- 6 large eggs
- 4½ cups cake flour
- 4 quarts water

SAUCE
- 2⅔ cups cubed peeled butternut squash
- ⅓ cup thinly sliced fresh basil leaves
- ⅓ cup water
- 2 tablespoons plus 2 teaspoons olive oil
- 2 garlic cloves, peeled and thinly sliced
- 1¼ teaspoons kosher salt
- ¾ teaspoon pepper
- 1⅓ cups heavy whipping cream
- ⅔ cup crumbled Gorgonzola cheese
- 1½ pounds fresh spinach, coarsely chopped

1. Preheat oven to 400°. Scrub and pierce potatoes. Bake for 50-55 minutes or until tender. Peel potatoes; press through a potato ricer or strainer into a large bowl. Cool slightly.
2. Add ricotta and Romano cheeses, oil and salt to potato pulp; beat on low speed until smooth. Beat in eggs, one at a time. Add flour; mix well. On a lightly floured surface, knead 10-12 times, forming a soft dough.
3. Divide dough into 16 portions. On a floured surface, roll each portion into a ½-in.-thick rope; cut into ¾-in. pieces. Press and roll each piece with a lightly floured fork.
4. In a Dutch oven, bring water to a boil. Cook gnocchi in batches until they float, 30-60 seconds. Remove with a slotted spoon and keep warm.
5. In a large saucepan, combine the squash, basil, water, oil, garlic, salt and pepper. Bring to a boil. Cover and cook until squash is tender, 4-6 minutes.
6. Stir in cream and Gorgonzola. Bring to a boil. Reduce heat; simmer, uncovered, for 2 minutes. Add spinach; cook until spinach is wilted. Serve with gnocchi.

SAUSAGE MANICOTTI

My classic Italian entree comes together in a snap, but tastes like it took hours. It's so tasty and easy to fix.
—**Carolyn Henderson** Maple Plain, MN

Prep: 15 min. • **Bake:** 65 min.
Makes: 7 servings

- 1 **pound uncooked bulk pork sausage**
- 2 **cups (16 ounces) 4% cottage cheese**
- 1 **package (8 ounces) manicotti shells**
- 1 **jar (24 ounces) marinara sauce**
- 1 **cup shredded part-skim mozzarella cheese**

1. Preheat oven to 350°. In a large bowl, combine sausage and cottage cheese. Stuff into uncooked manicotti shells. Place in a greased 13x9-in. baking dish. Top with marinara sauce.
2. Cover and bake for 55-60 minutes or until a thermometer inserted into the center of a shell reads 160°.
3. Uncover; sprinkle with mozzarella cheese. Bake 8-10 minutes longer or until cheese is melted. Let stand for 5 minutes before serving.

Freeze option: Transfer individual portions of cooled manicotti to freezer containers; freeze. To use, partially thaw in refrigerator overnight. Transfer to a microwave-safe dish and microwave on high, stirring occasionally and adding a little spaghetti sauce if necessary.

LEMONY ROASTED CHICKEN AND POTATOES

This one-dish meal tastes like it needs hours of hands-on time to put together, but it takes just minutes to prep the simple ingredients. The meat juices cook the veggies to perfection. So easy!
—**Sherri Melotik** Oak Creek, WI

Prep: 20 min. • **Bake:** 40 min.
Makes: 4 servings

- 1½ **pounds red potatoes, (about 5 medium), cut into ¾-inch cubes**
- 1 **large onion, coarsely chopped**
- 1 **medium lemon, halved and sliced**
- 3 **tablespoons olive oil, divided**
- 3 **garlic cloves, minced**
- 1¼ **teaspoon salt, divided**
- 1 **teaspoon dried rosemary, crushed, divided**
- 1 **teaspoon pepper, divided**
- 4 **bone-in chicken thighs (about 1½ pounds)**
- 4 **chicken drumsticks (about 1 pound)**
- 1 **teaspoon paprika**
- 6 **cups fresh baby spinach (about 5 ounces)**
  Lemon wedges, optional

1. Preheat oven to 425°. Place potatoes, onion and the lemon slices in a large bowl; toss with 2 tablespoons oil, garlic and ½ teaspoon each salt, rosemary and pepper. Spread evenly in a greased roasting pan. Roast on an upper oven rack for 20 minutes.
2. Meanwhile, toss chicken with paprika and the remaining salt, rosemary and pepper. In a large skillet, heat remaining oil over medium-high heat. Brown the chicken in batches.
3. Place chicken over the potato mixture. Roast until a thermometer inserted in chicken reads 170° and the potatoes are tender, 15-20 minutes. Remove chicken from pan. Immediately add spinach to the vegetables, stirring to wilt slightly. Serve vegetables with chicken and, if desired, lemon wedges.

APRICOT GINGER MUSTARD-GLAZED HAM

Although I usually buy spiral-sliced hams, I decided to do a home-baked ham with a gingery glaze. This is how you do special-occasion dining.
—**Ally Phillips** Murrells Inlet, SC

Prep: 15 min. • **Bake:** 2 hours
Makes: 16 servings

- 1 fully cooked bone-in ham (7 to 9 pounds)
- ½ cup apricot halves, drained
- ½ cup stone-ground mustard
- ⅓ cup packed brown sugar
- 2 tablespoons grated fresh gingerroot
- 1 tablespoon whole peppercorns
- ½ teaspoon sea salt
- ½ teaspoon coarsely ground pepper

1. Preheat oven to 325°. Place ham on a rack in a shallow roasting pan. Using a sharp knife, score surface of ham with ¼-in.-deep cuts in a diamond pattern. Cover and bake 1¾-2¼ hours or until a thermometer reads 130°.
2. Meanwhile, place the remaining ingredients in a food processor; process until blended. Remove ham from oven. Increase oven setting to 425°. Spread apricot mixture over the ham.
3. Bake ham, uncovered, 15-20 minutes longer or until a thermometer reads 140°. If desired, increase oven setting to broil; broil 2-4 minutes or until golden brown.

PORK SHEPHERD'S PIE

Of all the shepherd's pie recipes I've tried through the years, this one is definitely the best. I enjoy cooking for my family, who all agree this meat pie is a keeper.
—**Mary Arthurs** Etobicoke, ON

Prep: 30 min. • **Bake:** 45 min.
Makes: 6 servings

PORK LAYER
- 1 pound ground pork
- 1 small onion, chopped
- 2 garlic cloves, minced
- 1 cup cooked rice
- ½ cup pork gravy or ¼ cup chicken broth
- ½ teaspoon salt
- ½ teaspoon dried thyme

CABBAGE LAYER
- 1 medium carrot, diced
- 1 small onion, chopped
- 2 tablespoons butter or margarine
- 6 cups chopped cabbage
- 1 cup chicken broth
- ½ teaspoon salt
- ¼ teaspoon pepper

POTATO LAYER
- 2 cups mashed potatoes
- ¼ cup shredded cheddar cheese

Preheat oven to 350°. In a skillet over medium heat, brown pork until no longer pink. Add onion and garlic. Cook until vegetables are tender; drain. Stir in rice, gravy, salt and thyme. Spoon into a greased 11x7-in. baking dish. In the same skillet, saute carrot and onion in butter over medium heat for 5 minutes. Stir in cabbage; cook for 1 minute. Add broth, salt and pepper; cover and cook for 10 minutes. Spoon over pork layer. Spoon or pipe mashed potatoes on top; sprinkle with cheese. Bake, uncovered, for 45 minutes or until browned.

LEMON CHICKEN WITH ORZO

Here's a dish that's light and summery but still filling. My kids love all the veggies—for real! If you like a lot of lemon, stir in an extra splash of lemon juice just before serving.

—Shannon Humphrey Hampton, VA

Prep: 20 min. • **Cook:** 20 min.
Makes: 4 servings

⅓ cup all-purpose flour
1 teaspoon garlic powder
1 pound boneless skinless chicken breasts
¾ teaspoon salt, divided
½ teaspoon pepper
2 tablespoons olive oil
1 can (14½ ounces) reduced-sodium chicken broth
1¼ cups uncooked whole wheat orzo pasta
2 cups chopped fresh spinach
1 cup grape tomatoes, halved
3 tablespoons lemon juice
2 tablespoons minced fresh basil
Lemon wedges, optional

1. In a shallow bowl, mix flour and garlic powder. Cut chicken into 1½-in. pieces; pound each piece with a meat mallet to ¼-in. thickness. Sprinkle with ½ teaspoon salt and pepper. Dip both sides of chicken in the flour mixture to coat lightly; shake off excess.

2. In a large skillet, heat oil over medium heat. Add the chicken; cook 3-4 minutes on each side or until golden brown and the chicken is no longer pink. Remove from pan; keep warm. Wipe skillet clean.

3. In the same pan, bring the broth to a boil. Stir in the orzo and return to a boil. Reduce heat; simmer, covered, for 8-10 minutes or until tender. Stir in the spinach, tomatoes, lemon juice, basil and the remaining salt; remove from heat. Return chicken to the pan. If desired, serve with lemon wedges.

FREEZE IT PIZZA-STYLE MANICOTTI

Ham, pepperoni and string cheese make little bundles I stuff into manicotti shells. It's a fun, hands-on recipe that children can help prepare.
—**Judy Armstrong** Prairieville, LA

Prep: 20 min. • **Bake:** 25 min.
MAKES: 4 servings

- 8 uncooked manicotti shells
- 1 jar (24 ounces) spaghetti sauce
- 8 slices deli ham (about 6 ounces)
- 8 fresh basil leaves
- 8 pieces string cheese
- 24 slices pepperoni
- 1 can (2¼ ounces) sliced ripe olives, drained
- 1 cup shredded Parmesan cheese

1. Cook manicotti according to package directions for al dente; drain. Preheat oven to 350°.
2. Pour 1 cup sauce into an 11x7-in. baking dish. On a short side of each ham slice, layer one basil leaf, one piece string cheese and three slices of pepperoni; roll up. Insert ham rolls into the manicotti shells; arrange in a single layer in prepared baking dish.
3. Pour the remaining sauce over top. Sprinkle with olives and Parmesan cheese. Bake, uncovered, 25-30 minutes or until heated through.
Freeze option: Cover unbaked casserole and freeze for up to 3 months. Thaw in the refrigerator overnight. Remove from the refrigerator 30 minutes before baking. Cover and bake at 375° for 25-30 minutes or until the pasta is tender. Let stand for 10 minutes before serving.

FISH & FRIES

Dine like you're in a traditional British pub. These moist fish fillets from the oven have a fuss-free coating that's healthier but just as crunchy and golden as the deep-fried kind. Simply seasoned and baked, the crispy fries are perfect on the side.
—**Janice Mitchell** Aurora, CO

Prep: 10 min. • **Bake:** 35 min.
Makes: 4 servings

- 1 pound potatoes (about 2 medium)
- 2 tablespoons olive oil
- ¼ teaspoon pepper

FISH
- ⅓ cup all-purpose flour
- ¼ teaspoon pepper
- 1 large egg
- 2 tablespoons water
- ⅔ cup crushed cornflakes
- 1 tablespoon grated Parmesan cheese
- ⅛ teaspoon cayenne pepper
- 1 pound haddock or cod fillets
  Tartar sauce, optional

1. Preheat oven to 425°. Peel and cut potatoes lengthwise into ½-in.-thick slices; cut slices into ½-in.-thick sticks.
2. In a large bowl, toss potatoes with oil and pepper. Transfer to a 15x10x1-in. baking pan coated with cooking spray. Bake, uncovered, 25-30 minutes or until golden brown and crisp, stirring once.
3. Meanwhile, in a shallow bowl, mix flour and pepper. In another shallow bowl, whisk egg with water. In a third bowl, toss cornflakes with cheese and cayenne. Dip fish in flour mixture to coat both sides; shake off excess. Dip in egg mixture, then in cornflake mixture, patting to help the coating adhere.
4. Place fish on a baking sheet coated with cooking spray. Bake 10-12 minutes or until fish just begins to flake easily with a fork. Serve with potatoes and, if desired, tartar sauce.

GRECIAN PASTA & CHICKEN SKILLET

We love a homemade meal at the end of the day. But the prep involved? Not so much. My Greek-inspired pasta is lemony, herby and, thankfully, easy.

—**Roxanne Chan** Albany, CA

Prep: 30 min. • **Cook:** 10 min
Makes: 4 servings

- 1 can (14½ ounces) reduced-sodium chicken broth
- 1 can (14½ ounces) no-salt-added diced tomatoes, undrained
- ¾ pound boneless skinless chicken breasts, cut into 1-inch pieces
- ½ cup white wine or water
- 1 garlic clove, minced
- ½ teaspoon dried oregano
- 4 ounces multigrain thin spaghetti
- 1 jar (7½ ounces) marinated quartered artichoke hearts, drained and coarsely chopped
- 2 cups fresh baby spinach
- ¼ cup roasted sweet red pepper strips
- ¼ cup sliced ripe olives
- 1 green onion, finely chopped
- 2 tablespoons minced fresh parsley
- ½ teaspoon grated lemon peel
- 2 tablespoons lemon juice
- 1 tablespoon olive oil
- ½ teaspoon pepper
  Crumbled reduced-fat feta cheese, optional

1. In a large skillet, combine the first six ingredients; add spaghetti. Bring to a boil. Cook for 5-7 minutes or until chicken is no longer pink and spaghetti is tender.
2. Stir in artichoke hearts, spinach, red pepper, olives, green onion, parsley, lemon peel, lemon juice, oil and pepper. Cook and stir 2-3 minutes or until spinach is wilted. If desired, sprinkle with cheese.

Multigrain vs. Whole Grain

"Whole grain" means that all parts of the grain kernel are used, bringing added health benefits. "Multigrain" means that a food contains more than one type of grain—but these are not necessarily whole grain.

GRILLED SKIRT STEAK WITH RED PEPPERS & ONIONS

This fun dish is a welcome part of our family cookouts. It makes a quick and delicious steak and vegetable combo that's ideal for lunch or dinner.

—**Cleo Gonske** Redding, CA

Prep: 30 min. + marinating • **Grill:** 20 min.
Makes: 6 servings

- ½ cup apple juice
- ½ cup red wine vinegar
- ¼ cup finely chopped onion
- 2 tablespoons rubbed sage
- 3 teaspoons ground coriander
- 3 teaspoons ground mustard
- 3 teaspoons freshly ground pepper
- 1 teaspoon salt
- 1 garlic clove, minced
- 1 cup olive oil
- 1 beef skirt steak (1½ pounds), cut into 5-in. pieces
- 2 medium red onions, cut into ½-inch slices
- 2 medium sweet red peppers, halved
- 12 green onions, trimmed

1. In a small bowl, whisk the first nine ingredients until blended; gradually whisk in oil. Pour 1½ cups marinade into a large resealable plastic bag. Add beef; seal bag and turn to coat. Refrigerate overnight. Cover and refrigerate the remaining marinade.
2. In a large bowl, toss the remaining vegetables with ¼ cup of the reserved marinade. Grill red onions and peppers, covered, over medium heat, 4-6 minutes on each side or until tender. Grill the green onions 1-2 minutes on each side or until tender.
3. Drain beef, discarding the marinade in the bag. Grill, covered, over medium heat 4-6 minutes on each side or until meat reaches desired doneness (for medium-rare, a thermometer should read 135°; medium, 140°; medium-well, 145°); baste with the remaining marinade during the last 4 minutes of cooking. Let steak stand 5 minutes.
4. Chop the vegetables into bite-size pieces; transfer to a large bowl. Cut steak diagonally across the grain into thin slices; add to vegetables and toss to combine.

FREEZE IT MEXICAN CHICKEN ALFREDO

One family member likes Italian, another likes Mexican. They never have to argue when this rich and creamy sensation is on the menu!

—**Tia Woodley** Stockbridge, GA

Prep: 25 min. • **Bake:** 30 min.
Makes: 2 casseroles (4 servings each)

- 1 package (16 ounces) gemelli or spiral pasta
- 2 pounds boneless skinless chicken breasts, cubed
- 1 medium onion, chopped
- ¼ teaspoon salt
- ¼ teaspoon pepper
- 1 tablespoon canola oil
- 2 jars (15 ounces each) Alfredo sauce
- 1 cup grated Parmesan cheese
- 1 cup medium salsa
- ¼ cup 2% milk
- 2 teaspoons taco seasoning

1. Preheat oven to 350°. Cook pasta according to package directions.
2. Meanwhile, in a large skillet over medium heat, cook chicken, onion, salt and pepper in oil until chicken is no longer pink. Stir in Alfredo sauce; bring to a boil. Stir in the cheese, salsa, milk and taco seasoning.
3. Drain pasta; toss with the chicken mixture. Divide between two greased 8-in. square baking dishes. Cover and bake until bubbly, 30-35 minutes.

Freeze option: Cover and freeze unbaked casserole up to 3 months. To use, thaw in refrigerator overnight. Remove from refrigerator 30 minutes before baking. Preheat oven to 350°. Bake casserole, covered, until bubbly, 50-60 minutes.

Contest Winner

BAKED PUMPKIN GOAT CHEESE ALFREDO WITH BACON

This is a unique and delicious pasta, perfect for fall. I made this for my girlfriends, and everyone asked for the recipe!

—**Ashley Lecker** Green Bay, WI

Prep: 35 min. • **Bake:** 20 min.
MAKES: 10 servings

- 1 pound cellentani
- 4 tablespoons butter
- 1 tablespoon olive oil
- 3 garlic cloves, minced
- 2 shallots, minced
- 2 cups heavy whipping cream
- 1 cup whole milk
- 4 ounces crumbled goat cheese
- ½ cup grated Parmesan cheese
- ½ cup canned pumpkin
- ½ teaspoon white pepper
- 2 tablespoons chopped fresh sage

TOPPINGS

- 1 pound bacon strips, cooked and crumbled
- 2 ounces crumbled goat cheese
- ¼ cup grated Parmesan cheese

1. Preheat oven to 350°. Cook pasta according to package instructions.
2. Meanwhile, in a large saucepan, heat butter and olive oil over medium heat. Add garlic and shallots; cook and stir for 1-2 minutes. Add the next six ingredients. Reduce heat to low. Cook, stirring constantly, until reduced, 6-8 minutes. Add sage. Remove from heat.
3. Drain pasta; gently stir into cream sauce. Transfer to a greased 13x9-in. baking dish. Top with bacon, goat cheese and Parmesan. Bake, covered, for about 15 minutes. Remove cover; bake until cheeses are melted, about 5 minutes longer.

FREEZE IT SOUTHWESTERN CASSEROLE

I've been making this mild family-pleasing casserole for years. It tastes wonderful, fits nicely into our budget and, best of all, makes a second one to freeze and enjoy later.
—**Joan Hallford** North Richland Hills, TX

Prep: 15 min. • **Bake:** 40 min.
Makes: 2 casseroles (6 servings each)

- 2 cups (8 ounces) uncooked elbow macaroni
- 2 pounds ground beef
- 1 large onion, chopped
- 2 garlic cloves, minced
- 2 cans (14½ ounces each) diced tomatoes, undrained
- 1 can (16 ounces) kidney beans, rinsed and drained
- 1 can (6 ounces) tomato paste
- 1 can (4 ounces) chopped green chilies, drained
- 1½ teaspoons salt
- 1 teaspoon chili powder
- ½ teaspoon ground cumin
- ½ teaspoon pepper
- 2 cups shredded Monterey Jack cheese
- 2 jalapeno peppers, seeded and chopped

1. Cook macaroni according to package directions. Meanwhile, in a large saucepan, cook beef and onion over medium heat, crumbling beef, until meat is no longer pink. Add garlic; cook 1 minute longer. Drain. Stir in next eight ingredients. Bring to a boil. Reduce heat; simmer, uncovered, for 10 minutes. Drain macaroni; stir into beef mixture.

2. Preheat oven to 375°. Transfer macaroni mixture to two greased 2-qt. baking dishes. Top with cheese and jalapenos. Cover and bake for 30 minutes. Uncover; bake until bubbly and heated through, about 10 minutes longer.

Freeze option: Cool casserole, cover and freeze up to 3 months. To use, thaw in the refrigerator 8 hours or overnight. Preheat oven to 375°. Remove casserole from refrigerator 30 minutes before baking. Cover and bake, increasing time as necessary to heat through and for a thermometer inserted in center to read 165°, 20-25 minutes.

Note: Wear disposable gloves when cutting hot peppers; the oils can burn exposed skin. Avoid touching your face.

BACON & TOMATO-TOPPED HADDOCK

Bacon presents a compelling argument for anyone who doesn't like fish. And for those who do, it just got even better.
—**Sherri Melotik** Oak Creek, WI

Prep: 25 min. • **Bake:** 10 min.
Makes: 5 servings

- 6 bacon strips, chopped
- 1 medium onion, thinly sliced
- 1 garlic clove, minced
- 1 cup panko (Japanese) bread crumbs
- 2 plum tomatoes, chopped
- ¼ cup minced fresh parsley
- 2 tablespoons olive oil
- 1 tablespoon butter, melted
- 5 haddock fillets (6 ounces each)
- 2 tablespoons lemon juice
- ¼ teaspoon salt

1. In a skillet, cook bacon over medium heat until partially cooked but not crisp. Add onion and garlic; cook until golden, stirring occasionally, 10-15 minutes.

2. Remove from heat; stir in bread crumbs, tomatoes and parsley. Set aside. Preheat oven to 400°. Spread oil and butter in an ungreased 15x10x1-in. baking pan. Place fillets in pan. Drizzle with lemon juice and sprinkle with salt. Top with bread crumb mixture.

3. Bake, uncovered, 10-15 minutes or until fish flakes easily with a fork.

Meals in Minutes

Need to beat the clock? These main dishes come together in 30 minutes or less! Just because you're tight on time doesn't mean you can't enjoy pasta dinners, southwestern staples and pizzas loaded with the flavors everyone craves. You'll even find recipes that use your cast-iron skillet in delicious new ways.

CHICKEN PROVOLONE

This is one of my simplest dishes and also one of my husband's favorites. It's easy to prepare and looks fancy served on a dark plate with a garnish of fresh parsley or basil.
—**Dawn E. Bryant** Thedford, NE

Start to Finish: 25 min.
Makes: 4 servings

- 4 boneless skinless chicken breast halves (4 ounces each)
- ¼ teaspoon pepper
    Butter-flavored cooking spray
- 8 fresh basil leaves
- 4 thin slices prosciutto or deli ham
- 4 slices provolone cheese

1. Sprinkle chicken with pepper. Coat a large nonstick skillet with butter-flavored cooking spray; cook the chicken over medium heat for 4-5 minutes on each side or until a thermometer reads 170°.
2. Transfer to an ungreased baking sheet; top with the basil, prosciutto and cheese. Broil 6-8 in. from the heat for 1-2 minutes or until the cheese is melted.

FREEZE IT SKILLET SHEPHERD'S PIE

This is the best shepherd's pie I've ever tasted. It's quick to make, and I usually have most of the ingredients on hand.
—**Tirzah Sandt** San Diego, CA

Start to Finish: 30 min.
Makes: 6 servings

- 1 pound ground beef
- 1 cup chopped onion
- 2 cups frozen corn, thawed
- 2 cups frozen peas, thawed
- 2 tablespoons ketchup
- 1 tablespoon Worcestershire sauce
- 2 teaspoons minced garlic
- 1 tablespoon cornstarch
- 1 teaspoon beef bouillon granules
- ½ cup cold water
- ½ cup sour cream
- 3½ cups mashed potatoes (prepared with milk and butter)
- ¾ cup shredded cheddar cheese

1. In a large skillet, cook beef and onion over medium heat until meat is no longer pink; drain. Stir in the corn, peas, ketchup, Worcestershire sauce and garlic. Reduce heat to medium-low; cover and cook for 5 minutes.

2. Combine the cornstarch, bouillon and water until well blended; stir into the beef mixture. Bring to a boil over medium heat; cook and stir for 2 minutes or until thickened. Stir in sour cream and heat through (do not boil).
3. Spread mashed potatoes over the top; sprinkle with cheese. Cover and cook until potatoes are heated through and cheese is melted.

Freeze option: Prepare beef mixture as directed but do not add sour cream. Freeze cooled meat mixture in a freezer container. To use, partially thaw pie in refrigerator overnight. Heat through in a large skillet, stirring occasionally and adding a little water if necessary. Stir in sour cream; proceed as directed.

A Healthier Pie

For a colorful and healthy take on this shepherd's pie recipe, try using mashed butternut squash or sweet potato in place of regular mashed potatoes.

STEAK FAJITAS

Tender strips of steak and a zesty tomato and jalapeno relish make these traditional fajitas extra special.
—**Rebecca Baird** Salt Lake City, UT

Start to Finish: 30 min.
Makes: 6 servings

- 2 large tomatoes, seeded and chopped
- ½ cup diced red onion
- ¼ cup lime juice
- 1 jalapeno pepper, seeded and minced
- 3 tablespoons minced fresh cilantro
- 2 teaspoons ground cumin, divided
- ¾ teaspoon salt, divided
- 1 beef flank steak (about 1½ pounds)
- 1 tablespoon canola oil
- 1 large onion, halved and sliced
- 6 whole wheat tortillas (8 inches), warmed
  Sliced avocado and lime wedges, optional

1. For salsa, place first five ingredients in a small bowl; stir in 1 teaspoon cumin and ¼ teaspoon salt. Let stand until serving.
2. Sprinkle steak with remaining cumin and salt. Grill, covered, over medium heat or broil 4 in. from heat until meat reaches desired doneness (for medium-rare, a thermometer should read 135°), 6-8 minutes. Let stand 5 minutes.
3. In a skillet, heat oil over medium-high heat; saute onion until crisp-tender. Slice steak thinly across the grain; serve in tortillas with onion and salsa. If desired, serve with avocado and lime wedges.

SAUCY PEACH-BALSAMIC CHICKEN

I throw this sweet and savory chicken dish together in no time on a weeknight. With a side of broccoli and rice, it's a healthy meal my whole family enjoys.
—**Trisha Kruse** Eagle, ID

Start to Finish: 30 min.
Makes: 4 servings

- 4 boneless skinless chicken breast halves (4 ounces each)
- ½ teaspoon salt
- ¼ teaspoon pepper
- 2 tablespoons butter
- ¼ cup reduced-sodium chicken broth
- ¼ cup sherry or additional reduced-sodium chicken broth
- ⅓ cup peach preserves
- 2 garlic cloves, thinly sliced
- 2 teaspoons minced fresh tarragon
- 1 tablespoon balsamic vinegar

1. Sprinkle chicken with salt and pepper. In a large skillet, brown chicken on both sides in butter. Remove from the skillet and keep warm.
2. Add broth and sherry to skillet, stirring to loosen browned bits from pan. Stir in preserves, garlic and tarragon. Bring to a boil. Reduce heat; simmer, uncovered, for 5 minutes, stirring occasionally. Stir in vinegar. Return chicken to skillet; cover and cook over medium heat 8-10 minutes or until a thermometer reads 165°.

WEEKNIGHT PASTA SKILLET

This zesty pasta dish is ideal for busy weeknights. It's low on ingredients, easy to prep and tastes so comforting when the weather turns cool. A salad on the side makes it a meal.
—**Stacey Brown** Spring, TX

Start to Finish: 30 min.
Makes: 8 servings

- 1 package (19½ ounces) Italian turkey sausage links, casings removed
- 1 can (28 ounces) whole plum tomatoes with basil
- 1 can (14½ ounces) no-salt-added whole tomatoes
- 4 cups uncooked spiral pasta (about 12 ounces)
- 1 can (14½ ounces) reduced-sodium chicken broth
- ¼ cup water
- ½ cup crumbled goat or feta cheese

1. In a Dutch oven, cook and crumble sausage over medium-high heat until no longer pink, 5-7 minutes. Meanwhile, coarsely chop tomatoes, reserving juices.
2. Add tomatoes and the reserved juices to the sausage; stir in pasta, broth and water. Bring to a boil. Reduce heat to medium; cook, uncovered, until the pasta is al dente, 15-18 minutes, stirring occasionally. Top with cheese.

CRESCENT TURKEY CASSEROLE

How do you make a dinner of turkey and vegetables appealing to kids? You turn it into a pie, of course! My version tastes classic, but won't take any time at all.
—**Daniela Essman** Perham, MN

Start to Finish: 30 min.
Makes: 4 servings

- ½ cup mayonnaise
- 2 tablespoons all-purpose flour
- 1 teaspoon chicken bouillon granules
- ⅛ teaspoon pepper
- ¾ cup 2% milk
- 2 cups frozen mixed vegetables (about 10 ounces), thawed
- 1½ cups cubed cooked turkey breast
- 1 tube (4 ounces) refrigerated crescent rolls

1. Preheat oven to 375°. In a saucepan, mix first four ingredients until smooth; gradually stir in the milk. Bring to a boil over medium heat; cook and stir until thickened, about 2 minutes. Add vegetables and turkey; cook and stir until heated through. Transfer to a greased 8-in. square baking pan.
2. Unroll the crescent dough and separate into eight triangles; arrange over the turkey mixture. Bake until heated through and the topping is golden brown, 15-20 minutes.

Turkey Biscuit Potpie: Thaw vegetables; combine in a bowl with turkey breast, one 10¾-ounce can condensed cream of chicken soup and ¼ teaspoon dried thyme. Place in a deep-dish 9-in. pie plate. Mix 1 cup biscuit/baking mix, ½ cup milk and 1 egg; spoon over top. Bake at 400° for 25-30 minutes.

Turkey Asparagus Casserole: Thaw a 10-ounce package of frozen cut asparagus; combine in a bowl with turkey breast, one 10¾-ounce can condensed cream of chicken soup and ¼ cup water. Bake at 350° for 30 minutes, topping with a 2.8-ounce can of french-fried onions during last 5 minutes.

MEATBALL PIZZA

I always keep meatballs and pizza crusts in the freezer to make this specialty on the spur of the moment. Add a tossed salad, and you have a delicious dinner.

—**Mary Humeniuk-Smith** Perry Hall, MD

Start to Finish: 25 min.
Makes: 8 slices

- 1 prebaked 12-inch pizza crust
- 1 can (8 ounces) pizza sauce
- 1 teaspoon garlic powder
- 1 teaspoon Italian seasoning
- ¼ cup grated Parmesan cheese
- 1 small onion, halved and sliced
- 12 frozen fully cooked Italian meatballs (½ ounce each), thawed and halved
- 1 cup shredded part-skim mozzarella cheese
- 1 cup shredded cheddar cheese

1. Preheat oven to 350°. Place pizza crust on an ungreased 12-in. pizza pan or baking sheet.

2. Spread sauce over crust; sprinkle with garlic powder, Italian seasoning and Parmesan cheese. Top with onion and meatballs; sprinkle with the remaining cheeses. Bake for 12-17 minutes or until the cheese is melted.

GINGER HALIBUT WITH BRUSSELS SPROUTS

I moved to the United States from Russia and love cooking Russian food for my family and friends. Halibut with soy sauce, ginger and pepper is a favorite.

—**Margarita Parker** New Bern, NC

Start to Finish: 25 min.
Makes: 4 servings

- 4 teaspoons lemon juice
- 4 halibut fillets (4 to 6 ounces each)
- 1 teaspoon minced fresh gingerroot
- ¼ to ¾ teaspoon salt, divided
- ¼ teaspoon pepper
- ½ cup water
- 10 ounces (about 2½ cups) fresh Brussels sprouts, halved
  Crushed red pepper flakes
- 1 tablespoon canola oil
- 5 garlic cloves, sliced lengthwise
- 2 tablespoons sesame oil
- 2 tablespoons soy sauce
  Lemon slices, optional

1. Brush lemon juice over halibut fillets. Sprinkle with minced ginger, ¼ teaspoon salt and pepper.

2. Place fish on an oiled grill rack, skin side down. Grill, covered, over medium heat (or broil 6 in. from heat) until fish just begins to flake easily with a fork, 6-8 minutes.

3. In a large skillet, bring water to a boil over medium-high heat. Add Brussels sprouts, pepper flakes and, if desired, the remaining salt. Cook, covered, until Brussels sprouts are tender, 5-7 minutes. Meanwhile, in a small skillet, heat oil over medium heat. Add garlic; cook until golden brown. Drain on paper towels.

4. Drizzle sesame oil and soy sauce over halibut. Serve with the Brussels sprouts; sprinkle with the fried garlic. If desired, serve with lemon slices.

MUSHROOM-HERB STUFFED FRENCH TOAST

This recipe transforms traditionally sweet French toast into a savory delight with mushrooms and cheese. The ooey-gooey texture is irresistible!
—**Lisa Huff** Wilton, CT

Prep: 25 min. • **Cook:** 5 min./batch
Makes: 8 servings

- 1 **pound thinly sliced baby portobello mushrooms**
- 4 **tablespoons butter, divided**
- 1 **package (8 ounces) reduced-fat cream cheese**
- 2 **cups shredded Gruyere or Swiss cheese, divided**
- 4 **tablespoons minced chives, divided**
- 1 **tablespoon minced fresh tarragon or 1 teaspoon dried tarragon**
- 1 **garlic clove, minced**
- ⅛ **teaspoon salt**
- ⅛ **teaspoon pepper**
- 16 **slices Texas toast**
- 4 **large eggs**
- 2 **cups 2% milk**
- 2 **tablespoons butter, melted**

1. In a large skillet, saute mushrooms in 1 tablespoon butter until tender; set aside.

2. In a small bowl, beat cream cheese, 1 cup Gruyere cheese, 2 tablespoons chives, tarragon, garlic, salt and pepper until blended. Spread over bread slices. Spoon mushrooms over half of the slices; place remaining bread slices over the top, spread side down.

3. In a shallow bowl, whisk the eggs, milk and melted butter. Dip both sides of the sandwiches into the egg mixture.

4. In a large skillet, toast sandwiches in the remaining butter in batches for 2-3 minutes on each side or until golden brown. Sprinkle with the remaining cheese and chives.

BLUSHING PENNE PASTA

I reworked this recipe from an original that called for vodka and heavy whipping cream. My friends and family had a hard time believing a sauce this rich, flavorful and creamy could be light.
—**Margaret Wilson** San Bernardino, CA

Start to Finish: 30 min.
Makes: 8 servings

- 1 package (16 ounces) penne pasta
- 2 tablespoons butter
- 1 medium onion, halved and thinly sliced
- 2 tablespoons minced fresh thyme or 2 teaspoons dried thyme
- 2 tablespoons minced fresh basil or 2 teaspoons dried basil
- 1 teaspoon salt
- 1½ cups half-and-half cream, divided
- ½ cup white wine or reduced-sodium chicken broth
- 1 tablespoon tomato paste
- 2 tablespoons all-purpose flour
- ½ cup shredded Parmigiano-Reggiano cheese, divided

1. In a 6-qt. stockpot, cook the pasta according to package directions. Drain; return to pot.
2. Meanwhile, in a large nonstick skillet, heat butter over medium heat; saute onion until lightly browned, 8-10 minutes. Add herbs and salt; cook and stir for 1 minute. Add 1 cup cream, wine and tomato paste; cook and stir until blended.
3. Mix flour and the remaining cream until smooth; gradually stir into the onion mixture. Bring to a boil; cook and stir until thickened, about 2 minutes. Stir in ¼ cup cheese. Stir into the pasta. Serve with the remaining cheese.

Contest Winner

GRILLED RIBEYE WITH GARLIC BLUE CHEESE MUSTARD SAUCE

This simple steak gets a big flavor boost from two of my favorites: mustard and blue cheese. My husband and I make this recipe to celebrate our anniversary each year!
—**Ashley Lecker** Green Bay, WI

Prep: 20 min. • **Grill:** 10 min. + standing
Makes: 4 servings

- 1 cup half-and-half cream
- ½ cup Dijon mustard
- ¼ cup plus 2 teaspoons crumbled blue cheese, divided
- 1 garlic clove, minced
- 2 beef ribeye steaks (1½ inches thick and 12 ounces each)
- 1 tablespoon olive oil
- ¼ teaspoon salt
- ¼ teaspoon pepper

1. In a small saucepan over medium heat, whisk together cream, mustard, ¼ cup blue cheese and garlic. Bring to a simmer. Reduce heat to low; whisk occasionally.
2. Meanwhile, rub meat with olive oil; sprinkle with salt and pepper. Grill steaks, covered, on a greased rack over high direct heat for 4-6 minutes on each side until meat reaches desired doneness (for medium-rare, a thermometer should read 135°; medium, 140°; medium-well, 145°). Remove from grill; let stand for 10 minutes while sauce finishes cooking. When sauce is reduced by half, pour over steaks; top with remaining blue cheese.

CHICKEN-PEPPER ALFREDO

When I want a lighter dinner, I use lean turkey bacon in this recipe. It gives the pasta that richness you want without the extra fat.

—**Courtney Harris** Denton, TX

Start to Finish: 30 min.
Makes: 4 servings

- 8 ounces uncooked linguine
- 1½ pounds chicken tenderloins, cut into 1-inch cubes
- 1 teaspoon garlic powder
- 1 teaspoon pepper
- 2 tablespoons olive oil
- ½ cup sliced fresh mushrooms
- ¼ cup finely chopped red onion
- 4 turkey or pork bacon strips, chopped
- 1 garlic clove, minced
- 1 jar (15 ounces) roasted red pepper Alfredo sauce
- ¼ cup grated Parmesan cheese

1. Cook linguine according to the package directions. Meanwhile, sprinkle chicken with garlic powder and pepper. In a large skillet, heat oil over medium heat. Add chicken, mushrooms, onion, bacon and garlic; cook and stir for 8-10 minutes or until chicken is no longer pink.
2. Drain linguine; add to skillet. Stir in Alfredo sauce; heat through. Sprinkle with cheese.

COUNTRY CHICKEN WITH GRAVY

Here's a lightened-up take on classic southern comfort food. It's been a hit at our house since the first time we tried it!

—**Ruth Helmuth** Abbeville, SC

Start to Finish: 30 min.
Makes: 4 servings

- ¾ cup crushed cornflakes
- ½ teaspoon poultry seasoning
- ½ teaspoon paprika
- ¼ teaspoon salt
- ¼ teaspoon dried thyme
- ¼ teaspoon pepper
- 2 tablespoons fat-free evaporated milk
- 4 boneless skinless chicken breast halves (4 ounces each)
- 2 teaspoons canola oil
- GRAVY
- 1 tablespoon butter
- 1 tablespoon all-purpose flour
- ¼ teaspoon pepper
- ⅛ teaspoon salt
- ½ cup fat-free evaporated milk
- ¼ cup condensed chicken broth, undiluted
- 1 teaspoon sherry or additional condensed chicken broth
- 2 tablespoons minced chives

1. In a shallow bowl, combine the first six ingredients. Place milk in another shallow bowl. Dip chicken in milk, then roll in the cornflake mixture.
2. In a large nonstick skillet, cook chicken in oil over medium heat for 6-8 minutes on each side or until a thermometer reads 170°.
3. Meanwhile, in a small saucepan, melt butter. Stir in flour, pepper and salt until smooth. Gradually stir in the milk, broth and sherry. Bring to a boil; cook and stir for 1-2 minutes or until thickened. Stir in chives. Serve with the chicken.

TORTILLA PIE

My husband and I especially like this delicious dinner pie because it's lighter tasting than traditional lasagnas made with pasta. Even our two young daughters get excited when I bring these to the table!
—**Lisa King** Caledonia, MI

Start to Finish: 30 min.
Makes: 4 servings

- ½ **pound lean ground beef (90% lean)**
- ½ **cup chopped onion**
- 2 **garlic cloves, minced**
- 1 **teaspoon chili powder**
- ½ **teaspoon ground cumin**
- 1 **can (14½ ounces) Mexican diced tomatoes, drained**
- ¾ **cup reduced-fat ricotta cheese**
- ¼ **cup shredded part-skim mozzarella cheese**
- 3 **tablespoons minced fresh cilantro, divided**
- 4 **whole wheat tortillas (8 inches)**
- ½ **cup shredded cheddar cheese**

1. Preheat oven to 400°. In a large skillet, cook and crumble beef with onion and garlic over medium heat until no longer pink, 4-6 minutes. Stir in spices and tomatoes. Bring to a boil; remove from heat. In a small bowl, mix ricotta cheese, mozzarella cheese and 2 tablespoons of cilantro.

2. Place one tortilla in a 9-in. round baking pan coated with cooking spray. Layer with half of the meat sauce, one tortilla, ricotta mixture, another tortilla and the remaining meat sauce. Top with remaining tortilla; sprinkle with cheddar cheese and remaining cilantro.

3. Bake, covered, until heated through, 15-20 minutes.

Quick-Fix Pizzas

Is pizza the perfect food? Convenient, versatile and always a crowd pleaser, it might just be! With these tasty pizzas, you can choose the ingredients your family will love and get dinner on the table in record time.

EASY THREE-CHEESE PESTO PIZZA

Using a ready-made crust, pizza can be on a serving tray in half an hour. This triple-cheese version is meatless and makes a hearty appetizer for casual gatherings.

—Pat Stevens Granbury, TX

....

Start to Finish: 30 min.
Makes: 16 slices

- ½ cup finely chopped red onion
- ½ cup finely chopped sweet red pepper
- 1 tablespoon olive oil
- 1 prebaked 12-inch pizza crust
- ½ cup prepared pesto
- 1 cup crumbled feta cheese
- 1 cup shredded part-skim mozzarella cheese
- 1 cup shredded Parmesan cheese
- ⅓ cup chopped ripe olives
- 1 medium tomato, thinly sliced

1. Preheat oven to 400°. In a small skillet, saute onion and red pepper in oil until tender. Remove from heat; set aside.
2. Place crust on an ungreased 14-in. pizza pan. Spread pesto to within ½ in. of edges. Layer with cheeses, onion mixture, olives and tomato.
3. Bake 15-18 minutes or until the cheese is melted.

FREEZE IT CHICKEN PIZZA

Loaded with chicken and black beans, this fun twist on traditional pizza will fill your family up fast.

—Taste of Home Test Kitchen

....

Start to Finish: 30 min.
Makes: 6 servings

- 1 pound boneless skinless chicken breasts, cut into 1-inch pieces
- 1 tablespoon olive oil
- 1 prebaked 12-inch pizza crust
- ¼ cup prepared pesto
- 1 large tomato, chopped
- ½ cup canned black beans, rinsed and drained
- 1 cup shredded part-skim mozzarella cheese
- ½ cup shredded Parmesan cheese

1. In a large skillet over medium heat, cook chicken in oil for 10-15 minutes or until no longer pink.
2. Place the crust on a lightly greased 12-in. pizza pan. Spread with pesto; top with the chicken, tomato, beans and cheeses. Bake at 400° for 10-12 minutes or until the cheese is melted.
Freeze option: Securely wrap and freeze unbaked pizza. To use, unwrap pizza; bake as directed, increasing time as necessary.

STEAK & BLUE CHEESE PIZZA

Even my hubby, who doesn't normally like blue cheese, adores this scrumptious pizza! If time allows, cook the onion a bit longer, until it's rich and caramelized, for unbeatable flavor.

—**Kadija Bridgewater** Boca Raton, FL

Start to Finish: 30 min.
Makes: 6 servings

- ½ pound beef top sirloin steak, thinly sliced
- ¼ teaspoon salt
- ¼ teaspoon pepper
- 2 tablespoons olive oil, divided
- 2 cups sliced baby portobello mushrooms
- 1 large onion, sliced
- ½ cup heavy whipping cream
- ¼ cup crumbled blue cheese
- 1 prebaked 12-inch pizza crust
- 2 teaspoons minced fresh parsley

1. Preheat oven to 450°. Sprinkle beef with salt and pepper. In a large skillet, heat 1 tablespoon oil over medium heat. Add beef and mushrooms; cook 3-4 minutes or until beef is no longer pink. Remove from pan.

2. Cook onion in the remaining oil for 2-3 minutes or until tender. Add cream and blue cheese; cook 3-5 minutes longer or until slightly thickened.

3. Place crust on a 12-in. pizza pan or baking sheet. Spread with cream mixture; top with the beef mixture. Sprinkle with parsley. Bake 10-12 minutes or until sauce is bubbly and crust is lightly browned.

GRILLED SAUSAGE-BASIL PIZZAS

These easy little pizzas are a wonderful change of pace from the classic cookout menu. Let everybody go crazy with the toppings.

—**Lisa Speer** Palm Beach, FL

Start to Finish: 30 min.
Makes: 4 servings

- 4 Italian sausage links (4 ounces each)
- 4 naan flatbreads or whole pita breads
- ¼ cup olive oil
- 1 cup tomato basil pasta sauce
- 2 cups shredded part-skim mozzarella cheese
- ½ cup grated Parmesan cheese
- ½ cup thinly sliced fresh basil

1. Grill sausages, covered, over medium heat 10-12 minutes or until a thermometer reads 160°, turning occasionally. Cut into ¼-in. slices.

2. Brush both sides of flatbreads with oil. Grill, covered, over medium heat for 2-3 minutes or until bottoms are lightly browned.

3. Remove from grill. Layer grilled sides with sauce, sausage, cheeses and basil. Return to grill; cook, covered, until cheese is melted, 2-3 minutes longer.

GRILLED SALMON WITH CHORIZO-OLIVE SAUCE

Every one of the ingredients in this recipe brings a ton of flavor. Both chorizo and salmon cook in a hurry, and garlic and citrus go beautifully with them, too.
—**Charlene Chambers** Ormond Beach, FL

Start to Finish: 25 min.
Makes: 4 servings

- 3 links (3 to 4 ounces each) fresh chorizo
- 4 green onions, chopped
- 2 garlic cloves, minced
- 1 can (14½ ounces) diced tomatoes, drained
- ¼ cup chopped pitted green olives
- ½ teaspoon grated orange peel
- ¼ teaspoon salt
- ¼ teaspoon pepper
- 4 salmon fillets (6 ounces each)

1. Remove chorizo from casings. In a large ovenproof skillet on a stove or grill, cook and stir chorizo, green onions and garlic over medium-high heat, crumbling sausage. Cook until sausage is no longer pink, 4-6 minutes; drain.
2. Reduce heat to medium. Add the tomatoes, olives and orange peel; stir to combine. Sprinkle salt and pepper over salmon.
3. On a greased grill rack, grill salmon, covered, over medium heat 3-4 minutes per side, or until the fish just begins to flake easily with a fork. Top with the chorizo mixture.

ARTICHOKE BLUE CHEESE FETTUCCINE

When I'm in a rush, I use store-bought Alfredo sauce to speed along my blue-cheesy noodles with mushrooms. Fresh refrigerated fettuccine gets it done even faster.
—**Jolanthe Erb** Harrisonburg, VA

Start to Finish: 20 min.
Makes: 4 servings

- 1 package (12 ounces) fettuccine
- 1 cup sliced fresh mushrooms
- 1 can (14 ounces) water-packed artichoke hearts, drained and chopped
- 1½ cups Alfredo sauce
- ¼ cup crumbled blue cheese

1. Cook fettuccine according to the package directions.
2. Meanwhile, place a large nonstick skillet coated with cooking spray over medium-high heat. Add mushrooms and artichoke hearts; cook and stir until the mushrooms are tender. Stir in Alfredo sauce; bring to a boil over medium heat. Reduce heat; simmer, uncovered, for 5 minutes, stirring occasionally.
3. Drain the fettuccine, reserving ⅓ cup of the pasta water. Add fettuccine to the artichoke mixture; toss to combine, adding reserved pasta water if desired. Sprinkle with blue cheese.

Contest Winner

PIZZA IN A BOWL

On busy days, it's a comfort to know that my family can sit down to dinner minutes after we walk in the door. This recipe works in a slow cooker, too. Double it to wow at a potluck.

—**Virginia Krites** Cridersville, OH

Start to Finish: 25 min.
Makes: 6 servings

- 8 ounces uncooked rigatoni (about 3 cups)
- ¾ pound ground beef
- ½ cup chopped onion
- 1 can (15 ounces) pizza sauce
- ⅔ cup condensed cream of mushroom soup, undiluted
- 2 cups shredded part-skim mozzarella cheese
- 1 package (3½ ounces) sliced pepperoni
  Chopped fresh basil or arugula, optional

1. Cook rigatoni according to package directions; drain. Meanwhile, in a large skillet, cook beef and onion over medium heat 6-8 minutes or until beef is no longer pink, breaking up beef into crumbles; drain. Add pizza sauce, soup and cheese; cook and stir over low heat until cheese is melted.

2. Add rigatoni and pepperoni to the beef mixture. Heat through, stirring to combine. If desired, top with basil.

POTATO KIELBASA SKILLET

Smoky kielbasa steals the show in this hearty all-in-one meal. It adds instant coziness to chilly fall nights.

—*Taste of Home* Test Kitchen

Start to Finish: 30 min.
Makes: 4 servings

- 1 pound red potatoes (3-4 medium), cut into 1-inch pieces
- 3 tablespoons water
- 2 tablespoons brown sugar
- 2 tablespoons cider vinegar
- 1 tablespoon Dijon mustard
- 1½ teaspoons minced fresh thyme or ½ teaspoon dried thyme
- ¼ teaspoon pepper
- 1 tablespoon olive oil
- ½ cup chopped onion
- ¾ pound smoked kielbasa or Polish sausage, cut into ¼-inch slices
- 4 cups fresh baby spinach
- 5 bacon strips, cooked and crumbled

1. Place potatoes and water in a microwave-safe dish. Microwave, covered, on high until the potatoes are tender, 3-4 minutes; drain.

2. Meanwhile, mix brown sugar, vinegar, mustard, thyme and pepper. In a large skillet, heat oil over medium-high heat; saute onion and kielbasa until the onion is tender.

3. Add the potatoes; cook and stir until lightly browned, 3-5 minutes. Stir in the brown sugar mixture; bring to a boil. Reduce heat; simmer, uncovered, for 2 minutes, stirring occasionally. Stir in spinach until wilted. Stir in bacon.

SHRIMP AND GRITS

For a sweet and spicy meal, I serve shrimp and veggies in a honey-kissed sauce alongside creamy grits. It's my fresh spin on the southern classic.

—**Judith King** Madisonville, TN

Start to Finish: 30 min.
Makes: 4 servings

    2 cups water
    1 cup fat-free half-and-half
    4 teaspoons butter, divided
    ¼ teaspoon salt
    ¼ teaspoon pepper
    ¾ cup quick-cooking grits
    ¼ cup ketchup
    1 tablespoon honey
    2 teaspoons lemon juice
    ½ to 1 teaspoon hot pepper sauce
    3 celery ribs, chopped
    1 medium onion, chopped
    1 pound uncooked medium shrimp,
       peeled and deveined
    1 cup shredded reduced-fat
       cheddar cheese

1. In a large saucepan, bring water, half-and-half, 2 teaspoons butter, salt and pepper to a boil. Slowly stir in the grits. Reduce heat to medium-low; cook, covered, about 5 minutes or until thickened, stirring occasionally. Remove from heat.

2. Meanwhile, in a small bowl, mix ketchup, honey, lemon juice and pepper sauce. In a large skillet, heat the remaining butter over medium-high heat. Add the celery and onion; cook and stir until tender. Add shrimp; cook and stir until shrimp turn pink. Stir in ketchup mixture.

3. Stir cheese into grits. Serve shrimp mixture with grits.

SPINACH-PESTO WHITE PIZZA

When my kids were small, they tried to avoid veggies and I had to get creative. I figured that because pesto is already green, it would be the perfect place to add some spinach. The recipe gained a following right away.

—**Janet Burbach** North Platte, NE

Start to Finish: 30 min.
Makes: 6 slices

    1 teaspoon olive oil
    3 cups fresh baby spinach
    ¼ cup plus 1 tablespoon prepared
       pesto, divided
    1 package (6 ounces) ready-to-use
       grilled chicken breast strips
    1 prebaked 12-inch pizza crust
    2 cups shredded part-skim mozzarella
       cheese
    5 bacon strips, cooked and crumbled
    ½ cup part-skim ricotta cheese
    ¼ cup shredded Parmesan cheese

1. Preheat oven to 450°. In a large skillet, heat oil over medium-high heat. Add spinach; cook and stir just until wilted. Remove from heat; stir in ¼ cup pesto. In a small bowl, toss chicken with the remaining pesto.

2. Place crust on an ungreased baking sheet. Spread with spinach mixture; top with chicken, mozzarella cheese and bacon. Drop ricotta cheese by rounded teaspoonfuls over top; sprinkle with Parmesan cheese. Bake 8-10 minutes or until cheese is melted.

FREEZE IT TOMATO & GARLIC BUTTER BEAN DINNER

For those days when I get home late and just want a warm meal, I stir up tomatoes, garlic and butter beans. Ladle it over noodles if you're in the mood for pasta.
—**Jessica Meyers** Austin, TX

Start to Finish: 15 min.
Makes: 4 servings

- 1 tablespoon olive oil
- 2 garlic cloves, minced
- 2 cans (14½ ounces) no-salt-added petite diced tomatoes, undrained
- 1 can (16 ounces) butter beans, rinsed and drained
- 6 cups fresh baby spinach (about 6 ounces)
- ½ teaspoon Italian seasoning
- ¼ teaspoon pepper
  Hot cooked pasta and grated Parmesan cheese, optional

In a large skillet, heat oil over medium-high heat. Add garlic; cook and stir until tender, 30-45 seconds. Add tomatoes, beans, spinach, Italian seasoning and pepper; cook until spinach is wilted, stirring occasionally. If desired, serve with pasta and cheese.

Freeze option: Freeze cooled bean mixture in freezer containers. To use, partially thaw in refrigerator overnight. Heat through in a saucepan, stirring occasionally and adding a little water if necessary.

STRAWBERRY-TERIYAKI GLAZED SALMON

I'm always up for a good salmon dinner, but this is the best recipe I've ever made. Strawberry jam might seem like a surprise in an Asian-inspired dish, but it makes a sweet-savory glaze that impresses everyone—even my boyfriend, who doesn't like fish.
—**Krystina Cahalan** Winter Park, FL

Start to Finish: 25 min.
Makes: 4 servings

- ¼ cup seedless strawberry jam
- 2 tablespoons reduced-sodium soy sauce
- 1 garlic clove, minced
- ½ teaspoon ground ginger
- 4 salmon fillets (4 ounces each)
- ¼ teaspoon salt
- ¼ teaspoon pepper

1. Preheat broiler. In a small saucepan, combine jam, soy sauce, garlic and ginger; cook and stir until mixture comes to a boil. Reduce heat; simmer, uncovered, 6-8 minutes or until mixture is reduced by half.
2. Sprinkle salmon with salt and pepper. Place in an ungreased 15x10x1-in. baking pan. Broil 4-6 in. from heat 8-10 minutes or until fish just begins to flake easily with a fork, brushing with 2 tablespoons jam mixture during the last 2 minutes of cooking. Just before serving, brush with the remaining jam mixture.

CURRY CHICKEN AND RICE

I updated this chicken and rice dish by adding veggies and cashews to give it fresh and crunchy appeal. The green chilies in the tomatoes give it just the right little kick, but if you really like spice, add some diced jalapeno.

—Denise Klibert Shreveport, LA

Start to Finish: 30 min.
Makes: 4 servings

- 1¾ cups water
- 1 tablespoon olive oil
- 1 package (7.2 ounces) rice pilaf mix
- 1 teaspoon curry powder
- 2 cups shredded rotisserie chicken
- 1 can (14½ ounces) diced tomatoes with mild green chilies, undrained
- 1 cup frozen peas (about 4 ounces)
- ½ cup chopped lightly salted cashews

1. In a large saucepan, bring water and oil to a boil. Stir in pilaf mix, contents of seasoning packet and the curry powder. Return to a boil. Reduce heat; simmer, covered, 15 minutes.

2. Stir in chicken, tomatoes and peas. Cook, covered, 8-10 minutes longer or until liquid is almost absorbed and rice is tender. Sprinkle with cashews.

SPAGHETTI SQUASH & SAUSAGE EASY MEAL

I first created my son's favorite dish using homegrown squash, kielbasa and salsa. This variation uses only four ingredients. What could be easier?

—Pam Copeland Taylorsville, UT

Start to Finish: 30 min.
Makes: 6 servings

- 1 medium spaghetti squash
- 1 tablespoon olive oil
- 1 package (14 ounces) smoked sausage, halved lengthwise and sliced
- 1 cup pico de gallo
- ¼ teaspoon salt
- ⅛ teaspoon pepper

1. Cut squash lengthwise in half; discard the seeds. Place halves on a microwave-safe plate, cut side down. Microwave, uncovered, on high for 15-20 minutes or until tender.

2. Meanwhile, in a large skillet, heat oil over medium heat. Add sausage; cook and stir 4-5 minutes or until lightly browned.

3. When squash is cool enough to handle, use a fork to separate strands. Add the squash, pico de gallo, salt and pepper to sausage; heat through, tossing to combine.

Note: One cup cooked spaghetti squash has about 10 grams of carbohydrates, versus 45 grams for regular spaghetti.

CHORIZO PUMPKIN PASTA

This spicy-sweet pasta makes a perfect quick dinner. Even better, it works on a bigger scale to feed a bunch of friends.
—**Christine Yang** Syracuse, NY

Start to Finish: 30 min.
Makes: 6 servings

- 3 cups uncooked gemelli or spiral pasta (about 12 ounces)
- 1 package (12 ounces) fully cooked chorizo chicken sausage links or flavor of choice, sliced
- 1 cup canned pumpkin
- 1 cup half-and-half cream
- ¾ teaspoon salt
- ¼ teaspoon pepper
- 1½ cups shredded Manchego or Monterey Jack cheese
  Minced fresh cilantro, optional

1. Cook pasta according to the package directions. Drain, reserving ¾ cup of the pasta water.
2. Meanwhile, in a large skillet, saute sausage over medium heat until lightly browned; reduce heat to medium-low. Add pumpkin, cream, salt and pepper; cook and stir until heated through. Toss with pasta and enough pasta water to moisten; stir in cheese. If desired, sprinkle with cilantro.

MEDITERRANEAN CHICKEN

As special as it is simple to prepare, this moist, flavorful chicken is dressed in tomatoes, olives and capers. It's a knockout main dish for guests.
—**Mary Relyea** Canastota, NY

Start to Finish: 25 min.
Makes: 4 servings

- 4 boneless skinless chicken breast halves (6 ounces each)
- ¼ teaspoon salt
- ¼ teaspoon pepper
- 3 tablespoons olive oil
- 1 pint grape tomatoes
- 16 pitted Greek or ripe olives, sliced
- 3 tablespoons capers, drained

1. Preheat oven to 475°. Sprinkle chicken with salt and pepper. In a large ovenproof skillet, cook the chicken in oil over medium heat for 2-3 minutes on each side or until golden brown. Add the tomatoes, olives and capers.
2. Bake, uncovered, for 10-14 minutes or until a thermometer reads 170°.

Cooking for Two

Just because you're preparing meals for a small household doesn't mean you have to put up with lots of leftovers or settle for no-frills dishes. Check out these 26 ideas, sized right for a pair. In addition to suppers, you'll find desserts, breakfasts and soups that take the ho-hum out of cooking for two.

CHICKEN GYROS

These yummy Greek specialties are a cinch to prepare at home. Tender chicken and a creamy cucumber sauce are tucked into pitas.
—**Taste of Home** Test Kitchen

Prep: 20 min. + marinating • **Cook:** 10 min.
Makes: 2 servings

- ¼ cup lemon juice
- 2 tablespoons olive oil
- ¾ teaspoon minced garlic, divided
- ½ teaspoon ground mustard
- ½ teaspoon dried oregano
- ½ pound boneless skinless chicken breasts, cut into ½-inch strips
- ½ cup chopped peeled cucumber
- ⅓ cup plain yogurt
- ¼ teaspoon dill weed
- 2 whole pita breads
- ½ small red onion, thinly sliced

1. In a large resealable plastic bag, combine the lemon juice, oil, ½ teaspoon garlic, mustard and oregano; add chicken. Seal bag and turn to coat; refrigerate for at least 1 hour. In a small bowl, combine the cucumber, yogurt, dill and remaining garlic; cover and refrigerate until serving.
2. Drain and discard marinade. In a large nonstick skillet, cook and stir the chicken for 7-8 minutes or until no longer pink. Spoon onto pita breads. Top with yogurt mixture and onion; fold in half.

ASPARAGUS & SHRIMP WITH ANGEL HAIR

We've all heard that the way to a man's heart is through his stomach, so when I plan a romantic dinner, this is one dish I like to serve. It's easy on the budget and turns out perfectly for two.
—**Shari Neff** Takoma Park, MD

Start to Finish: 30 min.
Makes: 2 servings

- 3 ounces uncooked angel hair pasta
- 8 uncooked shrimp (16-20 per pound), peeled and deveined
- ¼ teaspoon salt
- ⅛ teaspoon crushed red pepper flakes
- 2 tablespoons olive oil, divided
- 8 fresh asparagus spears, trimmed and cut into 2-inch pieces
- ½ cup sliced fresh mushrooms
- ¼ cup chopped seeded tomato, peeled
- 4 garlic cloves, minced
- 2 teaspoons chopped green onion
- ½ cup white wine or chicken broth
- 1½ teaspoons minced fresh basil
- 1½ teaspoons minced fresh oregano
- 1½ teaspoons minced fresh parsley
- 1½ teaspoons minced fresh thyme
- ¼ cup grated Parmesan cheese

1. Cook pasta according to package directions. Meanwhile, sprinkle the shrimp with salt and pepper flakes. In a large skillet or wok, heat 1 tablespoon oil over medium-high heat. Add shrimp; stir-fry until pink, 2-3 minutes. Remove; keep warm.
2. In same skillet, stir-fry the next five ingredients in the remaining oil until the vegetables are crisp-tender, about 5 minutes. Add wine and seasonings. Return shrimp to pan.
3. Drain pasta; add to the shrimp mixture and toss gently. Cook and stir until heated through, 1-2 minutes. Sprinkle with Parmesan cheese.

COCOA MERINGUES WITH BERRIES

Meringues can be a challenge to make on a humid day, but if you can't make them, you can often buy them at your favorite bakery. Add this sweet sauce, and you're all set!
—**Raymonde Bourgeois** Swastika, ON

Prep: 20 min. • **Bake:** 50 min. + standing
Makes: 2 servings

- 1 large egg white
- ⅛ teaspoon cream of tartar
  Dash salt
- 3 tablespoons sugar, divided
- 1 tablespoon baking cocoa
- ¼ teaspoon vanilla extract
- 2 tablespoons finely chopped
  bittersweet chocolate

BERRY SAUCE

- 2 tablespoons sugar
- 1 teaspoon cornstarch
- 2 tablespoons orange juice
- 1 tablespoon water
- ½ cup fresh or frozen blueberries,
  thawed
- ½ cup fresh or frozen raspberries,
  thawed

1. Place the egg white in a small bowl; let stand at room temperature for 30 minutes.
2. Preheat oven to 275°. Add cream of tartar and salt; beat on medium speed until soft peaks form. Gradually beat in 2 tablespoons sugar.
3. Combine cocoa and remaining sugar; add to meringue with vanilla. Beat on high until stiff, glossy peaks form and sugar is dissolved. Fold in chopped chocolate.
4. Drop two mounds onto a parchment paper-lined baking sheet. Shape into 3-in. cups with the back of a spoon. Bake for 50-60 minutes or until set and dry. Turn oven off; leave meringues in oven for 1 hour.
5. In a small saucepan, combine sugar, cornstarch, orange juice and water. Bring to a boil; cook and stir 1 minute or until thickened. Remove from the heat; stir in berries. Cool to room temperature. Spoon into meringues.

CREAM OF SPINACH CHEESE SOUP

Give yourself a delicious calcium boost with this creamy, cheesy soup. I like to serve it with a green salad. You can also add 2 cups of cubed cooked chicken, if you wish.
—**Maria Regakis** Saugus, MA

Start to Finish: 15 min.
Makes: 2 servings

- 1 cup chicken broth
- 1 package (6 ounces) fresh baby
  spinach, chopped
- ½ teaspoon onion powder
- ⅛ teaspoon pepper
- 4 teaspoons all-purpose flour
- 1 can (5 ounces) evaporated milk
- 1 cup shredded cheddar cheese

In a small saucepan, combine the broth, spinach, onion powder and pepper. Bring to a boil. Combine flour and milk until smooth; gradually add to soup. Return to a boil. Reduce heat; cook and stir for 2 minutes or until thickened. Stir in the cheese until melted.

GREEK-STYLE RAVIOLI

I took an Italian dish and gave it a Greek twist with spinach, olives and feta. I like serving this easy weeknight ravioli with garlic cheese toast.

—**Hetti Williams** Rapid City, SD

Start to Finish: 25 min.
Makes: 2 servings

  12 **frozen cheese ravioli**
  ⅓ **pound lean ground beef (90% lean)**
  1 **cup canned diced tomatoes with basil, oregano and garlic**
  1 **cup fresh baby spinach**
  ¼ **cup sliced ripe olives**
  ¼ **cup crumbled feta cheese**

1. Cook ravioli according to the package directions; drain. Meanwhile, in a skillet, cook beef over medium heat 4-6 minutes or until no longer pink; drain. Stir in the tomatoes; bring to a boil. Reduce heat; simmer, uncovered, 10 minutes, stirring occasionally.
2. Add ravioli, spinach and olives; heat through, stirring gently to combine. Sprinkle with cheese.

Salad Bar Savings

Check the price per pound on a package of feta cheese; it might be cheaper at your store's salad bar. The salad bar is also helpful when you need a small amount, as with the ¼ cup in this recipe.

GREEK ISLANDS STEAK SALAD

I invented this recipe while watching a movie set on the Greek islands. I like the combination of warm grilled steak and sauteed mushrooms with cold salad ingredients.

—**Chris Wells** Lake Villa, IL

Start to Finish: 25 min.
Makes: 2 servings

  1 **boneless beef top loin steak (8 ounces)**
  1 **tablespoon A.1. steak sauce**
MUSHROOMS
  1½ **cups sliced fresh mushrooms**
  2 **tablespoons butter**
  1 **tablespoon sherry or chicken broth**
  ⅛ **teaspoon salt**
  ⅛ **teaspoon pepper**
SALAD
  4 **cups torn mixed salad greens**
  10 **grape tomatoes, halved**
  ⅔ **cup thinly sliced cucumber**
  10 **pitted Greek olives**
  ¼ **cup finely chopped red onion**
  ½ **cup crumbled feta cheese**
  ¼ **cup prepared balsamic vinaigrette**

1. Rub steak on both sides with steak sauce; let stand for 10 minutes.
2. Meanwhile, in a small skillet, saute mushrooms in butter until golden brown. Add the sherry, salt and pepper. Cook 1-2 minutes longer or until the liquid is evaporated. Set aside and keep warm.
3. Grill steak, covered, on a lightly oiled grill rack over medium heat or broil 4 in. from the heat for 5-6 minutes on each side or until the meat reaches desired doneness (for medium-rare, a thermometer should read 145°; medium, 160°; well-done, 170°). Let stand for 5 minutes before slicing.
4. Divide salad greens between two plates. Top with tomatoes, cucumber, olives, onion, steak and mushrooms. Sprinkle with cheese. Drizzle with vinaigrette. Serve immediately.
Note: Depending on your region, top loin steak may be labeled as strip steak, Kansas City steak, New York strip steak, ambassador steak or boneless club steak.

DESSERT BRUSCHETTA WITH NECTARINE SALSA

Here's a fresh no-cook dessert for hot summer days. The flavors work wonderfully together.
—**Sally Sibthorpe** Shelby Township, MI

Start to Finish: 15 min.
Makes: 2 servings

- 1 medium nectarine, chopped
- ¼ cup fresh or frozen raspberries, thawed
- 1 tablespoon thinly sliced fresh mint leaves
- 2 slices pound cake
- 3 tablespoons mascarpone cheese
- 2 teaspoons honey
  Whipped cream, optional

1. In a small bowl, combine the nectarine, raspberries and mint. Let stand for 5 minutes.
2. Spread cake slices with cheese; top with fruit mixture. Drizzle with honey. If desired, serve with whipped cream.

Contest Winner

MAPLE & BLUE CHEESE STEAK

This is a wonderful cheesy dish that nearly melts in your mouth. I love this traditional Canadian meal!
—**Susan Jerrott** Bedford, NS

Prep: 20 min. + marinating • **Grill:** 10 min.
Makes: 2 servings

- 6 tablespoons balsamic vinegar
- 6 tablespoons maple syrup, divided
- 2 tablespoons plus 1½ teaspoons Dijon mustard
- 1 tablespoon minced fresh thyme or ¼ teaspoon dried thyme
- ½ pound beef top sirloin steak
- 2 tablespoons chopped pecans
- 1½ teaspoons olive oil
- ⅛ teaspoon salt
- ⅛ teaspoon pepper
- ¼ cup crumbled blue cheese

1. In a small bowl, combine the vinegar, 5 tablespoons maple syrup, mustard and thyme. Pour ⅔ cup marinade into a large resealable plastic bag; add the steak. Seal bag and turn to coat; refrigerate for up to 3 hours. Cover and refrigerate remaining marinade.
2. Meanwhile, in a small skillet, saute pecans in oil until toasted. Stir in the remaining maple syrup. Bring to a boil; cook for 1 minute, stirring constantly. Remove from skillet and spread onto waxed paper to cool completely.
3. Drain and discard marinade. Sprinkle steak with salt and pepper. Grill, over medium heat, for 4-6 minutes on each side or until the meat reaches desired doneness (for medium-rare steak, a thermometer should read 145°; medium, 160°; well-done, 170°). Let stand for 5 minutes before slicing.
4. Place reserved marinade in small saucepan. Bring to a boil; cook until liquid is reduced to ¼ cup, about 2 minutes. Divide steak slices between two plates. Drizzle with sauce; sprinkle with blue cheese and pecans.

PINEAPPLE-STUFFED CORNISH HENS

My mother brought this recipe back with her from Hawaii about 25 years ago. The tender meat, tropical stuffing and sweet-sour sauce made it a favorite of family and friends. I always keep copies of the recipe on hand to share.
—Vicki Corners Rock Island, IL

....

Prep: 20 min. • **Bake:** 1 hour 25 min.
Makes: 2 servings

- ½ teaspoon salt, divided
- 2 Cornish game hens (20 to 24 ounces each)
- 1 can (8 ounces) crushed pineapple
- 3 cups cubed day-old bread (½-inch cubes), crusts removed
- 1 celery rib, chopped
- ½ cup sweetened shredded coconut
- ⅔ cup butter, melted, divided
- ¼ teaspoon poultry seasoning
- 2 tablespoons steak sauce
- 2 tablespoons cornstarch
- 2 tablespoons brown sugar
- 1 cup cold water
- 1 tablespoon lemon juice

1. Sprinkle ¼ teaspoon salt inside hens; set aside. Drain pineapple, reserving juice. In a large bowl, combine the pineapple, bread cubes, celery and coconut. Add ⅓ cup butter; toss to coat. Loosely stuff hens with mixture.

2. Tuck wings under hens; tie the legs together. Place hens on a rack in a greased shallow roasting pan. Place the remaining stuffing in a greased 1½-cup baking dish; cover and set aside. Add poultry seasoning and the remaining salt to the remaining butter.

3. Spoon some butter mixture over hens. Bake, uncovered, at 350° for 40 minutes, basting twice with the butter mixture.

4. Add steak sauce and the reserved pineapple juice to any remaining butter mixture; baste hens. Bake reserved stuffing with hens for 30 minutes, basting the hens occasionally with the remaining butter mixture.

5. Uncover stuffing; bake 15-20 minutes longer or until a thermometer reads 185° for hens and 165° for stuffing in hens. Remove hens from pan; keep warm.

6. Pour drippings into a saucepan; skim fat. Combine cornstarch, brown sugar, water and lemon juice; add to the drippings. Bring to a boil; cook and stir 1-2 minutes or until thickened. Serve with hens and stuffing.

SOURDOUGH TURKEY MELTS

When days feel rushed, these sandwiches with turkey and green chilies are one of my favorite standbys. They stack up in about 10 minutes, honestly!
—**Leah Carter** San Pedro, CA

Start to Finish: 10 min.
Makes: 2 servings

- 2 tablespoons mayonnaise
- 4 slices sourdough bread
- ¼ cup canned chopped green chilies
- ¼ pound thinly sliced deli turkey
- ¼ cup shredded Colby-Monterey Jack cheese
- 1 tablespoon butter, softened

1. Spread mayonnaise over two slices of bread. Layer with green chilies, turkey and cheese. Top with the remaining bread. Spread outsides of sandwiches with butter.
2. In a large skillet, toast sandwiches over medium heat 1-2 minutes on each side or until golden brown and cheese is melted.
Havarti-Mushroom Grilled Cheese: Layer two slices rye bread with 3 ounces sliced Havarti with dill cheese; top with 1 sliced tomato, ½ cup sliced fresh mushrooms, 3 more ounces Havarti with dill, and two slices rye. Butter sandwiches and cook as directed.

SPINACH AND FETA STUFFED CHICKEN

My chicken bundles are simple, clean and comforting. Serve them with wild rice and green beans for one of our favorite meals.
—**Jim Knepper** Mount Holly Springs, PA

Start to Finish: 30 min.
Makes: 2 servings

- 8 ounces fresh spinach (about 10 cups)
- 1½ teaspoons cider vinegar
- ½ teaspoon sugar
- ⅛ teaspoon pepper
- 2 boneless skinless chicken thighs
- ½ teaspoon chicken seasoning
- 3 tablespoons crumbled feta cheese
- 1 teaspoon olive oil
- ¾ cup reduced-sodium chicken broth
- 1 teaspoon butter

1. Preheat oven to 375°. In a large skillet, cook and stir spinach over medium-high heat until wilted. Stir in vinegar, sugar and pepper; cool slightly.
2. Pound the chicken thighs with a meat mallet to flatten slightly; sprinkle with chicken seasoning. Top chicken with the spinach mixture and cheese. Roll up chicken from a long side; tie securely with kitchen string.
3. In an ovenproof skillet, heat oil over medium-high heat; add the chicken and brown on all sides. Transfer pan to oven; roast until a thermometer inserted in chicken reads 170°, 13-15 minutes.
4. Remove the chicken from pan; keep warm. On the stovetop, add broth and butter to the skillet; bring to a boil, stirring to loosen browned bits from pan. Cook until slightly thickened, 3-5 minutes. Serve with chicken.
Note: This recipe was tested with McCormick's Montreal Chicken Seasoning.

VEGGIE SALMON CHOWDER

I wanted to use up odds and ends in my fridge (waste not, want not!) and came up with this chowder. I thought others might enjoy a recipe that began as an experiment but has become a mainstay for me.
—**Liv Vors** Peterborough, ON

Start to Finish: 30 min.
Makes: 2 servings

- 1 medium sweet potato, peeled and cut into ½-inch cubes
- 1 cup reduced-sodium chicken broth
- ½ cup fresh or frozen corn
- ½ small onion, chopped
- 2 garlic cloves, minced
- 1½ cups fresh spinach, torn
- ½ cup flaked smoked salmon fillet
- 1 teaspoon pickled jalapeno slices, chopped
- 1 tablespoon cornstarch
- ½ cup 2% milk
- 1 tablespoon minced fresh cilantro
  Dash pepper

1. In a large saucepan, combine the first five ingredients; bring to a boil. Reduce heat; simmer, covered, 8-10 minutes or until potato is tender.
2. Stir in spinach, salmon and jalapeno; cook 1-2 minutes or until the spinach is wilted. In a small bowl, mix cornstarch and milk until smooth; stir into the soup. Bring to a boil; cook and stir 2 minutes or until thickened. Stir in the cilantro and pepper.

BEEF BURGUNDY OVER NOODLES

I got this delightful recipe from my sister-in-law many years ago. Whenever I serve it to guests, they always request the recipe. The tender beef, mushrooms and flavorful sauce are delicious over noodles.
—**Margaret Welder** Madrid, IA

Prep: 10 min. • **Cook:** 1 hour 20 min.
Makes: 2 servings

- 2 teaspoons butter
- ½ pound beef top sirloin steak, cut into ¼-inch-thick strips
- 2 tablespoons diced onion
- 1½ cups quartered fresh mushrooms
- ¾ cup Burgundy wine or beef broth
- ¼ cup plus 2 tablespoons water, divided
- 3 tablespoons minced fresh parsley, divided
- 1 bay leaf
- 1 whole clove
- ¼ teaspoon salt
- ⅛ teaspoon pepper
- 2 cups uncooked medium egg noodles (about 4 ounces)
- 1 tablespoon all-purpose flour
- ½ teaspoon browning sauce, optional

1. In a Dutch oven or large nonstick skillet, heat butter over medium-high heat; saute beef and onion just until the beef is lightly browned, 1-2 minutes. Stir in mushrooms, wine, ¼ cup water, 2 tablespoons parsley and seasonings; bring to a boil. Reduce heat; simmer, covered, until beef is tender, about 1 hour.
2. Meanwhile, cook the egg noodles according to package directions. Drain.
3. In a small bowl, mix flour and the remaining water until smooth; stir into the beef mixture. Bring to a boil; cook and stir until thickened, about 2 minutes. Discard bay leaf and clove. If desired, stir in browning sauce. Serve over noodles. Sprinkle with remaining parsley.

CHICKEN AND DUMPLINGS

This is my most treasured, comforting main-dish classic. The recipe's a real keeper, so we pared it down to make it perfect for a pair. Enjoy!
—Willa Govoro Nevada, MO

Prep: 35 min. • **Cook:** 40 min.
Makes: 2 servings

- 2 bone-in chicken breast halves (8 ounces each)
- ⅓ cup all-purpose flour
- 2 teaspoons canola oil
- 1 celery rib, cut into 1-inch pieces
- 1 medium carrot, cut into 1-inch pieces
- 1 tablespoon minced fresh parsley or 1 teaspoon dried parsley flakes
- ¼ teaspoon salt
- ¼ teaspoon garlic powder
- ¼ teaspoon dried thyme
- ⅛ teaspoon pepper
- 6 to 8 cups water

DUMPLINGS
- ½ cup all-purpose flour
- ½ teaspoon baking powder
- ¼ teaspoon salt
- 2 tablespoons beaten egg

GRAVY
- 4½ teaspoons all-purpose flour
- ¼ teaspoon salt
- 3 tablespoons water

1. Coat chicken with flour. In a large saucepan, brown chicken in oil. Add the celery, carrot, parsley, salt, garlic powder, thyme and pepper. Add enough water to cover. Bring to a boil. Reduce heat; cover and simmer for 25-30 minutes or until chicken is tender. Remove chicken and vegetables to a serving dish; keep warm.

2. Set aside ¼ cup broth; cool. Bring remaining broth to a simmer. For the dumplings, combine the flour, baking powder and salt; stir in egg and reserved broth just until moistened. Drop batter in four mounds onto simmering broth. Cover and simmer for 5-7 minutes or until a toothpick inserted in a dumpling comes out clean (do not lift cover while simmering). Remove dumplings and keep warm.

3. For gravy, transfer 1⅓ cups broth to a small saucepan (save the remaining broth for another use). Bring to a boil. Combine the flour, salt and water until smooth; stir into broth. Bring to a boil; cook and stir for 2 minutes or until thickened. Pour over chicken, vegetables and dumplings. Serve immediately.

Breakfast for Two

A tasty, filling hot breakfast is more than an indulgence—it gives you energy to keep you going throughout the day. But when it's just for two, a delicious homemade breakfast feels like a special occasion!

PUMPKIN CREAM OF WHEAT

This autumn-inspired breakfast tastes like pumpkin pie...without the guilt! Just double the recipe if you feel like sharing.
—**Amy Bashtovoi** Sidney, NE

Start to Finish: 10 min.
Makes: 1 serving

- ½ cup 2% milk
- ¼ cup half-and-half cream
- 3 tablespoons cream of wheat
- ¼ cup canned pumpkin
- 2 teaspoons sugar
- ⅛ teaspoon ground cinnamon
  Additional 2% milk

In a small microwave-safe bowl, combine the milk, cream and cream of wheat. Microwave, uncovered, on high for 1 minute; stir until blended. Cover and cook for 1-2 minutes or until thickened, stirring every 30 seconds. Stir in the pumpkin, sugar and cinnamon. Serve with additional milk.

VEGGIE OMELET WITH GOAT CHEESE

We eat a lot of vegetables, so I usually just set aside some of whatever veggies I'm serving for dinner for the next morning's omelet. This cuts preparation time in half! This recipe can be made with any variety of veggies and cheeses.
—**Lynne Keast** Monte Sereno, CA

Start to Finish: 30 min.
Makes: 2 servings

- 4 large eggs
- ¼ cup whole milk
- ¼ teaspoon salt
- ⅛ teaspoon pepper
- 4 teaspoons olive oil, divided
- 1 cup thinly sliced zucchini
- 4 small fresh mushrooms, chopped
- ¼ cup finely chopped green pepper
- 1 cup fresh baby spinach
- 2 green onions, thinly sliced
- 2 garlic cloves, thinly sliced
- ¼ cup crumbled goat cheese
  Additional thinly sliced green onions

1. In a small bowl, whisk eggs, milk, salt and pepper. In a large nonstick skillet, heat 2 teaspoons oil over medium-high heat. Add zucchini, mushrooms and green pepper; cook and stir 3-5 minutes or until tender.

2. Add spinach, green onions and garlic; cook and stir 1-2 minutes longer or until the spinach is wilted and garlic is tender. Transfer vegetable mixture to a small bowl. In same pan, heat the remaining oil. Pour in egg mixture. Mixture should set immediately at edge.

3. As eggs set, push cooked portions toward the center, letting uncooked eggs flow underneath. When the eggs are thickened and no liquid egg remains, spoon vegetable mixture on one side; sprinkle with cheese. Fold omelet in half; cut in half and slide onto plates. Sprinkle with additional green onions.

FLUFFY PUMPKIN PANCAKES

My daughters love these tender, fluffy pancakes served with butter, syrup and whipped cream. We freeze the extras—for popping in the toaster.

—**Mindy Bauknecht** Two Rivers, WI

Prep: 15 min. • **Cook:** 10 min./batch
Makes: 6 pancakes

- ⅓ cup all-purpose flour
- ⅓ cup whole wheat flour
- 2 tablespoons sugar
- ½ teaspoon baking powder
- ½ teaspoon baking soda
- ¼ teaspoon pumpkin pie spice
- ⅛ teaspoon ground cinnamon
  Dash salt

- 1 large egg
- ½ cup fat-free milk
- ⅓ cup vanilla yogurt
- ⅓ cup canned pumpkin
- 1 tablespoon canola oil
- ⅛ teaspoon vanilla extract
  Maple syrup

1. In a bowl, whisk together first eight ingredients. In another bowl, whisk the next six ingredients until blended. Add to dry ingredients; stir just until moistened.

2. Lightly coat a griddle with cooking spray; preheat over medium heat. Pour batter by ⅓ cupfuls onto the griddle. Cook until bubbles on top begin to pop. Turn; cook until golden brown. Serve with syrup.

PESTO EGG WRAPS

I wanted to create an easy recipe that would use up some leftover pesto. I put a few ingredients together, and came up with a quick breakfast that really satisfies.

—**Lisa Waterman** Lewistown, MT

Start to Finish: 15 min.
Makes: 2 servings

- ¼ cup oil-packed sun-dried tomatoes, chopped
- 4 large eggs, lightly beaten
- 2 tablespoons crumbled feta cheese
- 2 tablespoons prepared pesto
- 2 whole wheat tortillas (8 inches), warmed

1. Heat a large skillet over medium heat. Add tomatoes; cook and stir until heated through. Pour in eggs; cook and stir until the eggs are thickened and no liquid egg remains. Remove from heat; sprinkle with cheese.

2. Spread 1 tablespoon pesto across center of each tortilla; top with the egg mixture. Fold bottom and sides of the tortilla over the filling and roll up.

WHITE CHILI

This chili for two goes over well at my house. Since I'm also frequently asked to bring it to gatherings, I just double or triple the recipe to make it work.
—Carol Swainston Sheridan, MI

Start to Finish: 25 min.
Makes: 2 servings

- 2 green onions, chopped
- 1 to 2 tablespoons chopped seeded jalapeno pepper
- 2 garlic cloves, minced
- 1½ teaspoons plus 1 tablespoon butter, divided
- ¼ teaspoon rubbed sage
- ¼ teaspoon ground cumin
- ⅛ teaspoon ground ginger
- ½ pound boneless skinless chicken breast, cut into 1-inch cubes
- 1 tablespoon all-purpose flour
- 1¼ cups chicken broth
- 2 tablespoons milk
- 1 can (15½ ounces) great northern beans, rinsed and drained
   Shredded cheddar cheese

1. In a skillet, saute the onions, jalapeno and garlic in 1½ teaspoons butter until crisp-tender. Add the sage, cumin and ginger; cook for 1 minute. Add chicken; cook and stir until lightly browned.
2. In a small saucepan, melt remaining butter. Stir in flour until smooth; gradually add broth and milk. Bring to a boil; cook and stir 2 minutes or until thickened. Add beans. Pour over the chicken mixture. Cook over medium heat until heated through. Sprinkle cheese on each serving.
Note: Wear disposable gloves when cutting hot peppers; the oils can burn exposed skin. Avoid touching your face.

CHICKEN REUBEN ROLL-UPS

My Nebraska-native husband loves Reuben sandwiches and anything chicken, so I combined his two favorites in a fun roll-up.
—Ashli Kottwitz Hermitage, TN

Start to Finish: 30 minutes
Makes: 2 servings

- 2 slices swirled rye and pumpernickel bread
- 2 boneless skinless chicken breast halves (4 ounces each)
- ¼ teaspoon garlic salt
- ¼ teaspoon pepper
- 2 slices Swiss cheese
- 2 slices deli corned beef
- 2 tablespoons Thousand Island salad dressing
   Additional Thousand Island salad dressing, optional

1. Preheat oven to 425°. Tear bread into 2-in. pieces; place in a blender or food processor. Cover and pulse to form coarse bread crumbs; transfer to a shallow bowl.
2. Pound chicken breasts with a meat mallet to ¼-in. thickness; sprinkle with garlic salt and pepper. Top with cheese and corned beef. Roll up chicken from a short side and secure with toothpicks. Brush outsides with dressing; roll in bread crumbs.
3. Place roll-ups on a greased baking sheet, seam side down. Bake for 20-25 minutes or until the chicken is no longer pink. Discard toothpicks; if desired, serve with additional dressing.

LI'L PECAN PIES

I love having all the rich, traditional flavors of a full-size pecan pie in an adorable size that's just perfect for my husband and me.
—**Christine Boitos** Livonia, MI

Prep: 15 min. + chilling
Bake: 35 min. + cooling
Makes: 2 servings

- ½ cup all-purpose flour
- ⅛ teaspoon salt
- 3 tablespoons shortening
- 4 teaspoons cold water

FILLING

- ⅓ cup pecan halves
- 1 large egg
- ⅓ cup packed brown sugar
- ⅓ cup corn syrup
- ½ teaspoon vanilla extract
   Whipped cream, optional

1. In a small bowl, combine flour and salt; cut in shortening until crumbly. Gradually add water, tossing with a fork until dough forms a ball. Cover and refrigerate for at least 30 minutes.
2. Preheat oven to 375°. Remove dough from refrigerator and divide in half. Roll each half into a 6-in. circle. Transfer to two 4½-in. tart pans. Fit pastry into pans; trim if needed. Arrange pecans in shells.
3. In another small bowl, whisk egg, brown sugar, corn syrup and vanilla. Pour over pecans. Place shells on a baking sheet. Bake for 35-40 minutes or until a knife inserted in the center comes out clean. Cool on a wire rack. If desired, top with whipped cream.

PERSONAL POT ROASTS

Do you want a pot roast that has big old-fashioned flavor but doesn't serve eight? Then try this one that I enjoy making for my husband, Art, and myself.
—**Marian Platt** Sequim, WA

Prep: 10 min. • **Bake:** 2 hours
Makes: 2 servings

- 2 beef shanks (about 1½ pounds)
- 3 tablespoons all-purpose flour, divided
- 1½ cups cold water, divided
- ½ cup beef broth
- 1 tablespoon onion soup mix
- 1 garlic clove, minced
- 1 teaspoon Worcestershire sauce
- ¼ teaspoon dried thyme
- 1 large potato, peeled and cut into eighths
- 2 medium carrots, cut into 2-inch pieces
- 6 pearl onions
   Salt and pepper to taste

1. Preheat oven to 325°. Sprinkle meat with 1 tablespoon flour; place in a shallow 2-qt. baking dish. Mix 1 cup water, broth, soup mix, garlic, Worcestershire sauce and thyme; pour over meat. Cover and bake for 1½ hours.
2. Turn meat; add the potato, carrots and onions. Cover; return to oven for 30-45 minutes or until the meat and vegetables are tender. Remove meat and vegetables and keep warm.
3. To prepare gravy, skim fat from pan juices. Measure 1 cup of the juices and place in a small saucepan. Combine remaining flour and cold water; stir into juices. Bring to a boil; cook and stir for 2 minutes or until thickened. Season with salt and pepper. Serve with meat and vegetables.

GOLDEN CHICKEN CORDON BLEU

For an entree that's as elegant as it is easy, try this tender chicken classic. It's a simple recipe that's also really special.
—***Taste of Home*** Test Kitchen

Prep: 20 min. • **Bake:** 20 min.
Makes: 2 servings

- 2 boneless skinless chicken breast halves (6 ounces each)
- 2 slices deli ham (¾ ounce each)
- 2 slices Swiss cheese (¾ ounce each)
- ½ cup all-purpose flour
- ¼ teaspoon salt
- ⅛ teaspoon paprika
- ⅛ teaspoon pepper
- 1 large egg
- 2 tablespoons 2% milk
- ½ cup seasoned bread crumbs
- 1 tablespoon canola oil
- 1 tablespoon butter, melted

1. Preheat oven to 350°. Flatten chicken to ¼-in. thickness; top each with a slice of ham and cheese. Roll up and tuck in ends; secure with toothpicks.
2. In a shallow bowl, combine the flour, salt, paprika and pepper. In another bowl, whisk egg and milk. Place bread crumbs in a third bowl. Dip chicken in flour mixture, then egg mixture; roll in crumbs.
3. In a small skillet, brown chicken in oil on all sides. Transfer to an 8-in. square baking dish coated with cooking spray.
4. Bake, uncovered, for 20-25 minutes or until a thermometer reads 170°. Discard toothpicks; drizzle with butter.

POACHED PEARS WITH ORANGE CREAM

End the meal with a flourish with this easy and elegant dessert. A hint of orange lends just enough sweetness to temper the wine's bold taste. This recipe can easily be doubled, tripled or even quadrupled to serve a dinner party.
—**Julianne Schnuck** Milwaukee, WI

Prep: 10 min. • **Cook:** 45 min. + cooling
Makes: 2 servings

- 2 firm medium pears
- 1½ cups water
- 1 cup dry red wine or red grape juice
- ½ cup sugar
- 2 teaspoons vanilla extract
- ¼ cup reduced-fat sour cream
- 2 teaspoons confectioners' sugar
- ½ teaspoon grated orange zest
- ⅛ teaspoon orange extract
  Additional grated orange zest, optional

1. Core pears from bottom, leaving stems intact. Peel pears; cut ¼ in. from bottom to level if necessary. Place pears on their sides in a large saucepan. Add water, wine, sugar and vanilla. Bring to a boil. Reduce heat; simmer, covered, turning once, until pears are almost tender, 35-40 minutes. (For more intense flavor and color, leave fruit in cooking liquid and refrigerate overnight.)
2. Meanwhile, combine sour cream, confectioners' sugar, orange zest and extract. Refrigerate until serving.
3. Remove the pears with a slotted spoon; pat dry and, if warm, cool to room temperature. Discard cooking liquid. Place pears on dessert plates. Serve with orange cream; if desired, top with additional grated orange zest.

Choose Your Wine

Red wine in the poaching liquid produces an intensely flavored pear with a rosy red color; you can also use a fruity white wine for a natural look. Sparkling wine or champagne will make a lightly flavored pear.

SKILLET STEAK SUPPER

With all the ingredients cooked in one skillet, this steak dish couldn't be quicker to prepare, or easier to clean up after! The wine and mushroom sauce makes it extra special.
—**Sandra Fisher** Missoula, MT

Start to Finish: 20 min.
Makes: 2 servings

- 1 beef top sirloin steak (¾ pound)
- ½ teaspoon salt, divided
- ½ teaspoon pepper, divided
- 1 tablespoon olive oil
- 1 to 2 tablespoons butter
- ½ pound sliced fresh mushrooms
- 2 tablespoons white wine or chicken broth
- 3 tablespoons chopped green onions
- 1 tablespoon Worcestershire sauce
- 1 teaspoon Dijon mustard

1. Sprinkle steak with ¼ teaspoon each salt and pepper. In a skillet, heat oil over medium-high heat; cook the steak to desired doneness (for medium-rare, a thermometer should read 145°; medium, 160°), 6-7 minutes per side. Remove from pan; keep warm.

2. In same skillet, heat butter over medium-high heat; saute mushrooms until tender. Stir in wine; bring to a boil, stirring to loosen browned bits from pan. Stir in green onions, Worcestershire sauce, mustard and the remaining salt and pepper. Cut steak in half; serve with mushroom mixture.

BART'S BLACK BEAN SOUP FOR 2

Every cook can appreciate a fresh, simple soup that's ready in minutes. Add a salad and dinner rolls or quesadillas for a complete meal that hits the spot.
—**Sharon Ullyot** London, ON

Start to Finish: 10 min.
Makes: 2 servings

- ¾ cup canned black beans, rinsed and drained
- ¾ cup chicken broth
- ⅓ cup salsa
- ¼ cup whole kernel corn
  Dash hot pepper sauce
- 1 teaspoon lime juice
- ½ cup shredded cheddar cheese
- 1 tablespoon chopped green onion

In a microwave-safe bowl, combine the first five ingredients. Cover and microwave on high for 2 minutes or until heated through. Pour into two serving bowls; drizzle each serving with lime juice and sprinkle with the cheese and green onions.

Slow Cooker

If there's one appliance today's family cooks can't do without, it's the slow cooker. After all, who can resist a hot and hearty meal simmered to perfection after a long day? Turn the page and you'll find the best in slow-cooked comfort as well as new ways to simmer a winner. Let's get (slow) cooking!

CHUNKY CREAMY CHICKEN SOUP

I am a stay-at-home mom who relies on my slow cooker for easy, nutritious meals with minimal prep time and cleanup. I knew this recipe was a hit when I didn't have any leftovers and my husband asked me to make it again.

—**Nancy Clow** Mallorytown, ON

Prep: 15 min. • **Cook:** 4½ hours
Makes: 7 servings

- 1½ pounds boneless skinless chicken breasts, cut into 2-inch strips
- 2 teaspoons canola oil
- ⅔ cup finely chopped onion
- 2 medium carrots, chopped
- 2 celery ribs, chopped
- 1 cup frozen corn
- 2 cans (10¾ ounces each) condensed cream of potato soup, undiluted
- 1½ cups chicken broth
- 1 teaspoon dill weed
- 1 cup frozen peas
- ½ cup half-and-half cream

1. In a large skillet over medium-high heat, brown chicken in oil. Transfer to a 5-qt. slow cooker; add the onion, carrots, celery and corn.
2. In a large bowl, whisk the soup, broth and dill until blended; stir into the slow cooker. Cover and cook on low for 4 hours or until chicken and vegetables are tender.
3. Stir in peas and cream. Cover and cook 30 minutes longer or until soup is heated through.

CUBANO PORK SANDWICHES

When a hungry crowd's coming over, we plan a day ahead to make our juicy pork sandwiches. The sauce is loaded with zingy flavors.

—**Theresa Yardas** Sheridan, IN

Prep: 1¾ hours + marinating • **Cook:** 8 hours
Makes: 24 servings

- ⅓ cup ground cumin
- ¼ cup sugar
- 2 tablespoons onion powder
- 1 tablespoon kosher salt
- ½ teaspoon pepper
- 1 boneless pork shoulder roast (6 to 7 pounds)
- 2 teaspoons olive oil
- 1 large onion, quartered
- 1 cup dry red wine or beef broth
- ⅔ cup lime juice
- ⅓ cup lemon juice
- ⅓ cup orange juice
- 1 bay leaf
- 1 teaspoon dried cilantro flakes
- 1 teaspoon dried oregano
- 1 teaspoon dried thyme
- 1 teaspoon ground allspice
- 4 teaspoons olive oil

SANDWICHES
- 2 loaves unsliced French bread (1 pound each)
- ¼ cup sweet pickle relish
- ¼ cup Dijon mustard
- 8 slices Swiss cheese

1. In a small bowl, mix the first five ingredients. Cut roast into thirds; rub with oil. Rub spice mixture over meat; wrap in plastic. Refrigerate, covered, 24 hours.
2. In a large saucepan, combine onion, wine, juices, bay leaf and seasonings. Bring to a boil. Reduce heat; simmer, covered, 45 minutes. Strain the sauce, discarding onion and seasonings.
3. In a large skillet, heat oil over medium heat; brown roast on all sides. Transfer roast to a 6-qt. slow cooker. Pour sauce over meat. Cook, covered, on low for 8-10 hours or until the meat is tender. Remove roast; cool slightly. Skim fat from the cooking juices. Shred pork with two forks. Return pork to the slow cooker; heat through.
4. Preheat oven to 325°. Split bread horizontally. Hollow out bottoms of loaves, leaving ¾-in. shells. Spread relish and mustard inside shells. Layer with meat and cheese. Replace tops.
5. Wrap sandwiches tightly in heavy-duty foil. Place on baking sheets. Bake for 20-25 minutes or until heated through. Cut each crosswise into 12 slices.

PROVENCAL HAM & BEAN SOUP

There is nothing quite like the wonderful feeling of opening the door to smell this delicious stew bubbling away in the slow cooker. To make preparation even easier, I like to start it the night before, and then all I have to do is turn on the slow cooker in the morning.

—Lyndsay Wells Ladysmith, BC

Prep: 15 min. + soaking • **Cook:** 7 hours
Makes: 10 servings (3½ quarts)

- 2 cups assorted dried beans for soup
- 1 can (28 ounces) whole plum tomatoes, undrained
- 2 cups cubed fully cooked ham
- 1 large Yukon Gold potato, peeled and chopped
- 1 medium onion, chopped
- 1 cup chopped carrot
- 1 celery rib, chopped
- 2 garlic cloves, minced
- 2 teaspoons herbes de Provence
- 1½ teaspoons salt
- 1 teaspoon pepper
- 1 carton (32 ounces) unsalted chicken stock
  French bread

1. Rinse and sort beans; soak according to package directions. Drain and rinse beans, discarding liquid.
2. Transfer the beans to a 6-qt. slow cooker. Add the tomatoes; crush with a wooden spoon until chunky. Stir in the ham, vegetables, garlic, seasonings and stock. Cook, covered, on low for 7-9 hours or until the beans are tender. Serve with bread.

PUMPKIN PIE PUDDING

My husband loves anything pumpkin, and this creamy, comforting dessert is one of his favorites. We make this super-easy pudding year-round, but it's especially nice in fall.

—Andrea Schaak Bloomington, MN

Prep: 10 min. • **Cook:** 6 hours
Makes: 6 servings

- 1 can (15 ounces) solid-pack pumpkin
- 1 can (12 ounces) evaporated milk
- ¾ cup sugar
- ½ cup biscuit/baking mix
- 2 large eggs, beaten
- 2 tablespoons butter, melted
- 2½ teaspoons pumpkin pie spice
- 2 teaspoons vanilla extract
  Sweetened whipped cream or vanilla ice cream, optional

1. Combine the first eight ingredients. Transfer to a greased 3-qt. slow cooker.
2. Cook, covered, on low until a thermometer reads 160°, 6-7 hours. If desired, serve with whipped cream.

CHEESY CAULIFLOWER SOUP

When a chill is in the air, I like to make soups for the family. Cheese adds flavor and heartiness to this one, which is my own recipe.
—**Ruth Worden** Massena, NY

Prep: 30 min. • **Cook:** 3¾ hours
Makes: 8 servings (2 quarts)

- 1 large head cauliflower, broken into florets
- 2 cups chicken broth
- 2 tablespoons reduced-sodium chicken bouillon granules
- 2 cups half-and-half cream
- 2 cups 2% milk
- 1 medium carrot, shredded
- 2 bay leaves
- ¼ teaspoon garlic powder
- ½ cup mashed potato flakes
- 2 cups shredded cheddar cheese
  Paprika

1. In a large saucepan, combine the cauliflower, broth and bouillon. Bring to a boil. Reduce heat; cover and cook for 20 minutes or until tender. Mash florets.
2. Transfer to a 3-qt. slow cooker. Stir in the cream, milk, carrot, bay leaves and garlic powder. Cover and cook on low for 3 hours. Stir in potato flakes.
3. Cook 30 minutes longer or until soup is thickened. Discard the bay leaves. Cool slightly.
4. In a blender, process the soup in batches until smooth. Return to slow cooker; stir in cheese. Cook until soup is heated through and cheese is melted. Garnish with paprika.

CHIPOTLE SHREDDED SWEET POTATOES WITH BACON

The smoky heat of chipotle peppers blends perfectly with these creamy, cheesy sweet potatoes.
—**Kathi Jones-DelMonte** Rochester, NY

Prep: 30 min. • **Cook:** 4 hours
Makes: 10 servings

- 2 tablespoons olive oil
- 1 large sweet onion, finely chopped
- 2 shallots, finely chopped
- ¼ cup minced fresh parsley
- 2 teaspoons ground chipotle pepper
- 1 teaspoon coarsely ground pepper
- ½ teaspoon kosher salt
- 3 pounds large sweet potatoes (about 4 large), peeled and shredded
- 1 package (8 ounces) cream cheese, softened
- 2 cups shredded Manchego or Monterey Jack cheese
- 2 cups shredded Muenster cheese
- 1 package (16 ounces) applewood smoked bacon, cooked and chopped
- ½ teaspoon paprika

TOPPING
- 1 cup sour cream
- 2 tablespoons maple syrup
- ¼ teaspoon ground chipotle pepper

1. In a large skillet, heat oil over medium heat. Add onion and shallots; cook and stir 4-6 minutes or until softened.
2. Transfer onion mixture to a large bowl; stir in parsley and seasonings. Add sweet potatoes and cheeses, mixing well. Fold in chopped bacon.
3. Transfer mixture to a greased 5- or 6-qt. slow cooker. Sprinkle with paprika. Cook, covered, on low 4-5 hours or until potatoes are tender.
4. In a small bowl, mix the topping ingredients. Serve with sweet potatoes.

CITRUS TURKEY ROAST

I was skeptical at first about making roast turkey in the slow cooker. But once I tasted this dish, I was hooked.
—**Kathy Kittell** Lenexa, KS

Prep: 15 min. • **Cook:** 5¼ hours
Makes: 12 servings

- 1 frozen boneless turkey roast, thawed (3 pounds)
- 1 tablespoon garlic powder
- 1 tablespoon paprika
- 1 tablespoon olive oil
- 2 teaspoons Worcestershire sauce
- ½ teaspoon salt
- ½ teaspoon pepper
- 8 garlic cloves, peeled
- 1 cup chicken broth, divided
- ¼ cup water
- ¼ cup white wine or additional chicken broth
- ¼ cup orange juice
- 1 tablespoon lemon juice
- 2 tablespoons cornstarch

1. Cut roast in half. Combine the garlic powder, paprika, oil, Worcestershire sauce, salt and pepper; rub over turkey. Place in a 5-qt. slow cooker. Add the garlic, ½ cup broth, water, wine, orange juice and lemon juice. Cover and cook on low for 5-6 hours or until a thermometer reads 175°.
2. Remove the turkey and keep warm. Discard garlic cloves. For gravy, combine cornstarch and remaining broth until smooth; stir into cooking juices. Cover and cook on high for 15 minutes or until thickened. Slice turkey; serve with gravy.

CHICKEN CASSOULET SOUP

After my sister spent a year in France as an au pair, I created this lighter, easier version of French cassoulet for her. It uses chicken instead of the traditional duck.
—**Bridget Klusman** Otsego, MI

Prep: 35 min. • **Cook:** 6 hours
Makes: 7 servings (2¾ quarts)

- ½ pound bulk pork sausage
- 5 cups water
- ½ pound cubed cooked chicken
- 1 can (16 ounces) kidney beans, rinsed and drained
- 1 can (15 ounces) black beans, rinsed and drained
- 1 can (15 ounces) garbanzo beans or chickpeas, rinsed and drained
- 2 medium carrots, shredded
- 1 medium onion, chopped
- ¼ cup dry vermouth or chicken broth
- 5 teaspoons chicken bouillon granules
- 4 garlic cloves, minced
- ½ teaspoon dried thyme
- ¼ teaspoon fennel seed, crushed
- 1 teaspoon dried lavender flowers, optional
- ½ pound bacon strips, cooked and crumbled

1. In a large skillet, cook sausage over medium heat until no longer pink; drain.
2. Transfer to a 4- or 5-qt. slow cooker. Add the water, chicken, beans, carrots, onion, vermouth, bouillon, garlic, thyme, fennel and, if desired, lavender. Cover and cook on low for 6-8 hours or until heated through.
3. Divide soup among bowls; sprinkle each serving with bacon.
Note: Look for dried culinary lavender in spice shops. If using lavender from the garden, make sure it hasn't been treated with chemicals.

VERY VANILLA SLOW COOKER CHEESECAKE

Cinnamon and vanilla give this cheesecake so much flavor, and making it in the slow cooker creates a silky, smooth texture.
—**Krista Lanphier** Milwaukee, WI

Prep: 40 min. • **Cook:** 2 hours + chilling
Makes: 6 servings

- ¾ cup graham cracker crumbs
- 1 tablespoon sugar plus ⅔ cup sugar, divided
- ¼ teaspoon ground cinnamon
- 2½ tablespoons butter, melted
- 2 packages (8 ounces each) cream cheese, softened
- ½ cup sour cream
- 2 to 3 teaspoons vanilla extract
- 2 large eggs, lightly beaten

TOPPING

- 2 ounces semisweet chocolate, chopped
- 1 teaspoon shortening
  Miniature peanut butter cups or toasted sliced almonds

1. Grease a 6-in. springform pan; place on a double thickness of heavy-duty foil (about 12 in. square). Wrap foil securely around pan.

2. Pour 1 in. water into a 6-qt. slow cooker. Layer two 24-in. pieces of foil. Starting with a long side, roll up foil to make a 1-in.-wide strip; shape into a circle. Place in bottom of slow cooker to make a rack.

3. In a small bowl, mix cracker crumbs, 1 tablespoon sugar and cinnamon; stir in butter. Press onto bottom and about 1 in. up sides of prepared pan.

4. In a large bowl, beat cream cheese and remaining sugar until smooth. Beat in sour cream and vanilla. Add eggs; beat on low speed just until combined. Pour into crust.

5. Place springform pan on foil circle without touching slow cooker sides. Cover slow cooker with a double layer of white paper towels; place lid securely over towels. Cook, covered, on high for 2 hours.

6. Without removing the lid, turn off slow cooker and let cheesecake stand, covered, in slow cooker 1 hour.

7. Remove springform pan from the slow cooker; remove foil around the pan. Cool cheesecake on a wire rack 1 hour longer. Loosen sides from pan with a knife. Refrigerate overnight, covering when completely cooled.

8. For topping, in a microwave, melt chocolate and shortening; stir until smooth. Cool slightly. Remove rim from the springform pan. Pour chocolate mixture over cheesecake; sprinkle with miniature peanut butter cups or almonds. **Note:** Cheesecake may be stored in the refrigerator 4-6 days before serving. Wrap securely before chilling; top just before serving.

BEEF BRISKET IN BEER

One bite of this super-tender brisket, and your family will be hooked! The rich gravy is perfect for spooning over creamy mashed potatoes.

—**Eunice Stoen** Decorah, IA

Prep: 15 min. • **Cook:** 8 hours
Makes: 6 servings

- 1 fresh beef brisket (2½ to 3 pounds)
- 2 teaspoons liquid smoke, optional
- 1 teaspoon celery salt
- ½ teaspoon pepper
- ¼ teaspoon salt
- 1 large onion, sliced
- 1 can (12 ounces) beer or nonalcoholic beer
- 2 teaspoons Worcestershire sauce
- 2 tablespoons cornstarch
- ¼ cup cold water

1. Cut brisket in half; rub with liquid smoke, if desired, and celery salt, pepper and salt. Place in a 3-qt. slow cooker. Top with onion. Combine beer and Worcestershire sauce; pour over meat. Cover and cook on low for 8-9 hours or until tender.

2. Remove brisket and keep warm. Strain the cooking juices; transfer to a small saucepan. In a small bowl, combine cornstarch and water until smooth; stir into juices. Bring to a boil; cook and stir for 2 minutes or until thickened. Serve beef with gravy.

Note: This is a fresh beef brisket, not corned beef.

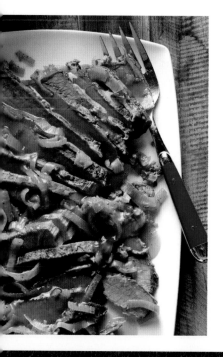

MEATY SLOW-COOKED JAMBALAYA

This recipe makes a big batch of delicious, meaty gumbo. The slow cooker gives the spices time to create a richly flavored Cajun dish.

—**Diane Smith** Pine Mountain, GA

Prep: 25 min. • **Cook:** 7¼ hours
Makes: 12 servings (3½ quarts)

- 1 can (28 ounces) diced tomatoes, undrained
- 1 cup reduced-sodium chicken broth
- 1 large green pepper, chopped
- 1 medium onion, chopped
- 2 celery ribs, sliced
- ½ cup white wine or additional reduced-sodium chicken broth
- 4 garlic cloves, minced
- 2 teaspoons Cajun seasoning
- 2 teaspoons dried parsley flakes
- 1 teaspoon dried basil
- 1 teaspoon dried oregano
- ¾ teaspoon salt
- ½ to 1 teaspoon cayenne pepper
- 2 pounds boneless skinless chicken thighs, cut into 1-inch pieces
- 1 package (12 ounces) fully cooked andouille or other spicy chicken sausage links
- 2 pounds uncooked medium shrimp, peeled and deveined
- 8 cups hot cooked brown rice

1. In a large bowl, combine the first 13 ingredients. Place chicken and sausage in a 6-qt. slow cooker. Pour tomato mixture over top. Cook, covered, on low for 7-9 hours or until chicken is tender.

2. Stir in shrimp. Cook, covered, for 15-20 minutes longer or until the shrimp turn pink. Serve with rice.

SLOW COOKER BEEF STEW

When there's a chill in the air, I love to make my slow-cooked stew. It's full of tender chunks of beef, potatoes and carrots.
—**Earnestine Wilson** Waco, TX

Prep: 25 min. • **Cook:** 8.5 hours
Makes: 8 servings

- 1½ pounds potatoes, peeled and cubed
- 6 medium carrots, cut into 1-inch slices
- 1 medium onion, coarsely chopped
- 3 celery ribs, coarsely chopped
- 3 tablespoons all-purpose flour
- 1½ pounds beef stew meat, cut into 1-inch cubes
- 3 tablespoons canola oil
- 1 can (14½ ounces) diced tomatoes, undrained
- ½ to 1 cup beef broth
- 1 teaspoon ground mustard
- ½ teaspoon salt
- ½ teaspoon pepper
- ½ teaspoon dried thyme
- ½ teaspoon browning sauce

1. Layer the potatoes, carrots, onion and celery in a 5-qt. slow cooker. Place flour in a large resealable plastic bag. Add stew meat; seal and toss to coat evenly. In a large skillet, brown the meat in oil in batches. Place over vegetables.
2. In a large bowl, combine tomatoes, broth, mustard, salt, pepper, thyme and the browning sauce. Pour over the beef. Cover and cook on high for 1½ hours. Reduce heat to low; cook 7-8 hours longer or until the meat and vegetables are tender.

SAVORY SAUSAGE STUFFING

I used to make the same old stuffing every year for Thanksgiving. About 10 years ago, I decided to jazz up my recipe by adding pork sausage. Now folks ask for this for every holiday meal.
—**Ursula Hernandez** Waltham, MN

Prep: 30 min. • **Cook:** 2 hours
Makes: 16 servings

- 1 pound sage pork sausage
- ½ cup butter, cubed
- ½ pound fresh mushrooms, finely chopped
- 6 celery ribs, finely chopped
- 2 small onions, finely chopped
- 2 garlic cloves, minced
- 1 loaf (13 ounces) French bread, cut into ½-inch cubes (about 17 cups)
- 4 cups cubed multigrain bread (½ inch)
- 1 tablespoon rubbed sage
- 1 cup chicken stock
- ½ cup white wine or chicken stock
- 1 cup dried cranberries
- ½ cup sunflower kernels, optional

1. In a large skillet, cook sausage over medium heat 4-6 minutes or until no longer pink, breaking into crumbles; drain. In a stockpot, melt butter over medium heat. Add mushrooms, celery and onions; cook and stir 3-4 minutes or until tender. Add garlic; cook 1 minute longer. Remove from heat.
2. Stir in the sausage. Add bread cubes and sage; toss to combine. Add chicken stock and wine. Stir in cranberries and, if desired, sunflower kernels. Transfer to a greased 6-qt. slow cooker. Cook, covered, on low 2-3 hours or until heated through, stirring once.

FREEZE IT STAMP-OF-APPROVAL SPAGHETTI SAUCE

My father is pretty opinionated, especially about food. This recipe received his nearly unattainable stamp of approval, and I have yet to hear any disagreement from anyone who has tried it!

—**Melissa Taylor** Higley, AZ

....

Prep: 30 min. • **Cook:** 8 hours
Makes: 12 servings (3 quarts)

- 2 **pounds ground beef**
- ¾ **pound bulk Italian sausage**
- 4 **medium onions, finely chopped**
- 8 **garlic cloves, minced**
- 4 **cans (14½ ounces each) diced tomatoes, undrained**
- 4 **cans (6 ounces each) tomato paste**
- ½ **cup water**
- ¼ **cup sugar**
- ¼ **cup Worcestershire sauce**
- 1 **tablespoon canola oil**
- ¼ **cup minced fresh parsley**
- 2 **tablespoons minced fresh basil or 2 teaspoons dried basil**
- 1 **tablespoon minced fresh oregano or 1 teaspoon dried oregano**
- 4 **bay leaves**
- 1 **teaspoon rubbed sage**
- ½ **teaspoon salt**
- ½ **teaspoon dried marjoram**
- ½ **teaspoon pepper**
  Hot cooked spaghetti

1. In a Dutch oven, cook the beef, sausage, onions and garlic over medium heat until meat is no longer pink; drain.

2. Transfer to a 5-qt. slow cooker. Stir in the tomatoes, tomato paste, water, sugar, Worcestershire sauce, oil and seasonings.

3. Cover and cook on low for 8-10 hours. Discard bay leaves. Serve with spaghetti.

Freeze option: Cool completely before placing in a freezer container. Cover and freeze for up to 3 months. To use, thaw in the refrigerator overnight. Place in a large saucepan; heat through, stirring occasionally. Serve with spaghetti.

Slow-Cooked Sandwiches

Slow cooking transforms a roast or a poultry cut into a delectable, ultra-tender mass of shredded or "pulled" meat—genius! These flavorful sandwiches simply can't be beat.

SHREDDED FRENCH DIP

A chuck roast slow-simmered in a beefy broth is delicious when shredded and spooned onto rolls. I serve the cooking juices in individual cups for dipping.
—**Carla Kimball** Callaway, NE

Prep: 5 min. • **Cook:** 6 hours
Makes: 10 servings

- 1 boneless beef chuck roast (3 pounds), trimmed
- 1 can (10½ ounces) condensed French onion soup, undiluted
- 1 can (10½ ounces) condensed beef consomme, undiluted
- 1 can (10½ ounces) condensed beef broth, undiluted
- 1 teaspoon beef bouillon granules
- 8 to 10 French or Italian rolls, split

1. Halve roast and place in a 3-qt. slow cooker. Combine the soup, consomme, broth and bouillon; pour over roast. Cover and cook on low for 6-8 hours or until meat is tender.
2. Remove meat and shred with two forks. Serve on rolls. Skim fat from cooking juices; serve juices on the side for dipping.

FREEZE IT ITALIAN TURKEY SANDWICHES

I hope you enjoy these tasty turkey sandwiches as much as our family does. The recipe makes plenty, so it's great for potlucks. Leftovers are just as good reheated the next day.
—**Carol Riley** Ossian, IN

Prep: 10 min. • **Cook:** 5 hours
Makes: 12 servings

- 1 bone-in turkey breast (6 pounds), skin removed
- 1 medium onion, chopped
- 1 small green pepper, chopped
- ¼ cup chili sauce
- 3 tablespoons white vinegar
- 2 tablespoons dried oregano or Italian seasoning
- 4 teaspoons beef bouillon granules
- 12 kaiser or hard rolls, split

1. Place the turkey breast in a greased 5-qt. slow cooker. Add the onion and green pepper.
2. Combine chili sauce, vinegar, oregano and bouillon; pour over the turkey and vegetables. Cover and cook on low for 5-6 hours or until the turkey is tender.
3. Shred turkey with two forks and return to the slow cooker; heat through. Spoon ½ cup onto each roll.
Freeze option: Place cooled meat and juice mixture in freezer containers. To use, partially thaw in refrigerator overnight. Microwave, covered, on high in a microwave-safe dish until heated through, gently stirring and adding a little water if necessary.

BBQ CHICKEN SLIDERS

Brining the chicken overnight helps it taste exceptionally good, making it so tender it melts in your mouth.
—**Rachel Kunkel** Schell City, MO

Prep: 25 min. + brining • **Cook:** 4 hours
Makes: 8 servings (2 sliders each)

BRINE
- 1½ quarts water
- ¼ cup packed brown sugar
- 2 tablespoons salt
- 1 tablespoon liquid smoke
- 2 garlic cloves, minced
- ½ teaspoon dried thyme

CHICKEN
- 2 pounds boneless skinless chicken breasts
- ⅓ cup liquid smoke
- 1½ cups hickory smoke-flavored barbecue sauce
- 16 slider buns or dinner rolls, split and warmed

1. In a large bowl, mix brine ingredients, stirring to dissolve the brown sugar. Reserve 1 cup of brine for cooking the chicken; cover and refrigerate.
2. Place chicken in a large resealable bag; add remaining brine. Seal bag, pressing out as much air as possible; turn to coat chicken. Place in a large bowl; refrigerate 18-24 hours, turning occasionally.
3. Remove chicken from brine and transfer to a 3-qt. slow cooker; discard brine in bag. Add the reserved brine and ⅓ cup liquid smoke to chicken. Cook, covered, on low 4-5 hours or until the chicken is tender.
4. Remove chicken; cool slightly. Discard cooking juices. Shred chicken with two forks and return meat to slow cooker. Stir in barbecue sauce; heat through. Serve on buns.

TEX-MEX SHREDDED BEEF SANDWICHES

You only need a few ingredients to make my delicious shredded beef. While the meat simmers to tender perfection, you will have time to do other things.
—**Kathy White** Henderson, NV

Prep: 5 min. • **Cook:** 8 hours
Makes: 8 servings

- 1 boneless beef chuck roast (3 pounds)
- 1 envelope chili seasoning
- ½ cup barbecue sauce
- 8 onion rolls, split
- 8 slices cheddar cheese

1. Cut roast in half; place in a 3-qt. slow cooker. Sprinkle with chili seasoning. Pour barbecue sauce over top. Cover and cook on low for 8-10 hours or until the meat is tender.
2. Remove roast; cool slightly. Shred the meat with two forks. Skim fat from the cooking juices. Return meat to the slow cooker; heat through. Using a slotted spoon, place ½ cup of the meat mixture on each roll bottom; top with cheese. Replace tops.

LOADED BAKED POTATO SOUP

The only thing that beats the taste of this comforting potato soup is the fact that it simmers on its own all day.

—**Barbara Bleigh** Colonial Heights, VA

Prep: 35 min. • **Cook:** 6 hours
Makes: 10 servings

- 2 large onions, chopped
- 3 tablespoons butter
- 2 tablespoons all-purpose flour
- 2 cups water, divided
- 4 cups chicken broth
- 2 medium potatoes, peeled and diced
- 1½ cups mashed potato flakes
- ½ pound sliced bacon, cooked and crumbled
- ¾ teaspoon pepper
- ½ teaspoon salt
- ½ teaspoon dried basil
- ⅛ teaspoon dried thyme
- 1 cup half-and-half cream
- ½ cup shredded cheddar cheese
- 2 green onions, sliced

1. In a large skillet, saute onions in butter until tender. Stir in flour. Gradually stir in 1 cup water. Bring to a boil; cook and stir for 2 minutes or until thickened. Transfer to a 5-qt. slow cooker.

2. Add the chicken broth, potatoes, potato flakes, bacon, pepper, salt, basil, thyme and the remaining water. Cover and cook on low for 6-8 hours or until the potatoes are tender. Stir in cream; heat through. Garnish with cheese and green onions.

FREEZE IT BEER-BRAISED PULLED HAM

To jazz up leftover ham, I slow-cooked it with a beer sauce. Buns loaded with ham, pickles and mustard are irresistible.

—**Ann Sheehy** Lawrence, MA

Prep: 10 min. • **Cook:** 7 hours
Makes: 16 servings

- 2 bottles (12 ounces each) beer or nonalcoholic beer
- ¾ cup German or Dijon mustard, divided
- ½ teaspoon coarsely ground pepper
- 1 fully cooked bone-in ham (about 4 pounds)
- 4 fresh rosemary sprigs
- 16 pretzel hamburger buns, split
  Dill pickle slices, optional

1. In a 5-qt. slow cooker, whisk together beer and ½ cup mustard. Stir in pepper. Add ham and rosemary. Cook, covered, on low until tender, 7-9 hours.

2. Remove ham; cool slightly. Discard rosemary sprigs. Skim fat. When ham is cool enough to handle, shred meat with two forks. Discard bone. Return to slow cooker; heat through.

3. Using tongs, place shredded ham on pretzel buns; top with remaining mustard and, if desired, dill pickle slices.

Freeze option: Freeze cooled ham mixture in freezer containers. To use, partially thaw in refrigerator overnight. Heat through in a covered saucepan, stirring gently and adding a little water if necessary.

SLOW-COOKED RANCH POTATOES

Even after seven years, my family still asks for this tasty potato and bacon dish. Try it once and I'll bet your family will be hooked, too.

—Lynn Ireland Lebanon, WI

Prep: 15 min. • **Cook:** 7 hours.
Makes: 10 servings

- 6 bacon strips, chopped
- 2½ pounds small red potatoes, cubed
- 1 package (8 ounces) cream cheese, softened
- 1 can (10¾ ounces) condensed cream of potato soup, undiluted
- ¼ cup 2% milk
- 1 envelope buttermilk ranch salad dressing mix
- 3 tablespoons thinly sliced green onions

1. In a large skillet, cook bacon over medium heat until crisp, stirring occasionally. Remove with a slotted spoon; drain on paper towels. Drain the drippings, reserving 1 tablespoon.
2. Place potatoes in a 3-qt. slow cooker. In a bowl, beat cream cheese, soup, milk, dressing mix and the reserved drippings until blended; stir into potatoes. Sprinkle with the bacon.
3. Cook, covered, on low 7-8 hours or until the potatoes are tender. Top with green onions.

SLOW COOKER SHORT RIBS

These tasty ribs are an easy alternative to traditionally braised short ribs—you don't need to pay any attention to them once you get them started!

—Rebekah Beyer Sabetha, KS

Prep: 30 min. • **Cook:** 6¼ hours
Makes: 6 servings

- 3 pounds bone-in beef short ribs
- ½ teaspoon salt
- ½ teaspoon pepper
- 1 tablespoon canola oil
- 4 medium carrots, cut into 1-inch pieces
- 1 cup beef broth
- 4 fresh thyme sprigs
- 1 bay leaf
- 2 large onions, cut into ½-inch wedges
- 6 garlic cloves, minced
- 1 tablespoon tomato paste
- 2 cups dry red wine or beef broth
- 4 teaspoons cornstarch
- 3 tablespoons cold water
  Salt and pepper to taste

1. Sprinkle ribs with salt and pepper. In a large skillet, heat oil over medium heat. In batches, brown ribs on all sides; transfer to a 4- or 5-qt. slow cooker. Add carrots, broth, thyme and bay leaf to ribs.
2. Add onions to the same skillet; cook and stir over medium heat 8-9 minutes or until tender. Add garlic and tomato paste; cook and stir 1 minute longer. Stir in wine. Bring to a boil; cook 8-10 minutes or until the liquid is reduced by half. Add to slow cooker. Cook, covered, on low 6-8 hours or until meat is tender.
3. Remove ribs and vegetables; keep warm. Transfer the cooking juices to a small saucepan; skim fat. Discard thyme and bay leaf. Bring juices to a boil. In a small bowl, mix cornstarch and water until smooth; stir into cooking juices. Return mixture to a boil; cook and stir for 1-2 minutes or until thickened. Season with salt and pepper to taste. Serve with ribs and vegetables.

SLOW-COOKED CARIBBEAN POT ROAST

This dish is definitely an all-year-round recipe. Sweet potatoes, orange zest and baking cocoa are my surprise ingredients.
—Jenn Tidwell Fair Oaks, CA

....

Prep: 30 min. • **Cook:** 6 hours
Makes: 10 servings

- 2 medium sweet potatoes, cubed
- 2 large carrots, sliced
- ¼ cup chopped celery
- 1 boneless beef chuck roast (2½ pounds)
- 1 tablespoon canola oil

- 1 large onion, chopped
- 2 garlic cloves, minced
- 1 tablespoon all-purpose flour
- 1 tablespoon sugar
- 1 tablespoon brown sugar
- 1 teaspoon ground cumin
- ¾ teaspoon salt
- ¾ teaspoon ground coriander
- ¾ teaspoon chili powder
- ½ teaspoon dried oregano
- ⅛ teaspoon ground cinnamon
- ¾ teaspoon grated orange zest
- ¾ teaspoon baking cocoa
- 1 can (15 ounces) tomato sauce

1. Place potatoes, carrots and celery in a 5-qt. slow cooker. In a large skillet, brown meat in oil on all sides. Transfer meat to the slow cooker.

2. In the same skillet, saute onion in drippings until tender. Add garlic; cook 1 minute longer. Combine flour, sugar, brown sugar, seasonings, orange zest and cocoa. Stir in tomato sauce; add to skillet and heat through. Pour over beef.

3. Cover and cook on low for 6-8 hours or until beef and vegetables are tender.

SLOW COOKER MASHED POTATOES

Sour cream and cream cheese add richness to these tasty make-ahead potatoes. They're wonderful when time is tight because they don't require any last-minute mashing.
—**Trudy Vincent** Valles Mines, MO

Prep: 20 min. • **Cook:** 2 hours
Makes: 8-10 servings

- 3 ounces cream cheese, softened
- ½ cup sour cream
- ¼ cup plus 1 tablespoon softened butter, divided
- 1 envelope ranch salad dressing mix
- 1 tablespoon minced fresh parsley
- 6 cups warm mashed potatoes (without added milk or butter)

In a large bowl, combine the cream cheese, sour cream, ¼ cup butter, salad dressing mix and parsley; stir in potatoes. Transfer to a 3-qt. slow cooker. Cover and cook on low for 2-3 hours. Top with remaining butter.
Note: This recipe was tested with fresh potatoes (not instant).

SLOW COOKER PEACH CRUMBLE

I look forward to going on our beach vacation every year, but I don't always relish the time spent cooking for everybody. This slow cooker dessert (or breakfast!) gives me more time to lie in the sun and enjoy the waves. Melty ice cream is a must.
—**Colleen Delawder** Herndon, VA

Prep: 20 min. • **Cook:** 3 hours
Makes: 8 servings

- 1 tablespoon butter, softened
- 6 large ripe peaches, peeled and sliced (about 6 cups)
- 2 tablespoons light brown sugar
- 1 tablespoon lemon juice
- 1 tablespoon vanilla extract
- 2 tablespoons coconut rum, optional

TOPPING

- 1 cup all-purpose flour
- ¾ cup packed light brown sugar
- 1½ teaspoons baking powder
- 1 teaspoon ground cinnamon
- ½ teaspoon baking soda
- ⅛ teaspoon salt
- 1 cup old-fashioned oats
- 6 tablespoons cold butter, cubed

1. Grease a 6-qt. oval slow cooker with 1 tablespoon softened butter. Toss the peaches with brown sugar, lemon juice, vanilla and, if desired, rum; spread evenly in slow cooker.
2. Whisk together the first six topping ingredients; stir in oats. Cut in butter until crumbly; sprinkle over peaches. Cook, covered, on low until peaches are tender, 3-4 hours.

EASY CORNED BEEF AND CABBAGE

I first tried this fuss-free way to cook traditional corned beef and cabbage for St. Patrick's Day a few years ago. Now it's a regular in my menu planning. It's terrific with Dijon mustard and crusty bread.
—**Karen Waters** Laurel, MD

Prep: 15 min. • **Cook:** 8 hours
Makes: 6-8 servings

- 1 medium onion, cut into wedges
- 4 large red potatoes, quartered
- 1 pound baby carrots
- 3 cups water
- 3 garlic cloves, minced
- 1 bay leaf
- 2 tablespoons sugar
- 2 tablespoons cider vinegar
- ½ teaspoon pepper
- 1 corned beef brisket with spice packet (2½ to 3 pounds), cut in half
- 1 small head cabbage, cut into wedges

1. Place the onion, potatoes and carrots in a 6- to 7-qt. slow cooker. Combine the water, garlic, bay leaf, sugar, vinegar, pepper and contents of spice packet; pour over vegetables. Top with brisket and cabbage.
2. Cover and cook on low for 8-9 hours or until the meat and vegetables are tender. Discard bay leaf before serving.

CINNAMON-RAISIN BANANA BREAD PUDDING

My family likes to change the toppings for this luscious dessert. We use berries, chopped nuts or fruits, ice cream, whipped cream or caramel topping. If I'm making the dessert for adults, I add a little rum to the milk mixture.
—**Aysha Schurman** Ammon, ID

Prep: 10 min. • **Cook:** 2½ hours
Makes: 8 servings

- 4 large eggs
- 2¼ cups 2% milk
- ¾ cup mashed ripe banana (about 1 large)
- ¼ cup packed brown sugar
- ⅓ cup butter, melted
- 1 teaspoon vanilla extract
- 1 loaf (1 pound) cinnamon-raisin bread, cut into 1-inch cubes
- ½ cup chopped pecans, toasted
  Vanilla ice cream, optional

1. In a large bowl, whisk the first six ingredients. Stir in the bread and pecans. Transfer to a greased 4-qt. slow cooker.
2. Cook, covered, on low 2½-3 hours or until a knife inserted in the center comes out clean. Serve warm, with ice cream if desired.

SLOW COOKER PORK POZOLE

I often make this heartwarming stew with pork ribs and hominy. It's a fill-you-up recipe of lightly spiced comfort.
—**Genie Gunn** Asheville, NC

Prep: 10 min. • **Cook:** 3 hours
Makes: 6 servings

- 1 can (15½ ounces) hominy, rinsed and drained
- 1 can (14½ ounces) diced tomatoes, undrained
- 1 can (14½ ounces) diced tomatoes with mild green chilies, undrained
- 1 can (10 ounces) green enchilada sauce
- 2 medium carrots, finely chopped
- 1 medium onion, finely chopped
- 3 garlic cloves, minced
- 2 teaspoons ground cumin
- ¼ teaspoon salt
- 1 pound boneless country-style pork ribs
  Lime wedges and minced fresh cilantro
  Corn tortillas, optional

1. In a 3- or 4-qt. slow cooker, combine the first nine ingredients; add pork. Cook, covered, on low 3-4 hours or until pork is tender.

2. Remove pork from slow cooker. Cut pork into bite-sized pieces; return to slow cooker. Serve with lime wedges and cilantro and, if desired, corn tortillas.

EASY CITRUS HAM

I created this recipe many years ago with items I already had on hand. The succulent ham has a mild citrus flavor. It was so popular at a church social that I knew I had a winner!
—**Sheila Christensen** San Marcos, CA

Prep: 15 min. • **Cook:** 4 hours + standing
Makes: 12 servings

- 1 boneless fully cooked ham (3 to 4 pounds)
- ½ cup packed dark brown sugar
- 1 can (12 ounces) lemon-lime soda, divided
- 1 medium navel orange, thinly sliced
- 1 medium lemon, thinly sliced
- 1 medium lime, thinly sliced
- 1 tablespoon chopped crystallized ginger

1. Cut ham in half; place in a 5-qt. slow cooker. In a small bowl, combine brown sugar and ¼ cup soda; rub over ham. Top with orange, lemon and lime slices. Add candied ginger and remaining soda to the slow cooker.

2. Cover and cook on low for 4-5 hours or until a thermometer reads 140°, basting occasionally with cooking juices. Let stand for 10 minutes before slicing.

Cookies, Bars & Candies

Pass the milk...or coffee or tea, because this chapter is loaded with sweet sensations! Perfect after-school snacks, bake-sale contributions, no-fuss desserts and late-night nibbles, these 30 treats come together in a pinch, travel well and brighten up any day. Turn to this chapter the next time your sweet tooth comes calling.

ALMOND BARS

This fast, delicious dessert always makes an appearance at Christmas celebrations. Everyone likes the rich almond flavor.
—**Cheryl Newendorp** Pella, IA

Prep: 15 min. • **Bake:** 30 min. + cooling
Makes: 4½ dozen

- 1 cup butter, softened
- 1 cup almond paste
- 2¼ cups sugar, divided
- 2 large eggs
- 1 teaspoon almond extract
- 2 cups all-purpose flour
- ½ cup slivered almonds

1. Preheat oven to 350°. In a large bowl, cream the butter, almond paste and 2 cups sugar until light and fluffy. Beat in eggs and extract. Gradually add flour, stirring just until moistened.
2. Spread into a greased 13x9-in. baking dish. Sprinkle with remaining sugar; top with almonds.
3. Bake for 30-35 minutes or until a toothpick inserted in the center comes out clean. Cool on a wire rack. Cut into squares. Store in the refrigerator.

BLOND BUTTERSCOTCH BROWNIES

Toffee and chocolate dot the golden brown batter of these delightful brownies. I do a lot of cooking for the police officers I work with, and they always line up for these treats.
—**Jennifer Ann Sopko** Battle Creek, MI

Prep: 15 min. • **Bake:** 20 min. + cooling
Makes: 2 dozen

- 2 cups all-purpose flour
- 2 cups packed brown sugar
- 2 teaspoons baking powder
- ¼ teaspoon salt
- ½ cup butter, melted and cooled
- 2 large eggs
- 1 teaspoon vanilla extract
- 1 cup semisweet chocolate chunks
- 4 Heath candy bars (1.4 ounces each), coarsely chopped

1. Preheat oven to 350°. In a large bowl, combine the flour, brown sugar, baking powder and salt. In another bowl, beat the butter, eggs and vanilla until smooth. Stir into the dry ingredients just until combined (batter will be thick).
2. Spread batter into a 13x9-in. baking pan coated with cooking spray. Sprinkle with chocolate chunks and chopped candy bars; press gently into batter.
3. Bake for 20-25 minutes or until a toothpick inserted in the center comes out clean. Cool on a wire rack. Cut into bars.

RUSTIC NUT BARS

My friends love crunching into the crust, so much like shortbread, and the wildly nutty topping on these chewy, gooey bars.
—**Barbara Driscoll** West Allis, WI

Prep: 20 min. • **Bake:** 35 min. + cooling
Makes: about 3 dozen

- 1 tablespoon plus ¾ cup cold butter, divided
- 2⅓ cups all-purpose flour
- ½ cup sugar
- ½ teaspoon baking powder
- ½ teaspoon salt
- 1 large egg, lightly beaten

TOPPING
- ⅔ cup honey
- ½ cup packed brown sugar
- ¼ teaspoon salt
- 6 tablespoons butter, cubed
- 2 tablespoons heavy whipping cream
- 1 cup chopped hazelnuts, toasted
- 1 cup salted cashews
- 1 cup pistachios
- 1 cup salted roasted almonds

1. Preheat oven to 375°. Line a 13x9-in. baking pan with foil, letting ends extend over sides by 1 in. Grease the foil with 1 tablespoon butter.

2. In a large bowl, whisk flour, sugar, baking powder and salt. Cut in the remaining butter until mixture resembles coarse crumbs. Stir in egg until blended (mixture will be dry). Press firmly onto bottom of prepared pan.

3. Bake 18-20 minutes or until edges are golden brown. Cool on a wire rack.

4. In a large heavy saucepan, combine honey, brown sugar and salt; bring to a boil over medium heat, stirring frequently to dissolve sugar. Boil 2 minutes without stirring. Stir in butter and cream; return to a boil. Cook and stir 1 minute or until smooth. Remove from heat; stir in nuts. Spread over crust.

5. Bake 15-20 minutes or until topping is bubbly. Cool completely in pan on a wire rack. Lifting with foil, remove from pan. Discard foil; cut into bars.

Note: To toast nuts, bake in a shallow pan in a 350° oven for 5-10 minutes or cook in a skillet over low heat until lightly browned, stirring occasionally.

TOFFEE PECAN BARS

Curl up with a hot cup of coffee and one of these oh-so-sweet treats. The golden topping and flaky crust give way to the heartwarming taste of old-fashioned pecan pie.
—**Dianna Croskey** Gibsonia, PA

Prep: 15 min. • **Bake:** 40 min. + chilling
Makes: 3 dozen

- 2 cups all-purpose flour
- ½ cup confectioners' sugar
- 1 cup cold butter, cubed
- 1 large egg
- 1 can (14 ounces) sweetened condensed milk
- 1 teaspoon vanilla extract
- 1 package English toffee bits (10 ounces) or almond brickle chips (7½ ounces)
- 1 cup chopped pecans

1. Preheat oven to 350°. In a large bowl, mix flour and confectioners' sugar; cut in butter until mixture is crumbly.

2. Press into a greased 13x9-in. baking pan. Bake 15 minutes. Meanwhile, in a small bowl, mix egg, milk and vanilla. Fold in toffee bits and pecans. Spoon over crust. Bake 24-26 minutes or until golden brown. Refrigerate until firm. Cut into bars.

Contest Winner

CHOCOLATE LINZER COOKIES

Living in the town of North Pole, it's no surprise that I enjoy holiday baking! My mom and I used to make these cookies together. Now I love to bake them for my own family. They remind me of home.
—**Heather Peters** North Pole, AK

Prep: 30 min. + chilling
Bake: 10 min./batch + cooling
Makes: 2 dozen

- ¾ cup butter, softened
- 1 cup sugar
- 2 large eggs
- ½ teaspoon almond extract
- 2⅓ cups all-purpose flour
- 1 teaspoon baking powder
- ½ teaspoon salt
- ½ teaspoon ground cinnamon
- 1 cup (6 ounces) semisweet chocolate chips, melted
  Confectioners' sugar
- 6 tablespoons seedless raspberry jam

1. Cream butter and sugar until light and fluffy. Add eggs, one at a time, beating well after each addition. Beat in extract. Combine flour, baking powder, salt and cinnamon; gradually add to the creamed mixture and mix well. Refrigerate for 1 hour or until easy to handle.
2. Divide the dough in half. On a lightly floured surface, roll out one portion to ⅛-in. thickness; cut with a floured 2½-in.

round cookie cutter. Roll out the rest of the dough; cut with a 2½-in. floured doughnut cutter so the center is cut out of each cookie.
3. Place 1 in. apart on ungreased baking sheets. Bake at 350° for 8-10 minutes or until edges are lightly browned. Remove to wire racks to cool.
4. Spread melted chocolate over the bottoms of solid cookies. Place cookies with cutout centers over chocolate. Sprinkle with confectioners' sugar. Spoon ½ teaspoon jam in center of each cookie.

TOFFEE ALMOND SANDIES

Loaded with crunchy chopped toffee and almonds, these crispy classics are my husband's favorite cookie. I used to bake them in large batches when our four sons lived at home. Now I whip them up for the grandchildren!
—**Alice Kahnk** Kennard, NE

Prep: 35 min. • **Bake:** 15 min./batch
Makes: about 12 dozen

- 1 cup butter, softened
- 1 cup sugar
- 1 cup confectioners' sugar
- 1 cup canola oil
- 2 large eggs
- 1 teaspoon almond extract
- 3½ cups all-purpose flour
- 1 cup whole wheat flour
- 1 teaspoon baking soda
- 1 teaspoon cream of tartar
- 1 teaspoon salt
- 2 cups chopped almonds
- 1 package (8 ounces) milk chocolate English toffee bits
  Additional sugar

1. Preheat oven to 350°. In a large bowl, cream butter and sugars until light and fluffy. Beat in the oil, eggs and extract. In another bowl, combine the flours, baking soda, cream of tartar and salt; gradually add to creamed mixture and mix well. Stir in almonds and toffee bits.
2. Shape dough into 1-in. balls; roll in sugar. Place balls on an ungreased baking sheet and flatten with a fork. Bake for 12-14 minutes or until lightly browned.

BIG SOFT GINGER COOKIES

These nicely spiced soft cookies are perfect for folks who like the flavor of ginger but don't care for the crunch of hard gingersnaps.
—**Barbara Gray** Boise, ID

Start to Finish: 25 min.
Makes: 2½ dozen

- ¾ cup butter, softened
- 1 cup sugar
- 1 large egg
- ¼ cup molasses
- 2¼ cups all-purpose flour
- 2 teaspoons ground ginger
- 1 teaspoon baking soda
- ¾ teaspoon ground cinnamon
- ½ teaspoon ground cloves
- ¼ teaspoon salt
  Additional sugar

1. Preheat oven to 350°. In a large bowl, cream butter and sugar until light and fluffy. Beat in egg and molasses. Combine the flour, ginger, baking soda, cinnamon, cloves and salt; gradually add to the creamed mixture and mix well.
2. Roll into 1½-in. balls, then roll in sugar. Place 2 in. apart on ungreased baking sheets. Bake until cookies are puffy and lightly browned, 10-12 minutes. Remove to wire racks to cool.

FROSTED ANISE SUGAR COOKIES

The anise flavor in these cookies is distinct but not overpowering. I add red and green sprinkles for Christmas, but you could decorate them to suit any occasion.
—**Janice Eanni** Willowick, OH

Prep: 30 min.
Bake: 10 min./batch + cooling
Makes: 7 dozen

- 1 cup butter, softened
- 1½ cups sugar
- 6 large eggs
- 1 teaspoon vanilla extract
- ¾ teaspoon anise extract
- 3½ cups all-purpose flour
- 4 teaspoons baking powder

GLAZE

- 3 cups confectioners' sugar
- 4 teaspoons butter, softened
- ¾ teaspoon vanilla extract
- ¼ to ⅓ cup whole milk
  Colored sprinkles, optional

1. Preheat oven to 350°. In a large bowl, cream butter and sugar until light and fluffy. Beat in the eggs and extracts. In another bowl, whisk flour and baking powder; gradually beat into the creamed mixture.
2. Drop by tablespoonfuls 2 in. apart onto greased baking sheets. Bake for 8-10 minutes or until cookies are light brown. Remove from pans to wire racks to cool completely.
3. For glaze, in a large bowl, mix the confectioners' sugar, butter, vanilla and enough milk to achieve spreading consistency. Dip tops of cookies into glaze. If desired, decorate with sprinkles. Let stand until set.

SUPER CHUNKY COOKIES

Chocolate lovers go crazy over these cookies that feature loads of chocolate! Whenever friends ask me to make "those cookies," I know exactly which recipe they're talking about.

—Rebecca Jendry Spring Branch, TX

Prep: 15 min. • **Bake:** 10 min./batch
Makes: about 6½ dozen

- ½ cup butter-flavored shortening
- ½ cup butter, softened
- 1 cup packed brown sugar
- ¾ cup sugar
- 2 large eggs
- 2 teaspoons vanilla extract
- 2½ cups all-purpose flour
- 1 teaspoon baking soda
- ⅛ teaspoon salt
- 1 cup miniature semisweet chocolate chips
- 1 cup milk chocolate chips
- 1 cup vanilla or white chips
- 4 ounces bittersweet chocolate, coarsely chopped
- ¾ cup English toffee bits or almond brickle chips
- ½ cup chopped pecans

1. Preheat oven to 350°. In a large bowl, cream the shortening, butter and sugars until light and fluffy. Add the eggs, one at a time, beating well after each addition. Beat in the vanilla. Combine the flour, baking soda and salt; gradually add to the creamed mixture and mix well. Stir in the remaining ingredients.

2. Drop by tablespoonfuls 3 in. apart onto ungreased baking sheets. Bake for 10-12 minutes or until lightly browned. Cool for 2-3 minutes before removing to wire racks to cool completely.

RED APPLE BUTTER BARS

Fall means apple-picking time. We love baking these bar treats using apples and apple butter with a crumbly good streusel on top.

—Nancy Foust Stoneboro, PA

Prep: 40 min. • **Bake:** 35 min. + cooling
Makes: 2 dozen

- 3 cups all-purpose flour
- 2 cups quick-cooking oats
- 2 cups packed brown sugar
- 1½ teaspoons baking soda
- ¾ teaspoon salt
- ¾ teaspoon ground cinnamon
- 1½ cups butter, melted
- 2 medium apples, chopped
- 1½ cups apple butter
- 1 cup chopped walnuts

1. Preheat oven to 350°. In a large bowl, combine the first six ingredients; stir in butter. Reserve 1⅓ cups crumb mixture for topping. Press the remaining mixture onto bottom of a greased 13x9-in. baking dish. Bake 15-20 minutes or until lightly browned. Cool completely on a wire rack.
2. Sprinkle apples over crust; spread with apple butter. Stir walnuts into reserved topping; sprinkle over apple butter. Bake 35-40 minutes or until lightly browned. Cool in pan on a wire rack. Cut into bars.
Note: This recipe was tested with commercially prepared apple butter.

FREEZE IT
MINT-FILLED COOKIES

I tuck a peppermint patty inside these treats for a surprise. The bites will melt in your mouth.

—Karen Nielson St. George, UT

Prep: 30 min. + chilling
Bake: 10 min./batch + cooling
Makes: about 3 dozen

- 1 cup butter, softened
- 4 ounces cream cheese, softened
- 1 cup sugar
- ½ cup packed brown sugar
- 2 large eggs
- 1 tablespoon 2% milk
- 1 teaspoon vanilla extract
- 4 cups all-purpose flour
- 1 teaspoon baking soda
- ½ teaspoon salt
- 40 chocolate-covered peppermint patties (1½ inches), unwrapped
- ¾ cup semisweet chocolate chips
- 1 tablespoon shortening

1. In a large bowl, cream butter, cream cheese and sugars until light and fluffy.

Beat in eggs, milk and vanilla. In another bowl, whisk flour, baking soda and salt; gradually beat into butter mixture.
2. Divide dough in half. Shape each into a disk; wrap in plastic. Refrigerate for 30 minutes or until firm enough to roll.
3. Preheat oven to 400°. On a lightly floured surface, roll each portion of dough to ¼-in. thickness. Cut with a floured 3-in. round cookie cutter. Place a mint patty in the center of each circle; fold the dough over the patty. Pinch to seal seams. Place on greased baking sheets, seam side down.
4. Bake for 8-10 minutes or until cookies are golden brown. Remove from pans to wire racks to cool completely.
5. In a microwave, melt chocolate chips and shortening; stir until smooth. Drizzle over cookies. Refrigerate until set. Store in an airtight container in the refrigerator.
Freeze option: Transfer disks of dough to a resealable plastic freezer bag; freeze. To use, thaw dough in refrigerator until soft enough to roll. Prepare, bake and decorate as directed.

SPICED RUM-NUT BRITTLE

Seasoned with cayenne pepper and cinnamon, this spicy brittle packs its own heat to warm up holiday visitors.
—**Terri McKitrick** Delafield, WI

Prep: 25 min. + cooling
Makes: about 1 pound

- 1 cup sugar
- ½ cup light corn syrup
- ½ cup chopped cashews
- ½ cup chopped pecans
- 1 teaspoon butter
- ½ teaspoon ground cinnamon
- ¼ teaspoon cayenne pepper
- ⅛ teaspoon salt
  Pinch ground nutmeg
- 1 teaspoon baking soda
- ½ teaspoon rum extract
- ½ teaspoon vanilla extract

1. Butter a 15x10 x1-in. pan; set aside. In a 2-qt. microwave-safe bowl, combine the sugar and corn syrup. Microwave, uncovered, on high for 3 minutes; stir. Microwave for 2½ minutes longer. Stir in cashews, pecans, butter, cinnamon, cayenne, salt and nutmeg.
2. Microwave, uncovered, on high for 2 minutes or until mixture turns a light amber color (mixture will be very hot). Quickly stir in baking soda and extracts until light and foamy. Immediately pour into prepared pan; spread with a metal spatula. Cool completely. Break into pieces; store in an airtight container.

CHOCOLATE BILLIONAIRES

I received this recipe while living in Texas. When we moved, I was sure to take it with me. These chocolate and caramel candies always get raves.
—**June Humphrey** Strongsville, OH

Prep: 45 min. + chilling
Makes: about 2 pounds

- 1 package (14 ounces) caramels
- 3 tablespoons water
- 1½ cups chopped pecans
- 1 cup crisp rice cereal
- 3 cups milk chocolate chips
- 1½ teaspoons shortening

1. Line two baking sheets with greased waxed paper; set aside. In a large heavy saucepan, combine caramels and water; cook and stir over low heat until smooth. Stir the in pecans and cereal. Drop by teaspoonfuls onto prepared pans. Refrigerate for 10 minutes or until firm.
2. In a microwave, melt chocolate chips and shortening; stir until smooth. Dip candy into the chocolate, coating all sides; allow excess to drip off. Place on prepared pans. Refrigerate until set. Store in an airtight container.

WHITE CHOCOLATE CRANBERRY BLONDIES

My family often requests these bars. For a fancier presentation for special occasions, cut them into triangles and drizzle chocolate over each individually.
—**Erika Busz** Kent, WA

....

Prep: 35 min. • **Bake:** 20 min. + cooling
Makes: 3 dozen

- ¾ **cup butter, cubed**
- 1½ **cups packed light brown sugar**
- 2 **large eggs**
- ¾ **teaspoon vanilla extract**
- 2¼ **cups all-purpose flour**
- 1½ **teaspoons baking powder**
- ¼ **teaspoon salt**
- ⅛ **teaspoon ground cinnamon**
- ½ **cup dried cranberries**
- 6 **ounces white baking chocolate, coarsely chopped**

FROSTING
- 1 **package (8 ounces) cream cheese, softened**
- 1 **cup confectioners' sugar**
- 1 **tablespoon grated orange zest, optional**
- 6 **ounces white baking chocolate, melted**
- ½ **cup dried cranberries, chopped**

1. Preheat oven to 350°. In a large microwave-safe bowl, microwave butter until melted; stir in the brown sugar. Cool slightly.

2. Beat in eggs, one at a time, and vanilla. In another bowl, whisk together flour, baking powder, salt and cinnamon; stir into the butter mixture. Stir in cranberries and the chopped chocolate (the batter will be thick). Spread into a greased 13x9-in. pan.

3. Bake until golden brown and a toothpick inserted in center comes out clean (do not overbake), 18-21 minutes. Cool completely on a wire rack.

4. For frosting, beat the cream cheese, confectioners' sugar and, if desired, orange zest until smooth. Gradually beat in half of the melted white chocolate; spread over blondies. Sprinkle with the cranberries; drizzle with the remaining melted chocolate.

5. Cut into triangles. Store in an airtight container in the refrigerator.

Crazy for Coconut

With the taste of the tropics and the look of a winter snowfall, coconut is the perfect addition to sweet treats all year round! These tasty confections make the most of this delicious ingredient by pairing it with chocolate, lemon and caramel.

SNOW-TOPPED WHITE CHOCOLATE MACADAMIA COOKIES

Just like snowflakes, these fluffy cookies will melt in your mouth. They're great served up plain, but you can set them in decorative cupcake liners for extra visual appeal.
—**Taste of Home** Test Kitchen

Prep: 35 min.
Bake: 15 min./batch + cooling
Makes: about 3 dozen

- 1 tube (16½ ounces) refrigerated sugar cookie dough
- ⅓ cup all-purpose flour
- ½ teaspoon vanilla extract
- ¾ cup white baking chips
- ½ cup finely chopped macadamia nuts, toasted

GLAZE
- 1½ cups confectioners' sugar
- 3 tablespoons 2% milk
- ½ teaspoon lemon extract
- 1½ cups sweetened shredded coconut

1. Preheat oven to 350°. Place cookie dough in a large bowl; let stand at room temperature 5-10 minutes to soften.
2. Add flour and vanilla to dough; beat until blended (dough will be slightly crumbly). Stir in baking chips and nuts.

Shape level tablespoons of dough into balls; place balls 2 in. apart on parchment paper-lined baking sheets.
3. Bake until cookie bottoms are lightly browned, 12-14 minutes. Remove to wire racks to cool completely.
4. For glaze, mix confectioners' sugar, milk and extract until smooth. Dip tops of cookies in glaze. Sprinkle with coconut, patting gently to adhere. Let stand until glaze is set.
Note: To toast nuts, bake in a shallow pan in a 350° oven for 5-10 minutes or cook in a skillet over low heat until lightly browned, stirring occasionally.

FUDGY MACAROON BARS

Sweet tooths make a beeline for my dessert tray whenever these rich squares show up. They're attractive on the platter and delectable with fudge and coconut.
—**Beverly Zdurne** East Lansing, MI

Prep: 25 min. • **Bake:** 35 min.
Makes: 3 dozen

- 4 ounces unsweetened chocolate
- 1 cup butter
- 2 cups sugar
- 1 cup all-purpose flour
- ¼ teaspoon salt

- 1 teaspoon vanilla extract
- 3 large eggs, lightly beaten

FILLING
- 3 cups sweetened shredded coconut
- 1 can (14 ounces) sweetened condensed milk
- 1 teaspoon vanilla extract
- ½ teaspoon almond extract

TOPPING
- 1 cup (6 ounces) semisweet chocolate chips
- ½ cup chopped walnuts

1. Preheat oven to 350°. In a microwave, melt the chocolate and butter; stir until smooth. Remove from the heat; cool slightly. Stir in the sugar, flour, salt, vanilla and eggs. Spread half of the batter into a greased 13x9-in. baking pan.
2. In a large bowl, combine the filling ingredients. Spoon over the chocolate layer. Carefully spread the remaining chocolate mixture over filling.
3. Bake for 35-40 minutes or until the sides pull away from the pan. Immediately sprinkle with chocolate chips. Allow chips to soften for a few minutes, then spread over the bars. Sprinkle with walnuts. Cool completely before cutting.

ALMOND-COCONUT LEMON BARS

Give traditional lemon bars a tasty twist with the addition of almonds and coconut.

—Taste of Home Test Kitchen

Prep: 10 min. • **Bake:** 40 min. + cooling
Makes: 2 dozen

1½ cups all-purpose flour
½ cup confectioners' sugar
⅓ cup blanched almonds, toasted
1 teaspoon grated lemon zest
¾ cup cold butter, cubed

FILLING

3 large eggs
1½ cups sugar
½ cup sweetened shredded coconut
¼ cup lemon juice
3 tablespoons all-purpose flour
1 teaspoon grated lemon zest
½ teaspoon baking powder
Confectioners' sugar

1. Preheat oven to 350°. In a food processor, combine flour, confectioners' sugar, almonds and lemon zest; cover and process until nuts are finely chopped. Add butter; pulse just until mixture is crumbly. Press into a greased 13x9-in. baking dish. Bake for 20 minutes.
2. Meanwhile, in a large bowl, whisk the eggs, sugar, coconut, lemon juice, flour, lemon zest and baking powder; pour over the hot crust. Bake until light golden brown, 20-25 minutes. Cool on a wire rack. Dust with confectioners' sugar. Cut into squares.

GO NUTS! COCONUT CARAMELS

I first got this recipe from a TV cooking show, but made some adjustments to suit our own tastes. We make the candy every Easter, and many more times throughout the year.

—Deanna Polito-Laughinghouse
Raleigh, NC

Prep: 10 min. • **Cook:** 5 min. + cooling
Makes: about ¾ pound

1 teaspoon butter
24 caramels
¾ cup plus 2 tablespoons sweetened shredded coconut, divided
½ cup white baking chips
½ cup salted peanuts

1. Line an 8x4-in. loaf pan with foil and grease the foil with butter; set aside.
2. In a microwave-safe bowl, combine the caramels, ¾ cup of the coconut, the baking chips and peanuts. Microwave on high, uncovered, for 1 minute; stir. Cook, uncovered, 30-60 seconds longer or until the caramels are melted; stir to combine. Press into the prepared pan. Sprinkle with the remaining coconut. Cool.
3. Using foil, lift the candy out of pan. Discard foil; cut candy into 1-in. squares.

FREEZE IT LEMON SNOWDROPS

I save my snowdrop cookies for special occasions. The crunchy, buttery sandwich cookie has a puckery lemon filling.
—**Bernice Martinoni** Petaluma, CA

Prep: 40 min. + chilling
Bake: 10 min./batch + cooling
Makes: 2 dozen

- 1 **cup butter, softened**
- ½ **cup confectioners' sugar**
- ¼ **teaspoon salt**
- 1 **teaspoon lemon extract**
- 2 **cups all-purpose flour**
  Granulated sugar

FILLING
- 1 **large egg, lightly beaten**
- ⅔ **cup granulated sugar**
- 2 **teaspoons grated lemon zest**
- 3 **tablespoons lemon juice**
- 4 **teaspoons butter**
  Additional confectioners' sugar, optional

1. Preheat oven to 350°. Cream butter, confectioners' sugar and salt until light and fluffy. Beat in extract. Gradually beat in flour. Shape teaspoonfuls of dough into balls (if necessary, refrigerate dough, covered, until firm enough to shape).

2. Place balls 1 in. apart on ungreased baking sheets; flatten slightly with bottom of a glass dipped in granulated sugar. Bake until light brown, 10-12 minutes. Remove cookies from pans to wire racks to cool completely.

3. For filling, whisk together the egg, granulated sugar, lemon zest and lemon juice in a small heavy saucepan over medium-low heat until blended. Add the butter; cook over medium heat, whisking constantly, until thickened and a thermometer reads at least 170°, about 20 minutes. Remove from the heat immediately (do not allow to boil). Transfer to a small bowl; cool. Press plastic wrap onto surface of the filling. Refrigerate until cold, about 1 hour.

4. Spread lemon filling on half of cookies; cover with remaining cookies. If desired, dust with confectioners' sugar. Store leftovers in refrigerator.

Freeze option: Freeze unfilled cookies in freezer containers. To use, thaw cookies in covered containers. Fill and decorate as directed.

CHEWY CHOCOLATE-CHERRY BARS

Colorful dried cherries and pistachios star in this take on seven-layer bars. To switch it up even more, try using cinnamon or chocolate graham cracker crumbs instead of plain and substitute pecans or walnuts for the pistachios.

—*Taste of Home* Test Kitchen

Prep: 10 min. • **Bake:** 25 min. + cooling
Makes: 3 dozen

- 1½ cups graham cracker crumbs
- ½ cup butter, melted
- 1 can (14 ounces) sweetened condensed milk
- 1½ cups dried cherries
- 1½ cups semisweet chocolate chips
- 1 cup sweetened shredded coconut
- 1 cup pistachios, chopped

1. Preheat oven to 350°. In a small bowl, mix cracker crumbs and butter. Press into a greased 13x9-in. baking pan. In a large bowl, mix the remaining ingredients until blended; carefully spread over crust.
2. Bake 25-28 minutes or until edges are golden brown. Cool in pan on a wire rack. Cut into bars.

PEANUT BUTTER CARAMEL BARS

When my husband and our three sons sit down to dinner, they ask, "What's for dessert?" I have a happy group of guys when I report that these rich bars are on the menu.

—**Lee Ann Karnowski** Stevens Point, WI

Prep: 50 min. + chilling
Bake: 20 min. + cooling
Makes: about 3 dozen

- 1 package yellow cake mix (regular size)
- ½ cup butter, softened
- 1 large egg
- 20 miniature peanut butter cups, chopped
- 2 tablespoons cornstarch
- 1 jar (12¼ ounces) caramel ice cream topping
- ¼ cup peanut butter
- ½ cup salted peanuts

TOPPING

- 1 can (16 ounces) milk chocolate frosting
- ½ cup chopped salted peanuts

1. Preheat oven to 350°. In a large bowl, combine cake mix, butter and egg; beat on low speed for 30 seconds. Beat on medium for 2 minutes or until no longer crumbly. Stir in peanut butter cups.
2. Press into a greased 13x9-in. baking pan. Bake for 18-22 minutes or until lightly browned.
3. Meanwhile, in a large saucepan, combine cornstarch, caramel topping and peanut butter; stir until smooth. Cook over low heat for 25-27 minutes or until mixture comes to a boil, stirring occasionally. Remove from the heat; stir in peanuts.
4. Spread evenly over warm crust. Bake 6-7 minutes longer or until almost set. Cool completely on a wire rack. Spread with frosting; sprinkle with peanuts. Cover and refrigerate for at least 1 hour before cutting. Store in the refrigerator.
Note: Reduced-fat peanut butter is not recommended for this recipe.

PEANUT BUTTER FUDGE

With three ingredients and a 10-minute prep time, this fudge couldn't be easier. It's a favorite "never fail" quickie recipe.
—**Eleanore Peterson** Fort Atkinson, WI

Prep: 10 min. + chilling
Makes: 1¾ pounds

- 1 pound white candy coating
- 1 cup creamy peanut butter
- 1 cup coarsely chopped walnuts

Melt coating in a saucepan over medium-low heat, stirring constantly until smooth. Remove from heat; stir in peanut butter and walnuts. Spread into a greased 8-in. square pan. Chill until firm. Cut in squares.

SALTED PEANUT ROLLS

A gift of homemade candy is always a hit! I dip these peanut rolls in chocolate, but they're yummy plain, too.
—**Elizabeth Hokanson** Arborg, MB

Prep: 1 hour + freezing
Makes: about 5 dozen

- 1 jar (7 ounces) marshmallow creme
- 2 to 2¼ cups confectioners' sugar, divided
- 1 package (14 ounces) caramels
- 2 tablespoons water
- 4 cups salted peanuts, chopped
- 2 cups (12 ounces) semisweet chocolate chips
- 2 teaspoons shortening

1. Line two 15x10x1-in. pans with waxed paper. In a large bowl, beat marshmallow creme and 1 cup confectioners' sugar until blended. Knead in enough remaining confectioners' sugar until smooth and easy to handle.

2. Divide mixture into four portions. Roll each into ½-in.-thick logs. Cut crosswise into 1½-in. pieces; place on one prepared pan. Freeze 15 minutes or until firm.

3. Meanwhile, heat caramels and water over low heat until melted, stirring occasionally. Working with one-fourth of the logs at a time, dip in caramel; roll in peanuts. Place on remaining prepared pan. Freeze coated logs until set.

4. In top of a double boiler or a metal bowl over barely simmering water, melt chocolate chips and shortening; stir until smooth. Dip bottom of rolls into melted chocolate; allow excess to drip off. Return to prepared pans. Refrigerate until set. Store between layers of waxed paper in an airtight container at room temperature.

WHITE PECAN FUDGE

Every Christmas, I package batches of this rich fudge to send to family and friends.
—**Marie Draper** Price, UT

Prep: 10 min. + chilling
Cook: 10 min.
Makes: about 3½ pounds (about 6½ dozen)

- 1 tablespoon plus ½ cup butter, divided
- 2½ cups miniature marshmallows
- 2¼ cups sugar
- 1 cup heavy whipping cream
- 16 ounces white baking chocolate, finely chopped
- 2 teaspoons vanilla extract
- 2 cups chopped pecans

1. Line a 9-in. square pan with foil; grease the foil with ½ tablespoon butter and set aside. Grease the sides of a large heavy saucepan with ½ tablespoon butter. Cut the remaining butter into small pieces and place in a large heatproof bowl; add marshmallows and set aside.

2. In the buttered saucepan, combine sugar and cream. Cook and stir over medium heat until mixture comes to a boil. Cover and cook for 2 minutes to dissolve any sugar crystals. Uncover; cook over medium heat, without stirring, until a candy thermometer reads 234° (soft-ball stage).

3. Remove from the heat. Pour over butter and marshmallows; stir until melted. Add the chocolate. Continue stirring until smooth. Stir in vanilla and nuts. Pour into prepared pan. Refrigerate until firm. Lift out of pan; remove foil and cut into 1-in. squares. Store in an airtight container at room temperature.

FROSTED BUTTER RUM BRICKLE BITES

The rum, real butter and toffee bits turned these cookies into my husband's new favorite. If you like them less sweet, instead of frosting, sprinkle them with confectioners' sugar while they're warm.
—**Cindy Nerat** Menominee, MI

Prep: 35 min.
Bake: 10 min./batch + cooling
Makes: about 4 dozen

- 1 cup butter, softened
- ¾ cup confectioners' sugar
- 2 teaspoons rum extract
- ½ teaspoon salt
- 2 cups all-purpose flour
- 1 package (8 ounces) brickle toffee bits

ICING
- ⅓ cup butter, cubed
- 2 cups confectioners' sugar
- ½ teaspoon rum extract
- 2 to 3 tablespoons 2% milk

1. Preheat oven to 375°. Beat first four ingredients until blended. Beat in flour. Stir in toffee bits. Shape dough into 1-in. balls; place 2 in. apart on parchment paper-lined baking sheets.
2. Bake until edges are light brown and toffee bits begin to melt, 8-10 minutes. Cool on pans 5 minutes. Remove to wire racks to cool completely.
3. In a small heavy saucepan, melt butter over medium heat. Heat until golden brown, about 5 minutes, stirring constantly. Remove from heat; stir in confectioners' sugar, rum extract and enough milk to reach desired consistency. Spread over cookies.

Contest Winner

CANDY BAR FUDGE

My manager at work shared this recipe with me. I've made this chewy and chocolaty fudge many times since. Packed with nuts and caramel, it's like a candy bar.
—**Lois Freeman** Oxford, MI

Prep: 20 min. + chilling
Makes: 2¾ pounds

- ½ cup butter
- ⅓ cup baking cocoa
- ¼ cup packed brown sugar
- ¼ cup milk
- 3½ cups confectioners' sugar
- 1 teaspoon vanilla extract
- 30 caramels, unwrapped
- 1 tablespoon water
- 2 cups salted peanuts
- ½ cup semisweet chocolate chips
- ½ cup milk chocolate chips

1. In a microwave-safe bowl, combine butter, cocoa, brown sugar and milk. Microwave on high until mixture boils, about 2 minutes. Stir in confectioners' sugar and vanilla. Pour into a greased 8-in. square dish.
2. In another microwave-safe bowl, heat caramels and water on high for 1¼ minutes or until melted. Stir in peanuts; spread over chocolate layer. Microwave chocolate chips on high for 30 seconds or until melted; spread over caramel layer. Chill until firm.

CHOCOLATE TRUFFLES

You may be tempted to save this recipe for a special occasion since these smooth, creamy chocolates are divine. But with just a few ingredients, they're easy to make any time.

—Darlene Wiese-Appleby *Creston, OH*

Prep: 20 min. + chilling
Makes: about 4 dozen

- 3 cups (18 ounces) semisweet chocolate chips
- 1 can (14 ounces) sweetened condensed milk
- 1 tablespoon vanilla extract
  Optional coatings: chocolate sprinkles, Dutch-processed cocoa, espresso powder and cocoa nibs

1. In a microwave, melt chocolate chips and milk; stir until smooth. Stir in vanilla. Refrigerate, covered, for 2 hours or until firm enough to roll.
2. Shape into 1-in. balls. Roll in coatings as desired.

CARAMEL TOFFEE BROWNIES

I love to make up recipes for foods that I am craving. In this case, chocolate, toffee and caramel came together in this brownie for one sensational treat. I frequently add these to care packages for family and friends.

—Brenda Caughell *Durham, NC*

Prep: 30 min. • **Bake:** 40 min. + cooling
Makes: 2 dozen
CARAMEL LAYER
- ½ cup butter, softened
- ⅓ cup sugar
- ⅓ cup packed brown sugar
- 1 large egg
- ½ teaspoon vanilla extract
- 1 cup all-purpose flour
- ½ teaspoon baking soda
- ¼ teaspoon salt
- ½ cup caramel ice cream topping
- 2 tablespoons 2% milk
- 1 cup toffee bits
BROWNIE LAYER
- 1 cup butter, cubed

- 4 ounces unsweetened chocolate
- 4 large eggs, lightly beaten
- 2 cups sugar
- 2 teaspoons vanilla extract
- 2 cups all-purpose flour

1. Preheat oven to 350°. In a large bowl, cream butter and sugars until light and fluffy; beat in egg and vanilla. Combine flour, baking soda and salt; gradually add to creamed mixture and mix well. In a small bowl, combine caramel topping and milk; add to batter and mix well. Fold in toffee bits; set aside.
2. In a microwave, melt the butter and chocolate. Beat in eggs, sugar and vanilla; gradually beat in flour.
3. Spread half of the brownie batter into a greased 13x9-in. baking pan. Drop the caramel batter by spoonfuls onto the brownie batter; swirl to combine. Drop the remaining brownie batter on top.
4. Bake for 40-45 minutes or until a toothpick inserted in center comes out clean. Cool on a wire rack.

TRUFFLE-FILLED COOKIE TARTS

I made chocolate truffles as a Christmas tradition for many years. I created this recipe to incorporate my truffles into the center of fudgy cookies. It was a hit with friends and family.

—Patricia Harmon Baden, PA

Prep: 65 min. + cooling
Cook: 20 min. + chilling
Makes: 2½ dozen

- ½ cup butter, softened
- ½ cup sugar
- ½ cup packed brown sugar
- 1 large egg
- 1 teaspoon vanilla extract
- 1½ cups all-purpose flour
- ⅓ cup baking cocoa
- ¼ teaspoon baking soda

FILLING

- 2 cups (12 ounces) semisweet chocolate chips
- ⅔ cup heavy whipping cream
- ¼ cup butter, cubed
- 2 large egg yolks
  Chocolate sprinkles

1. Preheat oven to 400°. In a large bowl, beat butter and sugars until blended. Beat in egg and vanilla. In another bowl, whisk flour, cocoa and baking soda; gradually beat into the creamed mixture.

2. Shape level tablespoons of dough into 2½-in.-wide patties. Press patties onto bottoms and up the sides of greased mini-muffin cups.

3. Bake cookies until set, 8-10 minutes. Immediately press a deep indentation in center of each with the end of a wooden spoon handle. Cool in pans 5 minutes. Remove to wire racks to cool completely.

4. For filling, in a small heavy saucepan, combine chocolate chips, cream and butter; cook and stir over medium heat until smooth. Remove from heat.

5. In a small bowl, whisk a small amount of hot mixture into egg yolks; return all to pan, whisking constantly. Cook over low heat, stirring constantly, until mixture is thickened and a thermometer reads at least 160°, 15-17 minutes. Do not allow to boil. Immediately transfer the filling to a bowl; cool 20 minutes, stirring occasionally.

6. Spoon 1 tablespoon filling into each crust. Top with sprinkles. Refrigerate until cold, about 1 hour.

CHOCOLATE FUDGE BROWNIES

These brownies are so rich and fudgy they don't need icing!

—Hazel Fritchie Palestine, IL

Prep: 15 min. • **Bake:** 35 min. + cooling
Makes: 16 servings

- 1 cup butter, cubed
- 6 ounces unsweetened chocolate, chopped
- 4 large eggs
- 2 cups sugar
- 1 teaspoon vanilla extract
- ½ teaspoon salt
- 1 cup all-purpose flour
- 2 cups chopped walnuts
  Confectioners' sugar, optional

1. Preheat oven to 350°. In a small saucepan, melt butter and chocolate over low heat. Cool slightly.

2. In a large bowl, beat eggs, sugar, vanilla and salt until blended. Stir in chocolate mixture. Add flour, mixing well. Stir in the walnuts.

3. Spread into a greased 9-in. square baking pan. Bake 35-40 minutes or until a toothpick inserted in center comes out with moist crumbs (do not overbake).

4. Cool completely in pan on a wire rack. If desired, dust with confectioners' sugar. Cut into bars.

Dazzling Desserts

Simply impressive desserts are hallmarks of country cooking, and this incredible selection of cakes, pies and tarts won't disappoint. You'll also discover cute cupcakes, lemony treats, fruity staples and other head-turning desserts that will have everyone asking for seconds—as well as your secrets!

MOLTEN PEPPERMINT-CHOCOLATE CAKES

I doctored up a recipe I found in the newspaper years ago. Top yours with crushed candy canes or chopped mint chocolates for a little extra wow.

—Genise Krause Sturgeon Bay, WI

Start to Finish: 30 min.
Makes: 4 servings

- ½ cup butter, cubed
- 4 ounces bittersweet chocolate, chopped
- 2 large eggs
- 2 large egg yolks
- ⅓ cup sugar
- ½ teaspoon peppermint extract
- ⅛ teaspoon salt
- ¼ cup all-purpose flour
  Confectioners' sugar

1. Preheat oven to 425°. In a small heavy saucepan, heat butter and chocolate over low heat until blended, stirring constantly; transfer to a large bowl.

2. Add eggs, egg yolks, sugar, extract and salt to chocolate mixture; mix well. Stir in flour. Pour into four greased 6-oz. custard cups or ramekins.

3. Place the custard cups on a baking sheet. Bake for 10-12 minutes or until a thermometer reads 160° and the edges of the cakes are set.

4. Remove cakes from oven; let stand 1 minute. Run a knife around sides of cakes; remove to dessert plates. Dust with confectioners' sugar. Serve immediately.

STRAWBERRIES & CREAM TORTE

This festive strawberry summer treat is one of my mom's favorites. It wows guests every time yet is simple to make.

—Cathy Branciaroli Wilmington, DE

Prep: 25 min. • **Bake:** 15 min. + cooling
Makes: 12 servings

- 2 large eggs, separated
- ¼ cup butter, softened
- ½ cup plus ½ teaspoon sugar, divided
- ½ teaspoon vanilla extract
- 1 cup all-purpose flour
- 1½ teaspoons baking powder
- ¼ teaspoon salt
- ½ cup 2% milk

ASSEMBLY

- 2 cups heavy whipping cream
- 1 pint fresh strawberries, hulled and sliced
- ½ teaspoon sugar
  Additional fresh strawberries

1. Place egg whites in a large bowl; let stand at room temperature 30 minutes.

Preheat oven to 350°. Line bottoms of two greased 8-in. round baking pans with parchment paper; grease paper.

2. In a large bowl, cream butter and ½ cup sugar until light and fluffy. Add egg yolks, beating well. Beat in vanilla.

3. In another bowl, whisk flour, baking powder and salt; add to creamed mixture alternately with milk, beating well after each addition. Transfer to prepared pans.

4. With clean beaters, beat egg whites on medium speed until foamy. Add the remaining sugar, beating on high until the sugar is dissolved. Continue beating until soft peaks form. Spread over batter in pans.

5. Bake for 12-15 minutes or until a toothpick inserted in the center comes out clean. Cool completely in pans on wire racks. (Cake layers will be thin.)

6. In a large bowl, beat cream until stiff peaks form. Loosen edges of cakes from pans with a knife. Carefully remove one cake to a serving plate, meringue side up.

7. Arrange sliced strawberries over top; sprinkle with sugar. Gently spread with half of the whipped cream. Top with the remaining cake layer, meringue side up; spread with remaining whipped cream. Top with whole strawberries. Refrigerate until serving.

RASPBERRY CHOCOLATE PUFFS

This chocolaty, flaky dessert is one of my favorite show-off recipes because it makes a spectacular presentation. The best part? It's actually surprisingly easy and quick to make.

—**Anneliese Deising** Plymouth, MI

Prep: 25 min. • **Bake:** 20 min. + cooling
Makes: 8 servings

- 1 cup milk chocolate chips
- 1 cup white baking chips
- 1 cup chopped pecans
- 1 package (17.3 ounces) frozen puff pastry, thawed
- 1 package (12 ounces) frozen unsweetened raspberries, thawed
- 1 cup confectioners' sugar
  Additional confectioners' sugar
  Optional ingredients: fresh raspberries and additional chocolate and white baking chips

1. Preheat oven to 425°. Toss together chocolate chips, baking chips and pecans. On a lightly floured surface, roll each pastry sheet into a 12-in. square; cut each sheet into quarters, making four 6-in. squares.

2. Place squares on ungreased baking sheets; top each with about ⅓ cup chocolate mixture. Lightly brush edges of pastry with water; bring together all corners, pinching the seams to seal.

3. Bake until golden brown, 18-20 minutes. Remove to a wire rack to cool slightly. Puree frozen raspberries with 1 cup confectioners' sugar in a food processor. Strain to remove seeds.

4. To serve, dust pastries with confectioners' sugar. Serve with raspberry sauce and, if desired, fresh berries and additional chips.

BILLIE'S SOUTHERN SWEET POTATO CAKE

I made this cake for my kids when they were younger and they told me, "Mommy, you're the best baker!" Little did they know that was Mommy's first attempt at homemade cake!

—**Billie Williams-Henderson** Bowie, MD

Prep: 25 min. • **Bake:** 40 min. + cooling
Makes: 20 servings

- 4 large eggs
- 2 cups sugar
- 2 cups canola oil
- 2 teaspoons vanilla extract

- 2 cups all-purpose flour
- 2 teaspoons baking soda
- 2 teaspoons ground cinnamon
- ½ teaspoon ground ginger
- ½ teaspoon ground allspice
- ½ teaspoon salt
- 3 cups shredded peeled sweet potatoes (about 2 medium)
- 1 cup finely chopped walnuts

FROSTING

- 1 package (8 ounces) cream cheese, softened
- ½ cup butter, softened
- 1 teaspoon vanilla extract
- 2 cups confectioners' sugar

1. Preheat oven to 350°. Grease a 13x9-in. baking pan.

2. In a large bowl, beat eggs, sugar, oil and vanilla until well blended. In another bowl, whisk flour, baking soda, spices and salt; gradually beat into egg mixture. Stir in sweet potatoes and walnuts.

3. Transfer to prepared pan. Bake until a toothpick inserted in center comes out clean, 40-45 minutes. Cool completely in pan on a wire rack.

4. In a small bowl, beat cream cheese, butter and vanilla until blended. Gradually beat in confectioners' sugar until smooth. Spread frosting over the cooled cake. Refrigerate leftovers.

Contest Winner

PEAR TART

This pretty pastry looks like it came from a fancy bakery. My sister-in-law brought this fruity dessert to dinner one night, and we all went back for seconds. It is truly scrumptious.

—**Kathryn Rogers** Suisun City, CA

Prep: 15 min. • **Bake:** 25 min. + chilling
Makes: 12 servings

- 3 tablespoons butter, softened
- ½ cup sugar
- ¾ teaspoon ground cinnamon
- ¾ cup all-purpose flour
- ⅓ cup finely chopped walnuts

FILLING

- 1 package (8 ounces) reduced-fat cream cheese
- ¼ cup plus 1 tablespoon sugar, divided
- 1 large egg
- 1 teaspoon vanilla extract
- 1 can (15 ounces) reduced-sugar sliced pears, drained well and thinly sliced
- ¼ teaspoon ground cinnamon

1. Preheat oven to 425°. Beat butter, sugar and cinnamon until crumbly. Beat in flour and walnuts. Press onto bottom and up sides of a 9-in. fluted tart pan with a removable bottom coated with cooking spray.

2. For filling, beat cream cheese and ¼ cup sugar until smooth. Beat in egg and vanilla. Spread into crust. Arrange pears over top. Mix cinnamon and remaining sugar; sprinkle over pears.

3. Bake 10 minutes. Reduce oven setting to 350°; bake until filling is set, 15-20 minutes. Cool 1 hour on a wire rack. Refrigerate at least 2 hours before serving.

APPLE DUMPLING BAKE

I received this recipe from a friend of mine, then tweaked it to suit my family's tastes. Mountain Dew is the secret ingredient in this rich apple dessert that's a snap to make.

—**Chris Shields** Monrovia, IN

Prep: 15 min. • **Bake:** 35 min.
Makes: 8 servings

- 2 medium Granny Smith apples
- 2 tubes (8 ounces each) refrigerated crescent rolls
- 1 cup sugar
- ⅓ cup butter, softened
- ½ teaspoon ground cinnamon
- ¾ cup Mountain Dew soda
  Vanilla ice cream

1. Preheat oven to 350°. Peel, core and cut each apple into eight wedges. Unroll both tubes of crescent dough; separate each into eight triangles. Wrap a triangle around each wedge. Place in a greased 13x9-in. baking dish.

2. In a bowl, mix sugar, butter and cinnamon until blended; sprinkle over dumplings. Slowly pour soda around the rolls (do not stir).

3. Bake, uncovered, until golden brown and apples are tender, 35-40 minutes. Serve warm with ice cream.

CARAMEL PEAR PUDDING

Don't expect this old-fashioned dessert to last long. The delicate pears and irresistible caramel topping make it a winner whenever I serve it.
—**Sharon Mensing** Greenfield, IA

Prep: 15 min. • **Bake:** 45 min.
Makes: 8 servings

- 1 cup all-purpose flour
- ⅔ cup sugar
- 1½ teaspoons baking powder
- ½ teaspoon ground cinnamon
- ¼ teaspoon salt
  Pinch ground cloves
- ½ cup whole milk
- 4 medium pears, peeled and cut into ½-inch cubes
- ½ cup chopped pecans
- ¾ cup packed brown sugar
- ¼ cup butter
- ¾ cup boiling water
  Vanilla ice cream or whipped cream, optional

1. Preheat oven to 375°. In a large bowl, combine the first six ingredients; beat in milk until smooth. Stir in pears and pecans. Spoon into an ungreased 2-qt. baking dish.
2. In another bowl, combine the brown sugar, butter and water; pour over batter. Bake, uncovered, 45-50 minutes. Serve warm with ice cream or whipped cream.

STRAWBERRY BLISS

My easy-to-make puff pastry crust is topped with a soft-set pudding layer that has a hint of strawberry flavor. It needs to chill for at least an hour, so it's your new go-to for a make-ahead brunch!
—**Candace Richter** Stevens Point, WI

Prep: 30 min. • **Bake:** 20 min. + chilling
Makes: 12 servings

- 1 cup water
- ½ cup butter, cubed
- 1 cup all-purpose flour
- 4 large eggs
- 1 package (8 ounces) cream cheese, softened
- ½ cup sugar
- 5 tablespoons seedless strawberry jam
- 3 cups cold milk
- 1 package (5.1 ounces) instant vanilla pudding mix
- ½ cup heavy whipping cream
- 3 cups quartered fresh strawberries

1. Preheat oven to 400°. In a large saucepan, bring water and butter to a rolling boil. Add flour all at once and beat until blended. Cook over medium heat, stirring vigorously until mixture pulls away from sides of pan and forms a ball. Remove from heat; let stand 5 minutes.
2. Add eggs, one at a time, beating well after each addition. Continue beating until mixture is smooth and shiny.
3. Spread into a greased 15x10x1-in. baking pan. Bake 20-25 minutes or until puffed and golden brown (surface will be uneven). Cool completely in pan on a wire rack.
4. In a large bowl, beat cream cheese, sugar and jam until smooth. Beat in milk and pudding mix until smooth. In a small bowl, beat cream until stiff peaks form; fold into pudding mixture. Spread over crust. Refrigerate at least 1 hour.
5. Just before serving, top with strawberries.

COCONUT ITALIAN CREAM CAKE

I'd never tasted an Italian cream cake before moving to Colorado. Now I bake for people in the area, and this beauty is one of my most requested treats.

—**Ann Bush** Colorado City, CO

Prep: 50 min. • **Bake:** 20 min. + cooling
Makes: 16 servings

- 5 large eggs, separated
- 1 cup butter, softened
- 1⅔ cups sugar
- 1½ teaspoons vanilla extract
- 2 cups all-purpose flour
- ¾ teaspoon baking soda
- ½ teaspoon salt
- 1 cup buttermilk
- 1⅓ cups sweetened shredded coconut
- 1 cup chopped pecans, toasted

FROSTING

- 12 ounces cream cheese, softened
- 6 tablespoons butter, softened
- 2¼ teaspoons vanilla extract
- 5⅔ cups confectioners' sugar
- 3 to 4 tablespoons heavy whipping cream
- ½ cup chopped pecans, toasted
- ¼ cup toasted sweetened shredded coconut, optional

1. Place egg whites in a small bowl; let stand at room temperature 30 minutes.
2. Preheat oven to 350°. Line bottoms of three greased 9-in. round baking pans with parchment paper; grease paper.
3. In a large bowl, cream butter and sugar until light and fluffy. Add egg yolks, one at a time, beating well after each addition. Beat in vanilla. In another bowl, whisk flour, baking soda and salt; add to creamed mixture alternately with the buttermilk, beating well after each addition. Fold in coconut and pecans.
4. With clean beaters, beat egg whites on medium speed until stiff peaks form. Gradually fold into batter. Transfer to prepared pans. Bake 20-25 minutes or until a toothpick inserted in center comes out clean. Cool in pans 10 minutes before removing to wire racks; remove paper. Cool completely.
5. For frosting, in a large bowl, beat the cream cheese and butter until smooth. Beat in vanilla. Gradually beat in confectioners' sugar and enough cream to reach spreading consistency. Spread frosting between layers and over the top and sides of cake. Sprinkle cake with pecans and, if desired, coconut. Refrigerate leftovers.
Note: To toast pecans and coconut, spread each, one at a time, in a 15x10x1-in. baking pan. Bake at 350° for 5-10 minutes or until lightly browned; stir occasionally.

CHOCOLATE PEANUT BUTTER CUPCAKES

I've been baking cakes for years and enjoy trying new combinations of flavors and textures. As soon as I took the first bite of these cupcakes, I knew I had created something divine! They are definitely worth the time it takes to make them.
—Ronda Schabes Vicksburg, MI

Prep: 55 min. • **Bake:** 20 min. + cooling
Makes: 2 dozen

- 2 cups sugar
- 1¾ cups all-purpose flour
- ¾ cup baking cocoa
- ½ teaspoon salt
- ½ teaspoon baking soda
- ½ teaspoon baking powder
- 1 cup buttermilk
- 1 cup strong brewed coffee, room temperature
- ½ cup canola oil
- 2 large eggs
- 1 teaspoon vanilla extract

FILLING

- ½ cup creamy peanut butter
- 3 tablespoons unsalted butter, softened
- 1 cup confectioners' sugar
- 2 to 4 tablespoons 2% milk

GANACHE

- 2 cups (12 ounces) semisweet chocolate chips
- ½ cup heavy whipping cream

PEANUT BUTTER FROSTING

- 1 cup packed brown sugar
- 4 large egg whites
- ¼ teaspoon salt
- ¼ teaspoon cream of tartar
- 1 teaspoon vanilla extract
- 2 cups unsalted butter, softened
- ⅓ cup creamy peanut butter

1. Preheat oven to 350°. In a large bowl, combine the first six ingredients. Whisk buttermilk, coffee, oil, eggs and vanilla until blended; add to the dry ingredients until combined. (Batter will be thin.) Fill paper-lined muffin cups two-thirds full.

2. Bake 18-20 minutes or until a toothpick inserted in the center comes out clean. Cool 10 minutes before removing from pans to wire racks to cool completely.

3. In a small bowl, cream peanut butter, butter, confectioners' sugar and enough milk to achieve piping consistency. Cut a small hole in the corner of a pastry or plastic bag; insert a small round tip. Fill with peanut butter filling. Insert tip into the top center of each cupcake; pipe about 1 tablespoon filling into each.

4. Place chocolate chips in a small bowl. In a small saucepan, bring cream just to a boil. Pour over the chocolate; whisk until smooth. Dip the top of each cupcake into ganache; place on wire racks to set.

5. In a large heavy saucepan, combine brown sugar, egg whites, salt and cream of tartar over low heat. With a hand mixer, beat on low speed for 1 minute. Continue beating on low over low heat until the frosting reaches 160°, about 8-10 minutes. Pour into a large bowl; add vanilla. Beat on high until stiff peaks form, about 5 minutes.

6. Add butter, 1 tablespoon at a time, beating well after each addition. If mixture begins to look curdled, place frosting bowl in another bowl filled with hot water for a few seconds. Continue adding butter and beating until smooth. Beat in peanut butter 1-2 minutes or until smooth.

7. Place frosting in a pastry or plastic bag with large star tip; pipe onto each cupcake. Store in an airtight container in the refrigerator. Let stand at room temperature before serving.

Filling a Pastry Bag

To fill a pastry bag without mess, place the bag tip-down into a tall glass. Fold the bag over the glass and fill it. Once it's three-fourths full, pull up the sides of the bag, lift it out of the glass, and twist the open end closed.

SPICED EGGNOG PUMPKIN PIE

With its 10-minute prep time and lovely blend of mild eggnog flavor and spices, this is a busy hostess' dream dessert! It's a staple for Thanksgiving and Christmas.
—**Patti Leake** Columbia, MO

Prep: 10 min. • **Bake:** 45 min. + cooling
Makes: 8 servings

       Pastry for single-crust pie (9 inches)
   1   can (15 ounces) solid-pack pumpkin
   1¼ cups eggnog
   ¾   cup sugar
   2   large eggs
   1   teaspoon ground cinnamon
   ½   teaspoon salt
   ½   teaspoon ground ginger
   ¼   teaspoon ground cloves
   ¼   teaspoon ground nutmeg

1. Preheat oven to 425°. Roll out pastry to fit a 9-in. pie plate. Transfer pastry to pie plate. Trim pastry to ½ in. beyond edge of plate; flute edges.
2. Place the remaining ingredients in a large bowl; beat just until smooth. Pour into pastry. Bake for 15 minutes. Reduce heat to 350°; bake 30-35 minutes longer or until a knife inserted in the center comes out clean. (Cover edges with foil during the last 15 minutes to prevent overbrowning if necessary.) Cool on a wire rack. Store in the refrigerator.
Pastry for single-crust pie: Combine 1¼ cups all-purpose flour and ¼ tsp. salt; cut in ½ cup cold butter until crumbly. Gradually add 3-5 tablespoons ice water, tossing with a fork until dough holds together when pressed. Wrap in plastic wrap and refrigerate 1 hour.

GLAZED SPICED RUM POUND CAKES

My recipe makes two loaf-sized treats, perfect for sharing. The spiced rum flavor in both the cake and the glaze really comes through.
—**Christine Russell** Littleton, NH

Prep: 30 min. • **Bake:** 45 min. + cooling
Makes: 2 loaves (8 slices each)

   1   cup butter, softened
   2   cups packed brown sugar
   5   large eggs
   ⅓   cup spiced rum
   2   teaspoons vanilla extract
   3½   cups all-purpose flour
   2   teaspoons baking powder
   ½   teaspoon baking soda
   ½   teaspoon salt
   ½   cup 2% milk
GLAZE
   ½   cup sugar
   ¼   cup butter, cubed
   2   teaspoons water
   2   teaspoons spiced rum
   ½   cup chopped pecans, toasted

1. Preheat oven to 350°. Grease and flour two 9x5-in. loaf pans. In a large bowl, cream butter and brown sugar until light and fluffy. Add eggs, one at a time, beating well after each addition. Beat in rum and vanilla. In another bowl, whisk flour, baking powder, baking soda and salt; add to creamed mixture alternately with milk, beating well after each addition.
2. Spoon batter into prepared pans. Bake for 45-50 minutes or until a toothpick inserted in center comes out clean. Cool in pans 10 minutes before removing to wire racks to cool.
3. Meanwhile, in a small saucepan, combine sugar, butter, water and rum. Bring to a boil. Remove from heat; drizzle over warm cakes. Sprinkle with pecans. Cool completely on wire racks.
Note: To toast nuts, bake in a shallow pan in a 350° oven for 5-10 minutes or cook in a skillet over low heat until lightly browned, stirring occasionally.

FUDGY TURTLE PIE

Everyone needs a truly decadent dessert recipe. We love to mix chocolate, caramel and crunchy candy bits in a pie that's ooey-gooey fabulous.

—**Dolores Vaccaro** Pueblo, CO

....

Prep: 55 min. + chilling
Makes: 16 servings

- 1½ cups chocolate wafer crumbs (32 wafers)
- ⅓ cup butter, melted
  FILLING
- 20 caramels
- ¼ cup heavy whipping cream
- 2 cups chopped pecans
- 4 Snickers candy bars (1.86 ounces each), chopped

TOPPING

- 2 cups (12 ounces) semisweet chocolate chips
- 1 cup heavy whipping cream
  Caramel ice cream topping, optional
  Additional chopped Snickers candy bars, optional

1. Preheat oven to 375°. In a small bowl, mix wafer crumbs and butter. Press onto bottom and up sides of a greased 9-in. fluted tart pan with removable bottom. Bake 8-10 minutes or until set. Cool on a wire rack.

2. For filling, in a small heavy saucepan, combine caramels and cream. Cook and stir over low heat until the caramels are melted. Stir in pecans. Remove from heat; pour into crust. Top with chopped candy.

3. For topping, place chocolate chips in a small bowl. In a small saucepan, bring cream just to a boil. Pour over chocolate; stir with a whisk until smooth. Pour and spread, if necessary, over top. Refrigerate 1 hour or until set.

4. If desired, drizzle ice cream topping over individual pieces and top with additional chopped candy.

Luscious Lemon Desserts

The flavor of lemon is ideal for desserts that are elegant without being fussy—and delicious without weighing you down. The tang cuts through sugary sweetness, and the freshness gives even dense, rich cheesecake a welcomed lightness.

LEMONADE ICEBOX PIE

You will detect a definite lemonade flavor in this refreshing pie. High and fluffy, it has a creamy, smooth consistency we really appreciate.
—**Cheryl Wilt** Eglon, WV

Prep: 15 min. + chilling
Makes: 8 servings

- 1 package (8 ounces) cream cheese, softened
- 1 can (14 ounces) sweetened condensed milk
- ¾ cup thawed lemonade concentrate
- 1 carton (8 ounces) frozen whipped topping, thawed
  Yellow food coloring, optional
- 1 graham cracker crust (9 inches)

In a large bowl, beat cream cheese and milk until smooth. Beat in lemonade concentrate. Fold in whipped topping and, if desired, food coloring. Pour into crust. Cover and refrigerate until set.
Orange Icebox Pie: Substitute ¾ cup thawed orange juice concentrate for the lemonade, add ½ teaspoon grated orange peel and omit food coloring.
Creamy Pineapple Pie: Substitute 1 can (8 ounces) crushed, undrained pineapple and ¼ cup lemon juice for lemonade. Omit food coloring.
Cool Lime Pie: Substitute ¾ cup thawed limeade concentrate for lemonade and use green food coloring instead of yellow.

MOIST LEMON CHIFFON CAKE

My fluffy cake is a real treat drizzled with a sweet-tart lemon glaze.
—**Rebecca Baird** Salt Lake City, UT

Prep: 15 min. • **Bake:** 45 min. + cooling
Makes: 16 servings

- ½ cup fat-free evaporated milk
- ½ cup reduced-fat sour cream
- ¼ cup lemon juice
- 2 tablespoons canola oil
- 2 teaspoons vanilla extract
- 1 teaspoon grated lemon peel
- 1 teaspoon lemon extract
- 2 cups cake flour
- 1½ cups sugar
- 1 tablespoon baking powder
- ½ teaspoon salt
- 1 cup large egg whites (about 7)
- ½ teaspoon cream of tartar

LEMON GLAZE
- 1¾ cups confectioners' sugar
- 3 tablespoons lemon juice

1. Preheat oven to 325°. In a large bowl, combine first seven ingredients. Sift together the flour, sugar, baking powder and salt; gradually beat into lemon mixture until smooth. In a small bowl, beat egg whites until foamy. Add cream of tartar; beat until stiff peaks form. Gently fold into the lemon mixture.
2. Pour into an ungreased 10-in. tube pan. Bake for 45-55 minutes or until cake springs back when lightly touched. Immediately invert the pan; cool cake completely. Remove cake to a serving platter. Combine glaze ingredients; drizzle over cake.

SHORTBREAD LEMON TART

For a change from ordinary lemon bars, we added orange peel to the crust and filling and turned the recipe into a tart.
—*Taste of Home* Test Kitchen

Prep: 20 min. • **Bake:** 25 min. + cooling
Makes: 10 servings

- 3 large eggs
- 1¼ cups granulated sugar
- ¼ cup lemon juice
- 1 tablespoon grated orange peel
- ¼ cup butter, melted

CRUST
- 1 cup all-purpose flour
- ⅓ cup confectioners' sugar
- ½ cup ground almonds
- 1 teaspoon grated lemon peel
- 1 teaspoon grated orange peel
- ½ cup cold butter, cubed
  Additional confectioners' sugar
  Fresh raspberries, optional

1. Let eggs stand at room temperature for 30 minutes.

2. Preheat oven to 350°. Whisk together eggs, sugar, lemon juice and orange peel. Whisk in butter until smooth. Set aside.

3. For crust, pulse first six ingredients in a food processor until mixture forms a ball. Press pastry onto the bottom and up the sides of an ungreased 9-in. fluted tart pan with removable bottom.

4. Pour lemon mixture into crust. Bake until center is almost set, 25-30 minutes. Cool on a wire rack. Just before serving, sprinkle with confectioners' sugar and, if desired, fresh raspberries.

LOVELY LEMON CHEESECAKE

Wait for the oohs and aahs when you present this luxurious cheesecake!
—**Margaret Allen** Abingdon, VA

Prep: 25 min. • **Bake:** 70 min. + chilling
Makes: 14 servings

- ¾ cup graham cracker crumbs
- 2 tablespoons sugar
- 3 teaspoons ground cinnamon
- 2 tablespoons butter, melted

FILLING
- 5 packages (8 ounces each) cream cheese, softened
- 1⅔ cups sugar
- ⅛ teaspoon salt
- ¼ cup lemon juice
- 1½ teaspoons vanilla extract
- 5 large eggs, lightly beaten
  Thin lemon slices, optional

1. Preheat oven to 325°. Place a greased 10-in. springform pan on a double thickness of heavy-duty foil (about 18 in. square). Wrap foil securely around pan.

2. In a small bowl, mix cracker crumbs, sugar and cinnamon; stir in butter. Press onto bottom of prepared pan; refrigerate while preparing filling.

3. In a large bowl, beat cream cheese, sugar and salt until smooth. Beat in lemon juice and vanilla. Add eggs; beat on low speed just until blended. Pour over crust. Place springform pan in a larger baking pan; add 1 in. of hot water to larger pan.

4. Bake 70-80 minutes or until center is just set and top appears dull. Remove springform pan from water bath. Cool cheesecake on a wire rack 10 minutes. Loosen sides from pan with a knife; remove foil. Cool 1 hour longer. Refrigerate overnight, covering when completely cooled.

5. Remove rim from pan. If desired, top cheesecake with lemon slices.

CHOCOLATE STRAWBERRY PUNCH BOWL TRIFLE

I threw this dessert together when I needed something quick to take to my in-laws'. Because it's beautiful, everyone thinks it requires a lot of effort. It's easy. And the recipe makes a lot, making this perfect for potlucks and large gatherings.
—Kristi Judkins Morrison, TN

Prep: 20 min. • **Bake:** 20 min.
Makes: 24-28 servings

- 1 package chocolate cake mix (regular size)
- 1 quart fresh whole strawberries, sliced
- 1 carton (13½ ounces) strawberry glaze
- 2 cartons (12 ounces each) frozen whipped topping, thawed, divided
- 1 cup chocolate frosting
  Shaved chocolate, optional

1. Prepare and bake chocolate cake according to package directions, using a 13x9-in. baking pan. Cool completely on a wire rack.
2. Cut cake into 1-in. cubes. Place half the cubes in a 6-qt. glass punch bowl. Top with half the sliced strawberries; drizzle with half the strawberry glaze. Spread with 3½ cups whipped topping.
3. In a microwave-safe bowl, heat frosting on high for 20-30 seconds or until pourable, stirring often; cool slightly. Drizzle half over the whipped topping. Repeat layers of cake, berries, glaze and whipped topping. If desired, drizzle with remaining frosting and sprinkle with shaved chocolate.

BLUEBERRY RHUBARB COUNTRY TART

When the rhubarb comes in, mix it with blueberries for a rustic and bubbly tart. Offer it to a friend with a warm cup of tea.
—Jeanne Ambrose Milwaukee, WI

Prep: 15 min. • **Bake:** 40 min.
Makes: 8 servings

- Pastry for single-crust pie
- ¾ cup sugar
- ¼ cup all-purpose flour
- 4 cups chopped fresh or frozen rhubarb, thawed
- 1 cup fresh or frozen blueberries, thawed
- 2 tablespoons 2% milk
- 1 tablespoon coarse sugar

1. On a lightly floured surface, roll dough into a 14-in. circle. Transfer to a parchment paper-lined baking sheet.

2. In a large bowl, mix sugar and flour. Add rhubarb and blueberries; toss to coat. Spoon filling over pastry to within 2 in. of edge. Fold pastry edge over filling, pleating as you go and leaving a 4-in. opening in the center. Brush folded pastry with milk; sprinkle with coarse sugar. Bake at 400° for 40-45 minutes or until crust is golden and filling is bubbly. Transfer tart to a wire rack to cool.

Pastry for single-crust pie: Combine 1¼ cups all-purpose flour and ¼ tsp. salt; cut in ½ cup cold butter until crumbly. Gradually add 3-5 tablespoons ice water, tossing with a fork until dough holds together when pressed. Wrap in plastic wrap and refrigerate 1 hour.
Note: If using frozen rhubarb, measure while still frozen, then thaw completely. Drain in a colander; do not press liquid out.

RHUBARB COBBLER

Crumbled macaroons are a distinctly different addition to this cobbler's topping. Serve hearty helpings alone or with vanilla ice cream.

—*Taste of Home* Test Kitchen

Start to Finish: 30 min.
Makes: 4 servings

- 4 cups sliced fresh or frozen rhubarb (1-inch pieces)
- 1 large apple, peeled and sliced
- ½ cup packed brown sugar
- ½ teaspoon ground cinnamon, divided
- 1 tablespoon cornstarch
- 2 tablespoons cold water
- 8 macaroons, crumbled
- 1 tablespoon butter, melted
- 2 tablespoons sugar
    Vanilla ice cream, optional

1. In a large skillet, combine rhubarb, apple, brown sugar and ¼ teaspoon cinnamon; bring to a boil. Reduce heat; cover and simmer 10-13 minutes or until rhubarb is tender. Combine cornstarch and water smooth; gradually add to the fruit mixture. Bring to a boil; cook and stir for 2 minutes or until thickened. Transfer to an ungreased 1-qt. baking dish.

2. In a small bowl, combine the crumbled cookies, butter, sugar and remaining cinnamon. Sprinkle over fruit mixture.

3. Broil 4 in. from the heat until lightly browned, 3-5 minutes. Serve warm with ice cream if desired.

Note: If using frozen rhubarb, measure while still frozen, then thaw completely. Drain in a colander, but do not press the liquid out.

BUTTERMILK PIE WITH PECANS

Branch out from the usual pecan pie with a creamy-crunchy version that comes out of the oven golden brown. Big slices are even better with a dollop of whipped cream.

—**Kathy Harding** Richmond, MO

....

Prep: 40 min. • **Bake:** 50 min. + cooling
Makes: 8 servings

    Pastry for single-crust pie (9 inches)
½ cup butter, softened
1¾ cups sugar
3 large eggs
3 tablespoons all-purpose flour
¼ teaspoon salt
1 cup buttermilk
2 teaspoons vanilla extract
1 cup chopped pecans
    Sweetened whipped cream,
      optional

1. Preheat oven to 425°. On a lightly floured surface, roll pastry to a ⅛-in.-thick circle; transfer to a 9-in. pie plate. Trim to ½ in. beyond rim of plate; flute edge. Line unpricked pastry with a double thickness of foil. Fill with pie weights, dried beans or uncooked rice.

2. Place on a baking sheet; bake for 20 minutes or until bottom is lightly browned. Remove foil and weights; bake 1-2 minutes longer or until golden brown. Cool crust on a wire rack. Reduce oven setting to 325°.

3. In a large bowl, beat butter and sugar until blended. Add eggs, one at a time, beating well after each addition. Beat in flour and salt. Gradually stir in buttermilk and vanilla.

4. Sprinkle pecans into crust; add filling. Bake 50-60 minutes or until center is set. Cover top loosely with foil during the last 15 minutes to prevent overbrowning if necessary.

5. Cool completely on a wire rack. If desired, serve with whipped cream. Serve or refrigerate within 2 hours.

Pastry for single-crust pie (9 inches): Combine 1¼ cups all-purpose flour and ¼ tsp. salt; cut in ½ cup cold butter until crumbly. Gradually add 3-5 tablespoons ice water, tossing with a fork until dough holds together when pressed. Wrap in plastic wrap and refrigerate 1 hour.

CREAMY LIME PIE WITH FRESH BERRIES

I combined the tangy taste of lime and cilantro with cream cheese for this berry pie that showcases seasonal fruit. The ginger cookies add zip to the crust.

—**Anneliese Barz** Fort Mill, SC

....

Prep: 30 min. + chilling
Bake: 10 min. + cooling
Makes: 8 servings

1¾ cups finely crushed gingersnap cookies (about 30 cookies)
¼ cup sugar
2 tablespoons all-purpose flour
⅓ cup butter, melted

FILLING
1 package (8 ounces) cream cheese, softened
4 teaspoons grated lime peel
2 tablespoons lime juice
1 cup confectioners' sugar
1 teaspoon vanilla extract
½ cup coarsely chopped fresh cilantro

TOPPING
2 cups fresh strawberries, sliced
2 cups fresh blueberries
2 tablespoons apricot preserves

1. Preheat oven to 375°. In a small bowl, mix crushed cookies, sugar and flour; stir in butter. Press onto bottom and up sides of a greased 9-in. pie plate. Bake until set, 8-10 minute. Cool crust completely on a wire rack.

2. In a small bowl, beat cream cheese, lime peel and lime juice until blended. Beat in confectioners' sugar and vanilla. Stir in cilantro. Transfer to crust. Refrigerate, covered, at least 4 hours or until filling is firm.

3. Just before serving, arrange berries over pie. In microwave, warm preserves just until melted. Brush over berries.

Contest Winner

SOUR CREAM APPLE PIE

A cool, creamy version of the original, this delicious dessert is the perfect finish to a satisfying summer meal. Its crumbly topping and smooth apple filling are crowd-pleasers—be prepared to serve seconds!
—**Sharon Bickett** Chester, SC

Prep: 15 min. • **Bake:** 35 min.
Makes: 8 servings

- 2 large eggs
- 1 cup (8 ounces) sour cream
- 1 cup sugar
- 6 tablespoons all-purpose flour, divided
- 1 teaspoon vanilla extract
- ¼ teaspoon salt
- 3 cups chopped peeled tart apples
- 1 unbaked pie shell (9 inches)
- ¼ cup packed brown sugar
- 3 tablespoons cold butter

1. Preheat oven to 375°. In a large bowl, beat eggs. Add sour cream. Stir in sugar, 2 tablespoons flour, vanilla and salt; mix well. Gently stir in apples. Pour into pie shell. Bake for 15 minutes.
2. Meanwhile, combine brown sugar and the remaining flour; cut in butter until mixture is crumbly. Sprinkle over top of pie. Bake 20-25 minutes longer or until filling is set. Cool completely on a wire rack. Serve or cover and refrigerate.

TART CHERRY LATTICE PIE

Whenever my mom is invited to a party, everyone requests her homemade double-crust fruit pies. In the summer, she uses fresh tart cherries for this recipe.
—**Pamela Eaton** Monclova, OH

Prep: 20 min. • **Bake:** 40 min. + cooling
Makes: 8 servings

- 1⅓ cups sugar
- ⅓ cup all-purpose flour
- 4 cups fresh or frozen pitted tart cherries, thawed and drained
- ¼ teaspoon almond extract
  Pastry for double-crust pie (9 inches)
- 2 tablespoons butter, cut into small pieces

1. Preheat oven to 400°. In a large bowl, combine sugar and flour; stir in cherries and extract.

2. On a lightly floured surface, roll one half of the pastry dough to a ⅛-in.-thick circle; transfer to a 9-in. pie plate. Trim pastry to ½ in. beyond rim of plate. Add filling; dot with butter.
3. Roll the remaining dough to a ⅛-in.-thick circle; cut into 1½-in.-wide strips. Arrange over filling in a lattice pattern. Trim and seal strips to edge of bottom pastry; flute edge. Cover edge loosely with foil.
4. Bake 40-50 minutes or until crust is golden brown and filling is bubbly. Remove foil. Cool on a wire rack.
Pastry for double-crust pie (9 inches): Combine 2½ cups all-purpose flour and ½ teaspoon salt; cut in 1 cup cold butter until crumbly. Gradually add ⅓- ⅔ cup ice water, tossing with a fork until dough holds together when pressed. Wrap in plastic wrap and refrigerate 1 hour.

ALMOND FUDGE CAKE

When it comes to decadent desserts, raspberries and chocolate always make a winning combination. People are amazed that this cake has fewer than 250 calories per slice.

—Mike Pickerel Columbia, MO

Prep: 20 min. • **Bake:** 55 min. + cooling
Makes: 12 servings

- 4 large egg whites
- 1 cup fat-free milk
- ¾ cup water
- ½ cup unsweetened applesauce
- 1 teaspoon almond extract
- 1¾ cups all-purpose flour
- 1½ cups sugar
- ¾ cup baking cocoa
- 1½ teaspoons baking powder
- 1½ teaspoons baking soda
- ½ teaspoon salt
- ¼ cup miniature semisweet chocolate chips

RASPBERRY SAUCE

- 2 cups fresh or frozen raspberries, thawed
- 1 tablespoon sugar
- 1 teaspoon lemon juice
- ¾ cup reduced-fat whipped topping
- 12 fresh raspberries

1. Preheat oven to 325°. In a large bowl, beat egg whites, milk, water, applesauce and extract until well blended. In a small bowl, combine the flour, sugar, cocoa, baking powder, baking soda and salt; gradually beat into the egg white mixture until blended (batter will be thin). Pour

into a 9-in. springform pan coated with cooking spray. Sprinkle with chips. Place pan on a baking sheet.

2. Bake for 55-60 minutes or until a toothpick inserted in the center comes out clean. Cool for 30 minutes. Carefully run a knife around edge of pan to loosen; remove sides of pan. Cool completely.

3. For sauce, puree the raspberries in a blender; strain to remove seeds. Stir in sugar and lemon juice. Spoon sauce onto dessert plates; top with cake wedges. Garnish each with 1 tablespoon whipped topping and a raspberry.

STRAWBERRY PRETZEL DESSERT

A salty pretzel crust nicely contrasts cream cheese and gelatin layers.

—Aldene Belch Flint, MI

Prep: 20 min. • **Bake:** 10 min. + chilling
Makes: 16 servings

- 2 cups crushed pretzels (about 8 ounces)
- ¾ cup butter, melted
- 3 tablespoons sugar

FILLING

- 2 cups whipped topping
- 1 package (8 ounces) cream cheese, softened
- 1 cup sugar

TOPPING

- 2 packages (3 ounces each) strawberry gelatin
- 2 cups boiling water
- 2 packages (16 ounces each) frozen sweetened sliced strawberries, thawed
  Additional whipped topping and pretzels, optional

1. In a bowl, combine pretzels, butter and sugar. Press into an ungreased 13x9-in. baking dish. Bake at 350° for 10 minutes. Cool on a wire rack.

2. For filling, in a small bowl, beat the whipped topping, cream cheese and sugar until smooth. Spread over pretzel crust. Refrigerate until chilled.

3. For topping, dissolve the gelatin in boiling water in a large bowl. Stir in the strawberries with syrup; chill until partially set. Carefully spoon over filling. Chill for 4-6 hours or until firm. Cut into squares; serve with whipped topping if desired.

Stop Gelatin Spread

Nobody likes gelatin that wanders. Using an offset spatula or the back of a spoon, spread cream cheese all the way to the edges so the gelatin stays put.

SANDY'S CHOCOLATE CAKE

Years ago, I drove 4½ hours to a cake contest, holding my entry on my lap the whole way. But it paid off. One bite and you'll see why this velvety beauty won first prize!
—**Sandy Johnson** Tioga, PA

Prep: 30 min. • **Bake:** 30 min. + cooling
Makes: 16 servings

- 1 cup butter, softened
- 3 cups packed brown sugar
- 4 large eggs
- 2 teaspoons vanilla extract
- 2⅔ cups all-purpose flour
- ¾ cup baking cocoa
- 3 teaspoons baking soda
- ½ teaspoon salt
- 1⅓ cups sour cream
- 1⅓ cups boiling water

FROSTING
- ½ cup butter, cubed
- 3 ounces unsweetened chocolate, chopped
- 3 ounces semisweet chocolate, chopped
- 5 cups confectioners' sugar
- 1 cup (8 ounces) sour cream
- 2 teaspoons vanilla extract

1. Preheat oven to 350°. Grease and flour three 9-in. round baking pans.

2. In a large bowl, cream butter and brown sugar until light and fluffy. Add eggs, one at a time, beating well after each addition. Beat in vanilla. In another bowl, whisk flour, cocoa, baking soda and salt; add to creamed mixture alternately with sour cream, beating well after each addition. Stir in water until blended.

3. Transfer to prepared pans. Bake until a toothpick comes out clean, about 30-35 minutes. Cool in pans 10 minutes; remove to wire racks to cool completely.

4. For frosting, in a metal bowl over simmering water, melt butter and chocolates; stir until smooth. Cool slightly.

5. In a bowl, combine confectioners' sugar, sour cream and vanilla. Add chocolate mixture; beat until smooth. Spread the frosting between layers and over top and sides of cake. Refrigerate leftovers.

WALNUT TOFFEE TART

I usually serve this scrumptious tart on Christmas and New Year's Day. It really showcases walnuts and is so pretty!.
—**Patricia Green** Yuba City, CA

Prep: 30 min. • **Bake:** 20 min.
Makes: 8-10 servings

- 2 cups all-purpose flour
- 3 tablespoons sugar

- ¾ cup cold butter
- 2 large egg yolks, lightly beaten
- ¼ cup cold milk

FILLING
- 1½ cups sugar
- 1½ cups heavy whipping cream
- ½ teaspoon ground cinnamon
- ¼ teaspoon salt
- 2 cups coarsely chopped walnuts

1. Preheat oven to 375°. Combine flour and sugar. Cut in butter until mixture resembles coarse crumbs. In a second bowl, combine egg yolks and milk; stir into flour mixture until blended. With lightly floured hands, press dough onto the bottom and 1 in. up the sides of a 12-in. tart pan with removable bottom. Line unpricked shell with a double thickness of heavy-duty foil. Fill with pie weights. Place pan on a baking sheet. Bake until edges are lightly browned, 12-15 minutes.

2. Meanwhile, in a saucepan, combine the sugar, cream, cinnamon and salt. Bring to a boil over medium heat, stirring constantly. Remove from the heat; stir in walnuts. Remove foil from pastry shell; pour filling into pastry. Bake until golden brown, 20-25 minutes. Cool on a wire rack. Store in the refrigerator.

Substitutions & Equivalents

EQUIVALENT MEASURES

3 teaspoons	= 1 tablespoon	16 tablespoons	= 1 cup
4 tablespoons	= ¼ cup	2 cups	= 1 pint
5⅓ tablespoons	= ⅓ cup	4 cups	= 1 quart
8 tablespoons	= ½ cup	4 quarts	= 1 gallon

FOOD EQUIVALENTS

GRAINS

Macaroni	1 cup (3½ ounces) uncooked	= 2½ cups cooked
Noodles, medium	3 cups (4 ounces) uncooked	= 4 cups cooked
Popcorn	⅓ - ½ cup unpopped	= 8 cups popped
Rice, long grain	1 cup uncooked	= 3 cups cooked
Rice, quick-cooking	1 cup uncooked	= 2 cups cooked
Spaghetti	8 ounces uncooked	= 4 cups cooked

CRUMBS

Bread	1 slice	= ¾ cup soft crumbs, ¼ cup fine dry crumbs
Graham crackers	7 squares	= ½ cup finely crushed
Buttery round crackers	12 crackers	= ½ cup finely crushed
Saltine crackers	14 crackers	= ½ cup finely crushed

FRUITS

Bananas	1 medium	= ⅓ cup mashed
Lemons	1 medium	= 3 tablespoons juice, 2 teaspoons grated peel
Limes	1 medium	= 2 tablespoons juice, 1½ teaspoons grated peel
Oranges	1 medium	= ¼ -⅓ cup juice, 4 teaspoons grated peel

VEGETABLES

Cabbage	1 head	= 5 cups shredded	Green pepper	1 large	= 1 cup chopped
Carrots	1 pound	= 3 cups shredded	Mushrooms	½ pound	= 3 cups sliced
Celery	1 rib	= ½ cup chopped	Onions	1 medium	= ½ cup chopped
Corn	1 ear fresh	= ⅔ cup kernels	Potatoes	3 medium	= 2 cups cubed

NUTS

Almonds	1 pound	= 3 cups chopped	Pecan halves	1 pound	= 4½ cups chopped
Ground nuts	3¾ ounces	= 1 cup	Walnuts	1 pound	= 3¾ cups chopped

EASY SUBSTITUTIONS

When you need...		Use...
Baking powder	1 teaspoon	½ teaspoon cream of tartar + ¼ teaspoon baking soda
Buttermilk	1 cup	1 tablespoon lemon juice or vinegar + enough milk to measure 1 cup (let stand 5 minutes before using)
Cornstarch	1 tablespoon	2 tablespoons all-purpose flour
Honey	1 cup	1¼ cups sugar + ¼ cup water
Half-and-half cream	1 cup	1 tablespoon melted butter + enough whole milk to measure 1 cup
Onion	1 small, chopped (⅓ cup)	1 teaspoon onion powder or 1 tablespoon dried minced onion
Tomato juice	1 cup	½ cup tomato sauce + ½ cup water
Tomato sauce	2 cups	¾ cup tomato paste + 1 cup water
Unsweetened chocolate	1 square (1 ounce)	3 tablespoons baking cocoa + 1 tablespoon shortening or oil
Whole milk	1 cup	½ cup evaporated milk + ½ cup water

Cooking Terms

Here's a quick reference for some of the most common cooking terms used in recipes:

BASTE To moisten food with melted butter, pan drippings, marinades or other liquid to add more flavor and juiciness.

BEAT A rapid movement to combine ingredients using a fork, spoon, wire whisk or electric mixer.

BLEND To combine ingredients until just mixed.

BOIL To heat liquids until bubbles form that cannot be stirred down. In the case of water, the temperature will reach 212°.

BONE To remove all meat from the bone before cooking.

CREAM To beat ingredients together to a smooth consistency, usually in the case of butter and sugar for baking.

DASH A small amount of seasoning, less than ⅛ teaspoon. If using a shaker, a dash would be a quick flick of the container.

DREDGE To coat foods with flour or other dry ingredients. Most often done with pot roasts and stew meat before browning.

FOLD To incorporate several ingredients by careful and gentle turning with a spatula. Used generally with beaten egg whites or whipped cream when mixing into the rest of the ingredients to keep the batter light.

JULIENNE To cut foods into long thin strips much like matchsticks. Used most often for salads and stir-fry dishes.

MINCE To cut into very fine pieces. Used often for garlic or fresh herbs.

PARBOIL To cook partially. Usually used in the case of chicken, sausages and vegetables.

PARTIALLY SET Describes the consistency of gelatin after it has been chilled for a short amount of time. Mixture should resemble the consistency of egg whites.

PUREE To process foods to a smooth mixture. Can be prepared in an electric blender, food processor, food mill or sieve.

SAUTE To fry quickly in a small amount of fat, stirring almost constantly. Most often done with onions, mushrooms and other chopped vegetables.

SCORE To cut slits partway through the outer surface of foods. Often used with ham or flank steak.

STIR-FRY To cook meats and/or vegetables with a constant stirring motion in a small amount of oil in a wok or skillet over high heat.

Alphabetical Index